Crossing Boundaries in Public Policy and Management

Crossing Boundaries shifts the level of the debate by offering engaging and real challenges to those who both research and promote multi-disciplinary work.
—**John Diamond**, *Edge Hill University, UK*

This book fills a gap in boundary-spanning collaboration in the public sector. It consolidates and integrates current theory and practice from leading scholarly thought and countless practitioner experiences. Then it translates lessons learned from action research into new insights on good practice. The book reaches out to academics, students, and practitioners alike who study and practice collaborative leadership.
—**John Wilkins**, *York University, Canada*

This book aims to develop four key challenges that remain unresolved in the boundary-spanning literature, which span from the conceptual, to the practice, to the translational. In doing so, it tackles the question of boundary-spanning from four different angles, providing an in-depth investigation of the current state of the field in each of these realms, in addition to new directions for solving the identified challenges. Finally, the book synthesises the lessons from each of these challenges into a coherent and integrated final piece of the boundary dilemma. In doing so, it will provide depth and a clearer agenda for future research and practice.

Crossing Boundaries in Public Policy and Management digs into the heart of enduring questions and challenges for cross-boundary working, providing in-depth conceptual contributions on the fundamental challenges of boundary work. It displays the latest state of knowledge on the topic and will be of interest to researchers, academics, practitioners and students in the fields of public management, public policy, public administration, public-private relationships and coordination and collaboration.

Luke Craven is a Research Fellow in the Public Service Research Group at UNSW Canberra.

Helen Dickinson is Associate Professor of Public Service Research and Director of the Public Service Research Group UNSW Canberra.

Gemma Carey is Associate Professor and the Research Director of the Centre for Social Impact UNSW and an NHMRC Fellow.

Routledge Critical Studies in Public Management
Edited by Stephen Osborne

The study and practice of public management has undergone profound changes across the world. Over the last quarter century, we have seen

- increasing criticism of public administration as the over-arching framework for the provision of public services,
- the rise (and critical appraisal) of the 'New Public Management' as an emergent paradigm for the provision of public services,
- the transformation of the 'public sector' into the cross-sectoral provision of public services, and
- the growth of the governance of inter-organizational relationships as an essential element in the provision of public services

In reality these trends have not so much replaced each other as elided or co-existed together—the public policy process has not gone away as a legitimate topic of study, intra-organizational management continues to be essential to the efficient provision of public services, whist the governance of inter-organizational and inter-sectoral relationships is now essential to the effective provision of these services.

Further, whilst the study of public management has been enriched by contribution of a range of insights from the 'mainstream' management literature it has also contributed to this literature in such areas as networks and inter-organizational collaboration, innovation and stakeholder theory.

This series is dedicated to presenting and critiquing this important body of theory and empirical study. It will publish books that both explore and evaluate the emergent and developing nature of public administration, management and governance (in theory and practice) and examine the relationship with and contribution to the over-arching disciplines of management and organizational sociology.

Books in the series will be of interest to academics and researchers in this field, students undertaking advanced studies of it as part of their undergraduate or postgraduate degree and reflective policy makers and practitioners.

Crossing Boundaries in Public Policy and Management
Tackling the Critical Challenges
Edited by Luke Craven, Helen Dickinson, and Gemma Carey

For a full list of titles in this series, please visit www.routledge.com

Crossing Boundaries in Public Policy and Management

Tackling the Critical Challenges

Edited by
Luke Craven,
Helen Dickinson, and
Gemma Carey

Routledge
Taylor & Francis Group

LONDON AND NEW YORK

First published 2019 by Routledge

2 Park Square, Milton Park, Abingdon, Oxon, OX14 4RN
605 Third Avenue, New York, NY 10017

Routledge is an imprint of the Taylor & Francis Group, an informa business

First issued in paperback 2020

Library of Congress Cataloging-in-Publication Data
Names: Craven, Luke, editor. | Dickinson, Helen, editor. |
   Carey, Gemma, editor.
Title: Crossing boundaries in public policy and management :
   tackling the critical challenges / edited by Luke Craven,
   Helen Dickinson, and Gemma Carey.
Description: New York City: Routledge, 2019. | Series: Routledge
   critical studies in public management | Includes index.
Identifiers: LCCN 2018046825 | ISBN 9781138636026
   (hardback) | ISBN 9781315206271 (ebook)
Subjects: LCSH: Public administration.
Classification: LCC JF1351 .C76 2019 | DDC 351—dc23
LC record available at https://lccn.loc.gov/2018046825

ISBN: 978-1-138-63602-6 (hbk)
ISBN: 978-0-367-73257-8 (pbk)

Typeset in Sabon
by Apex CoVantage, LLC

Contents

Contributor Biographies   vii

Introduction: The Inexorable Appeal of Boundaries
in Public Policy and Management   1
LUKE CRAVEN, GEMMA CAREY, AND HELEN DICKINSON

PART 1
The Concept Challenge   13

1 The Rise of Boundaries   15
   HELEN DICKINSON AND CATHERINE SMITH

2 Classifications of Boundaries   23
   HELEN DICKINSON AND CATHERINE SMITH

3 Boundary Concepts   38
   HELEN DICKINSON AND CATHERINE SMITH

4 Where Next for Boundaries?   53
   HELEN DICKINSON AND CATHERINE SMITH

PART 2
The Practical Challenge   63

5 The Challenges of Crossing Boundary Practice   67
   PAUL WILLIAMS

6 Lesson for Policy and Practice   70
   PAUL WILLIAMS

7 Training and Development   104
   PAUL WILLIAMS

8 Conclusions 108
PAUL WILLIAMS

PART 3
The Craft Challenge 119

9 Boundary Spanners: Toward a Theory of Practice 121
GEMMA CAREY, KERRY JACOBS, ELLIE MALBON, FIONA BUICK,
ANNA LI, AND PAUL WILLIAMS

10 The Theory Underpinning Crossing-Boundary Facilitation 135
CHRISTINE FLYNN

11 Towards the Craft and Practice of Facilitation Across
Collaborative Boundaries 165
CHRISTINE FLYNN

12 Conclusion 186
GEMMA CAREY, LUKE CRAVEN, AND HELEN DICKINSON

PART 4
The Methodology Challenge 191

13 Review, Methodological Approaches to Understanding
Collaborative Practice 193
LUKE CRAVEN, GEMMA CAREY, HELEN DICKINSON, AND
IONA RENNIE

14 A Spotlight on Systems Methodologies: Methods to
Understand Complex Issues 211
LUKE CRAVEN, GEMMA CAREY, HELEN DICKINSON, AND
IONA RENNIE

Conclusion: The Future of Boundary Spanning
Research and Practice 241
GEMMA CAREY, LUKE CRAVEN, AND HELEN DICKINSON

Index 257

Contributor Biographies

Fiona Buick is a Lecturer at the University of New South Wales, Canberra. Her research focuses on how human resource management can enable group and organisational effectiveness in the public sector. Research projects have explored the impact of organisational culture on joined-up working; how performance management can enable high performance; the factors that enable middle management capacity; and the factors that impede and enable structural change in the public sector.

Gemma Carey is Associate Professor and Research Director at the Centre for Social Impact UNSW. Dr Carey has investigated processes of 'joining up' within government and between government and non-government organisations. Her current research focuses on the design and implementation of the Australian National Disability Insurance Scheme and the challenges of quasi-markets in disability. Dr Carey has published over 60 articles on different aspects of public administration and health. Recent books include: "Grassroots to Government: Joining-up in Australia," and "Designing and Implementing Public Policy: Cross-sectoral Debates," "Managing and Leading in Inter-agency Settings."

Luke Craven is a Research Fellow in the Public Service Research Group at the University of New South Wales, Canberra. Luke's research focuses on developing new tools to understand and address complex policy challenges. He works with a range of public sector organisations to adapt and apply systems frameworks to support policy design, implementation and evaluation. Luke is known for developing the System Effects methodology, which is widely used to analyse complex causal relationships in participatory and qualitative data. He is also involved in number of collaborative projects that are developing innovative solutions to complex policy challenges, which includes work focused on food insecurity, health inequality and climate resilience. Luke holds a PhD in Political Science at the University of Sydney, where he remains affiliated with the Sydney Environment Institute and the Charles Perkins Centre.

Helen Dickinson is Associate Professor Public Service Research and Director of the Public Service Research Group at the School of Business, University of New South Wales, Canberra. Her expertise is in public services, particularly in relation to topics such as governance, leadership, commissioning and priority setting and decision-making. Helen has published 17 books and over 60 peer-reviewed journal articles on these topics and is also a frequent commentator within the mainstream media. She is co-editor of the Journal of Health, Organization and Management and Australian Journal of Public Administration. Helen is also a board member of the Consumer Policy Research Centre. In 2015 Helen was made a Victorian Fellow of the Institute of Public Administration Australia and she has worked with a range of different levels of government, community organisations and private organisations in Australia, UK, New Zealand and Europe on research and consultancy programmes.

Christine Flynn is a highly experienced consultant in organisational development, public sector governance and executive leadership in Australia. She is currently working with a range of national organisations on systems leadership, organisation change, leadership development and governance issues. She has been a senior executive in Commonwealth and state public services and has held several board roles. She is an accredited facilitator for the Australian Institute of Company Directors programmes for Board Chairs and Directors, Chief Executives and executive management. Christine is an experienced facilitator who designs and facilitates complex, multi-organisational processes for collaboration, co-design and co-creation where competing policies, values and cultures demand agile responses. Christine has worked with executive teams of public sector organisations in New Zealand and Australia, at the national, state and local government levels. Her fields of expertise are organisational development, board review and governance, strategy, leadership and senior executive development. Christine is an active researcher in the emerging public management space of connecting researchers and practitioners for improved connections and outcomes.

Kerry Jacobs, late of University of New South Wales Canberra, was a leading international researcher in public sector accounting and accountability. His many books and papers on public sector accountability and governance have made a profound contribution to our discipline. His research interests were focused on issues of public sector accountability, governance, audit, financial management and reform, particularly the relationship between accounting and politics.

Anna N. Li is a Postdoctoral Fellow at the Public Service Research Group, School of Business, UNSW Canberra. Her prior research has focused on regulation and contextual complexity in social welfare delivery, and the development of the third sector in Greater China. She currently examines inter-organisational relationships in policy implementation, and widely engages in collaboration with scholars on projects relating to public sector innovation in Australia and China.

Eleanor Malbon is a Research Fellow at the University of New South Wales. She holds a Combined Bachelor of Arts and Science from the ANU with first class honours in Human Ecology. Her specialisation within Human Ecology is system thinking methods to support public policy. Her work to date focuses on the insights that systems science can bring to policy that impacts upon the social determinants to health and to health equity. She is passionate about teaching. She has tutored for multiple courses within the Fenner School of Environment and Society and currently tutors for the course Complex Environmental Problems in Action.

Catherine Smith is an experienced educator and researcher in education, policy and community development, with international experience working in Canada, UK, Guinea-Bissau and Australia. In schools, she has specialised in teaching science, health and wellbeing, information technologies, learning interventions including EAL support, trauma recovery and assessment. Catherine's research and teaching explores the changing role of 'care' in policy and practice in state-society relationships. She focuses on the use of evidence in inclusive preventative health and well-being practices, and social emotional learning in different health promoting settings, particularly in schools. This work has also informed consultancy, course development and facilitation of executive education projects in public policy and management with public service participants and NGOs from Thailand and Indonesia. She is currently the project manager and research fellow on an ARC Linkage Researching Implementation Factors in Social Emotional Learning and a CI on a project Researching Policy Implications for the Use of Robots in Care Settings.

Paul Williams worked as a public sector manager for over 20 years in Welsh local government, before moving into academia where his career encompassed research, teaching and consultancy in public policy and management. He has undertaken a wide selection of research studies at local and national government levels in Wales on topics such as managing equality, sustainable development, community strategies, and working in collaboration. He has a track record of publications, reports and books in these areas and his particular research interests centre on collaboration, especially leadership, learning and knowledge management, integration of health and social care, and the role of individual agents—boundary spanners—in processes of collaboration.

Introduction

The Inexorable Appeal of Boundaries in Public Policy and Management

Luke Craven, Gemma Carey,
Helen Dickinson

Boundary work has always been an inevitable part of the discourse in public administration and public services. Boundaries, in their various forms, serve to mark what is in and out and where divisions are between things, whether they be policies, departments or ideas, lie. Although long recognised as important, the 1990s saw a worldwide push to more actively acknowledge and address these as an attempt to grapple with the 'wicked' public and social policy issues that implicate multiple government departments (Pollitt, 2003). Boundaries have, therefore, come centre stage in the fields of public policy and public administration—and have stayed central to many policy agendas since this time. Different forms of boundary work have been important in driving more efficient and/or effective policy development, implementation and service delivery. As Kelman (2008, p. 45) suggests, "topics of collaboration across government agencies and between government, private and non-government organisations are the most discussed questions" in public administration. Today we use a range of different terms to refer to this broad trend. The field of public administration has also expanded its treatment of boundaries to support policy and practice more effectively. Yet, there is little that is agreed on in this literature, beyond the idea that boundary work is necessary and is largely a good thing.

In the field of practice, governments internationally have become increasingly focused on designing ways and means of connecting across boundaries to achieve governmental and societal goals. Whether issues are complex and challenging—e.g. climate change, international terrorism, biosecurity, intergenerational poverty, health care or responding to global financial crisis—or the more straightforward provision of a single point of entry to government or delivering social security—governments around the world increasingly advocate the use of more collaborative, joined-up approaches that require cross-boundary connections. Connecting across government ministries or departments, across jurisdictions and across sectors all feature heavily in these developments. Yet, the fact remains that there is little examination of what practices are best practices, or what kind of boundary work is suited to many of the complex and emerging challenges that increasingly face governments in this century, what boundaries matter most and how should we approach them.

This book builds on the earlier collection "*Crossing Boundaries in Public Management and Policy*" from which it takes its name and inspiration. "*Crossing Boundaries in Public Management and Policy*" brought together what had been, to date, a highly fragmented and disorganised literature. It synthesised and crystallised challenges into boundary work in research and practice, drawing on diverse experiences. It emphasised that boundary spanners have consistently been shown to be important players in public policy and administration, which has come to be understood as characterised by plurality of processes, organisations and actors (Osborne, 2006). They enable better cross-sectoral and cross-departmental working (Head, 2014; Parston and Timmins, 1998) and are central for overcoming sub-cultural boundaries within government departments (Carey et al., 2017).

But, as O'Flynn et al. (2014) highlighted in the conclusion to the "*Crossing Boundaries in Public Management and Policy*" collection, we must be careful not to generalise when it comes to the practice or impact of crossing boundaries:

> Whilst there are zealous voices arguing that this is the 'one best way' of operating, our contributors are more pragmatic. Many note that there needs to be more focus on where this type of operating may be most effective, but that it is rarely *the* answer to governmental problems. As we have seen, there are various imperatives to the adoption of cross-boundary approaches, different forms are adopted in practice, and there are a range of factors that can inhibit or facilitate cross-boundary working. Trying to answer the fundamental questions demonstrates that this remains a complex field of study, and a profoundly complicated area of practice.
>
> (p. 303)

In this book we aim to provide an in-depth investigation of the boundary spanning literature, beginning from where O'Flynn and colleagues left off. Our goal is to synthesise and critique more recent developments, while emphasising that more can be done to understand the *complexity* of boundary crossing in research, policy and practice. As O'Flynn made clear in the earlier collection, one of the key frontiers for scholars of boundary spanning is taking a cross-disciplinary approach to understanding its operation in theory and practice. Put simply, there are important insights to be gained from a range of disciplines, and researchers may find that engaging with these different areas provides ways to move the field forward.

This book digs into the heart of enduring questions and challenges for cross-boundary working, providing in-depth conceptual and practical contributions on the fundamental challenges of boundary work. It arms readers with in-depth knowledge of the conceptual and practical challenges that sit at the heart of cross-boundary practice and research,

Aims of the Book

This book develops four key challenges that remain unresolved in the boundary-spanning literature, which reflect the complexity of the boundary-spanning field of study that O'Flynn made clear. These challenges span from the conceptual, to the practical, to the translational. In doing so, it tackles the question of boundary-spanning from four different angles— providing an in-depth investigation of the current state of the field in each of these realms, in addition to new directions for solving the identified challenges. Finally, the book synthesises the lessons from each of these (overlapping) challenges into a coherent and integrated final piece of the boundary problem. In doing so, it addresses both the fragmentation of the literature and provides a clearer agenda for future research and practice.

In line with the four major areas of focus for the book, it is oriented into four parts:

1. *The concept challenge*: what do we know about working across boundaries? How robust are our concepts? Where are the next conceptual developments to be found?
2. *The practice challenge*: how effective have we been at understanding practice and developing conceptual and theoretical understanding from it? How successfully have we translated this back into the practice of public management? How do boundary spanners work across and within different contexts or domains?
3. *The craft challenge*: do we understand the craft of working across boundaries? What areas of the practice of working across boundaries have been missed? What are the next areas for exploration in the practice of working across boundaries?
4. *The methodology challenge*: do our methodological approaches enable us to understand working across boundaries and build robust conceptual understanding? What methodological challenges do we face in understanding working across boundaries? What are the next methodological developments in the field?

These four areas, and the questions that underpin them, provide the connecting framework for the contributions to the book. Each of the authors has deliberately drawn from a broad range of literatures, in order to extend the boundary-crossing conversation beyond its usual suspects. Each Challenge is longer than a typical chapter, in a book of this type, reflecting our aspiration that the book provide both an in-depth investigation of the current state of the field in each of these realms, in addition to identifying new directions for solving these challenges. To not overwhelm the reader, these Parts are divided into a number of sections to aid the reading process. Relatedly, the editors made a deliberate choice to invite a diverse range of individuals to contribute to the book, both academics and practitioners, as well as from a range of geographic contexts. Each Part can be read as its own standalone piece of analysis, or as a cohesive collection, recognising that there is some inevitable overlap between these different domains.

The book is aimed at the many researchers, students and public servants who are confronting how to manage and relate across boundaries of organisations, sectors (public, private, third), and levels of government. We have attempted to draw on case studies and make some difficult material accessible, and there are also a number of sources cited so that those interested can read further. We now move on to provide a brief overview of the various parts and the arguments that they set out.

An Overview of the Parts

The Concept Challenge

Dickinson and Smith explore the conceptual literature around the ideas of boundaries and boundary work from a number of angles, drawing together a range of disciplinary perspectives. In doing so, they explore the various different ways that boundaries have been conceptualised within the literature from the material, stable, constraining and structural attributes suggested of the mainstream economics and commerce literature, through the symbolic, shifting, enabling facets outlined in the more interpretive accounts of decentred governance. Dickson and Smith argue that the way boundaries are conceptualised is not value neutral. Instead the choices that public policy and management scholars make about how to think about boundaries and their key features has significant implications for how boundary crossing emerges as a concept, practice and craft, a theme we return to throughout this volume. To make this argument they draw on the public management literature, as well as from insights in broader social theory literature (e.g. geography, sociology, international relations). In doing so, it aims to provide a new synthesis and critique of some of the potential conceptual resources we might draw on to understand boundaries and those that work across them.

As Dickinson and Smith note, greater evidence needs to be developed in relation to the most effective forms of boundary work for particular types of boundaries, with different aspirations in terms of changing or working across boundaries. They argue that while many of us can draw a range of conceptual resources from beyond public policy and management, more work remains necessary to be done to ensure that they are portable across these boundaries. In addition, although some have argued that 'boundary work' is the *modus operandi* of the 21st-century public servant (O'Flynn, 2014), the public administration literature is not well placed to support boundary work or those carrying out these tasks. There are surprisingly few works within public administration where boundaries are given exclusive attention as an object of analysis or inquiry in their own right. Instead, boundaries tend to be seen as the result of organising processes, or they are relegated to a secondary role in relation to the existing order. As the survey that Dickinson and Smith set out makes clear, what has been written is situated in a time when collaboration was an anomaly and structures affecting the everyday work of public servants were clear, static and singular (see also Bevir and Rhodes, 2011).

While much of the literature emphasises the idea of stable boundaries, for example, public/private, federal/state, citizen/bureaucrat, Dickinson and Smith's analysis makes clear that this notion of stability is no longer sufficient. They show that the dynamic nature of policy systems and subsystems—and the complexities of the many of the problems faced by modern societies—demands that we embrace a more dynamic and complex conceptualisation of boundaries themselves. In practice, boundaries are anything but the singular, static and immutable entities they are typically presented to be. Many of the challenges that arise in working collaboratively come from the interaction of multiple boundaries that change and shift over time, creating an ever more complicated environment in which public servants operate. This static structural approach also fails to account for important factors that drive dynamic, complex, unstable boundary-spaces.

This Part argues that continuing to treat boundaries in a static way limits the explanatory power of public administration theories and hinders the ability of public servants to work productively in a time where their practice demands the creation and curation of more collaborative environments to respond to increasingly complex problems (Dickinson et al., 2015). It acts as a continued call to the boundary-spanning community that we must rethink boundary notions to account for developments in practice, building on the work of Hernes and Paulsen (2003) almost a decade ago. As they make clear, there remains a "significant need for boundaries to be rediscovered and respecified" (pp. 2–3). Ultimately Dickinson and Smith make clear that we must move beyond assumptions of stability and developing more dynamic notions of boundaries can advance knowledge in the field of public administration. And, crucially, they show that this goal is not beyond our reach if we engage productively and critically across disciplines to explore the varied and multifaceted conceptualisations of boundaries present in the literature. In doing so, this Part lays the groundwork for the Parts that follow in exploring the practice of boundary work, methodologies for exploring boundary work and how we might translate theory into practice.

The Practice Challenge

In this Part, Williams explores how working across boundaries is understood in policy and practice. As he notes, the international public policy landscape is littered with numerous and diverse expressions of collaborative working, driven by frequent exhortations by policy makers and politicians to work in this mode of governance designed to tackle societal wicked issues. However, despite an accumulated body of practice and collective intent, collaborative working continues to be highly challenging in policy and practice with outcomes often less than optimum.

Taking this as his starting point, Williams re-examines and synthesises what we know about the determinants of effective collaboration including 'what works' and which levers are the most appropriate and effective to foster cross-boundary working. He draws on evidence from different policy areas, from different parts of the world and different stages of the policy process. In particular, he examines whether working between different sectors—public, private, third sector—presents any particular challenges and highlights areas of inter-sectoral learning. He asks what learning and knowledge management methods and carriers are the most effective, and how best to convert and translate what is known for the training, education and development of boundary-spanning agents. In doing so, the Practice challenge reflects on the question of whether leading and managing in collaboration is similar to or different from that in hierarchical forms of governance.

Williams frames his contribution within a practical framework that helps to understand the complicated interweaving and alchemy between structural and agential factors—particularly the manner in which different factors constrain and enable actions and interventions. Why is it that politicians and policy makers often reach for structural levers (reconfiguration, statutory powers, financial incentives) in an attempt to direct and manage the course of collaboration? Are these easier than attending to issues that relate to agency and culture? Or are these the most instrumental in determining outcomes?

Williams argues that we must develop approaches that can more explicitly frame what an effective boundary infrastructure might comprise—the key anchors and bridges and conversely the barricades and mazes that inhibit future collaboration. In particular, he focuses on exploring the challenges associated with working across the boundaries between academia and practice: what do practitioners want from research and how can the respective constituencies communicate most effectively with each other? Williams argues that it is important for practice to be translated into forms that are timely and digestible for practitioners through practice guides, workshops, training, consultancy and other mechanisms. By suggesting answers to this question, Williams consolidates and highlights what we know, and identifies future and fruitful areas of exploration for an interdisciplinary body of academic and practitioner interests.

The Craft Challenge

This Part explores boundary spanning, collaboration and transdisciplinary process as a craft that is practiced by those that cross boundaries. It is made of three sections that draw together contributions and perspectives from a range of authors. The first section has been contributed by a group of authors with an academic focus (led by Gemma Carey), and outlines a new theoretical and conceptual approach to exploring different types of boundary-spanning individuals based on their motivations and ways of operating. To do so, it draws on a range of social theories of the relationship between structure and agency to develop a theoretical typology of boundary-spanning individuals, which theorises why and how different boundary spanners operate and the likelihood that they produce institutional gains. As Carey et al. suggest, theorising boundary spanners in this way opens up the possibility that boundary spanners may act in ways that are counterproductive or counterintuitive, a point that has been seldom made in a literature that tends to cast boundary spanners in a positive light. By showing that boundary spanners can have constructive, neutral *and* deconstructive effects on institutional structure and responsiveness, the authors demonstrate that more attention needs to be paid to the complexities of boundary-spanning practice.

Sections 2 and 3 are contributed by Christine Flynn, and help extend our understanding of these same practical complexities by providing her own example of how boundary-spanning practitioners undertake their work. Drawing on public management case studies from her own practice, Flynn explores dimensions of boundary-spanning capability as a craft required to work across boundaries and create a safe space in which to achieve positive outcomes, while recognising that positive outcomes are not always a given.

Flynn's particular practice focuses on that of cross-boundary facilitation, which is a commonly used process to establish and build collaboration. The foundation of such a process is to invite a broad mix of stakeholders into a shared space, with the intent of establishing a collaborative network. The aspiration is that the network can continue to come together in various ways to build mutuality, reciprocity and trust in order to influence policy thinking and service implementation. Building collaborative capacity can be attempted through large and small group processes such as conferences, workshops, forums and meetings, as well as multiple communication channels. As Flynn shows, however, a number of questions about these processes, though, remains unanswered. How effective have we been at understanding practice and developing conceptual and theoretical understanding from it? How successfully have we translated this back into the practice of public management? These questions are at the heart of the Craft challenge.

Flynn argues that while we must acknowledge the existence of boundaries as real and powerful elements of governing a complex world, public management practitioners have developed different perspectives on what boundaries are and how to use them. These varying uses often reflect the political reality and systemic context in which a practitioner is working, which includes how different boundaries are valued by policy makers. Flynn argues that these uses range from boundary as a weapon, boundary as an excuse against innovation or positive risk, and boundary as a safety perimeter in which to engage in mutual learning.

This Part provides a comprehensive practical and theoretical overview of 'how' boundary spanners go about their practice, and draws clear links between the theory and practice of *being* a boundary spanner. By focusing on the practices and capabilities that underpin engagement and collaborative efforts between academics, citizens, community bodies and others, it shows that good practice requires boundary spanners integrate a range of research and strategic insights, on a broad range of public management challenges and themes into their craft. Finally, by exploring two recent Australian case studies where these practices worked, with uneven results, and critically analysing the current research discussions around the craft of boundary crossing, it provides a range of new models and tools to support boundary crossers as they go about their practice.

The Methodology Challenge

In this part, Craven et al. explore the methodological challenges of research on boundary spanning issues, by asking what *can* we know about crossing boundaries based on current research approaches? Through a detailed review and synthesis of these existing approaches, it suggests a range of strategies and innovations that address their limitations, as well as more readily respond to the complex realities of boundary crossing that the other Parts identify.

First, Craven et al. suggest much of the research on boundary issues reflects more general limitations in studies on wicked and complex policy problems. To make this point, they present a systematic review of methodological approaches used by empirical research that analyses boundary spanning at either the organisational, team or individual level. The review emphasises that the field is predominately comprised of single case studies from which authors hope to generalise, using mixed methods or social network analyses, and of studies that use the reflections of boundary- spanning practitioners. As Craven et al. argue, the result is that empirical research on boundary crossing is often caught between being too specific (i.e. the generalisation challenge) or not specific enough, seeking to describe specific cases without in-depth and nuanced investigation into the social practices and contextual complexities that sit at the core of boundary work. Following the review, the Part explores a range of strategies that can be used to simultaneously address the generalisation challenge, while maintaining a level of fidelity to the context of particular boundary-spanning initiatives, such as meta-synthesis and meta-analyses, comparative analysis and systems approaches that go beyond the current use of socio-metrics.

Second, Craven et al. review a range of methodologies that can help researchers and practitioners conceptualise issues, problems and social conditions that themselves cross boundaries and domains. Much of the work in public policy and administration is premised on the idea that the challenges we face are inter-sectoral, but to more effectively utilise boundary-crossing strategies we need methods to understand the *how* of wickedness and complexity. They provide a detailed overview of complexity theory, how it relates to theories of governance and 'wicked problems,' and what needs to be done to effectively operationalise it in practice. By emphasising a number of concrete strategies to operationalise complexity theory in practice—including approaches to modelling systems dynamics, group model building and other approaches to generating systems models from qualitative data—Craven et al. argue that it can and should be mobilised to understand the various inter-sectoral issues that scholars of public policy and management are interested in addressing.

They key point here is that the Methodological Challenge requires us to cross boundaries in and seek out disciplines which can offer new methodological tools, as well as conceptual and theoretical insights. As Craven et al. show, if we are committed to understanding the complexity of crossing boundaries in theory and practice, we must continue to critically examine boundaries between disciplines and their normative standards and approaches to knowledge, and how these might be overcome in order for us to capture, examine and progress the boundary problems faced by policy makers.

Overlapping Challenges: More Than the Sum of Their Parts

Drawing each of these challenges together, our overall aim is synthesise the lessons from each into a coherent and integrated final piece of the boundary problem. In doing so, we aim to address the fragmentation of the literature and provide a clearer agenda for future research and practice. Across these Challenges, we see a number of key questions that should orient our inquiry and engagement with the practice of boundary crossing: what types of boundaries are there? Why do we care about some boundaries more than others? What is it exactly we want to do with boundaries? What do we need to know about boundary crossers? What is the process and practice of crossing boundaries?

The point O'Flynn and colleagues made in the earlier collection *"Crossing Boundaries in Public Management and Policy"* resonates throughout this text: boundaries are complex. We argue that in order to more actively address that complexity in research, policy and practice, we need to explore the overlaps and interdependencies of the four challenges. Because boundary crossing as an object of inquiry crosses its own geographic, scalar, administrative and disciplinary boundaries, detail of one part of a given system can tell you little of the whole. Understanding the *complexity* of boundary crossing requires a broad field of vision, one that takes into consideration the conceptual, the methodological, and how they are operationalised as practice and craft. Changes in practice need to be studied and, ideally, can draw on the rich insights driven by methodological innovations. However, both of these need to start from a more robust conceptual basis that takes account of the multi-dimensions and dynamic nature of boundaries and boundary work. Put another way, any engagement with boundary spanning must recognise that we cannot separate theory from how it is operationalised in practice. Our understanding of boundary spanning extends only as far as the tools used to comprehend it, just as our capacity to act on particular understandings is bound up in those same means of comprehension. Certain methods do more than represent certain realities, but rather intervene and create them. And in the opposite direction, theories become real in their consequences because they constrain methodological possibilities, set the limits of normative reflection, and give direction to practical action. Without a robust conceptual starting point, research and practice will continue to miss critical elements of boundary problems.

We anticipate that the contributions found in this book will help advance our conceptualisations of boundaries and in turn, drive innovation in both research and practice. At the outset, there is no doubt that accepting boundaries and boundary work as complex raises its own set of challenges, but ultimately this is no cause for alarm. An approach that takes complexity seriously, while remaining critical and reflexive about what we know and how, can help move us toward an understanding of boundaries to address these challenges.

References

Bevir, M., & Rhodes, R. A. W. 2011, 'The stateless state', in M. Bevir (ed.), *The SAGE handbook of governance*, Sage Publications Ltd, London, pp. 203–217.

Carey, G., Buick, F., & Malbon, E. 2017, *The unintended consequences of structural change: When formal and informal institutions collide in efforts to address wicked problems*. www.tandfonline.com/doi/full/10.1080/01900692. 2017.1350708.

Dickinson, H., Sullivan, H., & Head, G. 2015, 'The future of the public service workforce: A dialogue', *Australian Journal of Public Administration*, vol. 74, no. 1, pp. 23–32.

Head, Brian W. 2014, 'The collaboration solution? Factors for collaborative success', in Janine O'Flynn, Deborah Blackman & John Halligan (eds.), *Crossing boundaries in public management and policy: The international experience*, Routledge, Abingdon, Oxon, pp. 142–157.

Hernes, T., & Paulsen, N. 2003, 'Introduction: Boundaries and organization', in N. Paulsen & T. Hernes (eds.), *Managing boundaries in organizations: Multiple perspectives*, Palgrave Macmillan, Basingstoke.

Kelman, S. 2007. 'The transformation of government in the decade ahead', in D. Kettl & S. Kelman (eds.), *Reflections on 21st century government management*, IBM Center for the Business of Government, Washington, DC.

O'Flynn, J. 2014, 'Crossing boundaries: The fundamental questions in public management and policy', in J. O'Flynn, D. Blackman & J. Halligan (eds.), *Crossing boundaries in public management and policy: The international experience*, Routledge, London.

Osborne, S. P. 2006, 'The new public governance?' *Public Management Review*, vol. 8, no. 3, pp. 377–387.

Parston, G., & Timmins, N. 1998, *Joined-up management*, Public Management Foundation, London.

Pollitt, C. 2003, *The essential public manager*, McGraw-Hill Education, United Kingdom.

Part 1

The Concept Challenge

Introduction

A large proportion of the critical work of public services takes place in and around the spaces that lie between jurisdictions, sectors, organisations and actors. These and other boundaries work to mark the limits of different problems, interests and activities and can create immense challenges—in skill, time and emotion—for those working across boundaries. As a result, 'boundary-work' is often considered the *modus operandi* of the modern public servant (O'Flynn, 2014). Yet, although the terminologies of boundaries and boundary-crossing are well embedded in the policy and academic literatures, there is often a failure to critically consider what it is that we mean by boundaries, what form they take and what we want to do in working across these. The familiarity of boundaries and the role that they play within our world may be partly responsible for the lack of critical attention spent conceptualising these entities. Boundaries are such a fundamental component of processes of human cognition and such a familiar idea they hide in plain sight.

Much of what has been written about boundaries in the public policy and public management literatures is situated in a time when collaboration was an anomaly and structures affecting the everyday work of public servants were clear, static and singular (Bevir and Rhodes, 2011). Such perspectives typically view boundaries as inhibiting the delivery of high quality public services and therefore something to be conquered, removed or overcome. The mainstream literature is congested with accounts of the challenges of working across boundaries, an activity that many public service organisations are reported to struggle with (Dickinson, 2014b). In recent years there have been frequent calls in the public policy and public management literatures to rethink and re-specify boundaries in order to improve the quality of public services and the ability of governments to meet the needs of their various constituencies (Heracleous, 2004; Hernes and Paulsen, 2003b; Lanham, 2006). This chapter aims to contribute to the process of this re-specification through an exploration of the conceptual basis of boundaries. In doing so we draw on a wide variety of different disciplinary contributions that go beyond the kinds of traditional literatures that are drawn on in the public policy and public management fields to develop a more inclusive set of ways that boundaries may be conceptualised.

This Part is organised into a series of chapters that explore the various ways that boundaries have been conceptualised within the literature: from the material, stable, constraining and structural attributes suggested of the mainstream economics and commerce literatures; through the symbolic, shifting, enabling facets outlined in the more interpretive accounts of decentred governance. In doing so, it explores: the different ways in which boundaries have been conceptualised; the key features of various boundary forms; and the implications of ways of viewing boundaries for the possibilities of working across them. Although there is at least a limited acceptance that a range of different forms of boundaries exist, there is typically more attention paid to some forms of these. Moreover, the solutions offered often involve the removal of boundaries, rather than working in and around these entities. The literature suggests that such interventions can cause new problems to emerge in and around boundaries, resulting in greater challenges than existed before. Ultimately the intention is that this Part lays the groundwork for those that follow in exploring the practice of boundary work, methodologies for exploring boundary work and how we might translate theory into practice.

The material in this Part is set out in four main chapters. The first deals with a number of issues relating to the rise of boundaries such as: why boundaries have gained prominence in recent years, why boundary work is important and what effective boundary blurring looks like. The second chapter moves on to consider how we can classify different types of boundaries and the impact of various boundary forms. The case is made that boundaries are entities that do more than just impede activity, as the more conventional literature would suggest, but they also do undertake important work that has implications for individuals and organisations. This is important to take into consideration when we think about what we are actually attempting to 'do' to boundaries when working in collaborative arrangements.

Chapter 3 focuses on 'boundary concepts,' providing an account of a range of terminology and ideas that have developed in relation to boundaries and boundary work. Definitions of these concepts are provided as are their relative merit and application within different settings. Chapter 4 considers where next for boundaries, arguing that the fields of public policy and public management are in need of a more dynamic means of conceptualising boundaries that will take into account a range of boundary types and an evidence base capable of supporting more effective boundary work. Taken together the four chapters of this Part provide a broad base in terms of the ways in which boundaries have been conceptualised which sets up the background for the discussions set out in the remaining Parts of the book.

1 The Rise of Boundaries

Helen Dickinson and Catherine Smith

Boundaries: Ubiquitous and Inevitable

A key part of the argument set out in this part is that boundaries are an ever-present and necessary part of our lives: be they physical boundaries (roads, doors), cultural boundaries (how to greet someone, what dress is appropriate), linguistic boundaries (which languages or words are appropriate), geographic boundaries (country border, mountain ranges), emotional boundaries (fear or affection for particular items or issues) or others. These boundaries vary in the degree to which there can be difficulties or even dangers in our attempts to break down or traverse these entities. As will be outlined in greater detail, where boundaries appear in the public policy and public management literatures it is typically alongside a discussion of their inherently problematic nature. This line of argument has somewhat of an enduring quality over both time and space. Perri 6 (1997) notes that from the start of the 20th century, UK politicians have argued for more inter-departmental working to overcome the challenges posed by administrative boundaries. Similar arguments have been made across a range of other geographical jurisdictions where the existence of boundaries has been argued to impede the effectiveness of public service systems (e.g. Schermerhorn, 1975; Sullivan and Skelcher, 2002; O'Flynn, Blackman, and Halligan, 2013).

What we find in the public policy and public management literature is that boundaries are described as being exceptional. However, boundaries exist all around us and are inevitable in the sense that they are necessary to the ways we make sense of the world around us. In fact, boundaries surround us and are a fundamentally important process in human cognition. In navigating everyday life, humans organise the things we encounter into 'discrete chunks,' e.g. 'normal,' 'perverse,' 'business,' 'pleasure' (Zerubavel, 1991). As Zerubavel (1996) describes, what is being done here is not the identification of natural groups but a series of mental clusters. This is an active process where individuals construct similarity between entities (through a process of 'lumping') and difference between things (through a process of 'splitting'). This process is not entirely subjective in the sense that it is learned as part of our cognitive socialisation (Zerubavel, 1997). To this extent, boundary-making is a form of relational work (Cabrera, Cabrera, and Powers, 2015). As an example of this, the rise of social media has led to often quite visible forms of boundary work as individuals actively work on their personal boundaries through their self-presented and cultivated public personas (Johnson and Ranzini, 2018). As we interact with others we refine our mental clusters through language and everyday experiences. We often take these mental structures for granted, particularly where they are reinforced by spatial or physical proximities—for example the division in our homes between culture (dining room) from nature (bathroom) and formal (living room) from informal (family room) (Zerubavel, 1996).

The ability to classify entities and to lump and split these into different groups is crucial in being able to navigate contemporary life. At their most basic we can think of boundaries as being mechanisms that categorise or distinguish one thing from another; whether those things are people, practices, places, objects, time or space. Boundaries are in essence a tool of demarcation (Gieryn, 1983). Akkerman and Bakker (2011) describe how boundaries simultaneously suggest a "sameness and continuity in the sense that within discontinuity two or more sites are relevant to one another in a particular way" (p. 133). Boundaries are, in this way, something that determine whether a bridge or a bond exists between two places, people, things or ideas. Boundaries, then, are something that is essential to life and our ability to navigate through it. However, once we move beyond a rather simplistic definition of boundaries being something that categorises or distinguishes or demarcates a particular terrain, they are described and treated in a number of different ways depending on the viewpoint or perspective adopted by those identifying these entities.

Our ability to understand what is happening around us is dependent on our capability to build boundaries along the axes of different social continua. However, the ubiquity and necessity of boundaries to our everyday activity may actually serve to hide these. Outside of the public policy and public management literatures, boundaries have a rich academic history, appearing in seminal works such as Marx (1963), Durkheim (1933) and Bourdieu (1979), amongst others. Boundaries have emerged as a crucial topic of study within a number of different disciplines including history, political science, sociology, anthropology, philosophy, organisational studies, economics, law, social psychology and even theoretical physics. However, in a review of the literature on boundaries in social sciences, Lamont and Molnár (2002) find that researchers who draw on this concept are often unaware of studies of boundaries beyond their own specialties across the social sciences. This chapter takes an expansive approach to the conceptualisation of boundaries in order to provide a more effective account of these entities than is found within the present literature.

Why is Boundary Work Important?

Over the years, the concept of boundaries has received sustained attention within public management and public policy circles. However, the level of interest and volume of discussion has accelerated over the past few decades, prompted by a number of drivers. It is not the intention of this chapter to explore these in detail as they are well-rehearsed elsewhere (e.g. O'Flynn, 2014; Dickinson, 2016). In conceptualising boundaries it is important that we consider the forces that have contributed to this increased focus on boundary work in public services. In this part, three major drivers that have contributed to this trend are considered: increased specialisation of work; increasingly disaggregated policy design and delivery contexts; and the complexity of problems that policy is seeking to deal with.

Across many different industries there has been a gradual trend towards specialisation. As Nicolini et al. (2012) observe, one of the "most notable characteristics of post-industrial society is that work is increasingly accomplished through collaboration among independent groups of disciplinary specialists" (p. 612). The rise of specialisation has created professionals who focus on particular areas (e.g. finance, information technology, administration, human resources) and agencies with narrow remits around a set of functions (e.g. regulatory and oversight, service delivery, policy development). The implication of this is associated boundaries around specialised knowledge and functions. These boundaries can be temporal, and defined by institutional memory and the mechanisms (or lack thereof) that facilitate an accessible history of what has been done before. This can be seen as stratified in the hybridisation of tools or practices, where the knowledge and the logic of the foundation on which tools and practices are scaffolded (Roberts and Beamish, 2017). Although this can be a helpful way to build specialised knowledge and expertise, if we do not have a full account of the constituent components of this knowledge it can limit its applications. The use of software systems, databases and other technologies is one example of this, where processes of the past can limit the functionality that can be built in the present and future. In practice, multiple different professionals and groups are required to work together to bring their expertise to bear on public service design and delivery. We have therefore seen an increasing amount of boundary work become necessary in order to overcome the challenges raised by the increasing specialisation of work.

In addition to the increasing specialisation of work, we have also seen the development of far more disaggregated policy design and delivery contexts in many systems around the world. This trend is often attributed to the influence that the New Public Management (NPM) philosophy has had in terms of who delivers public services within a contemporary context. NPM is often cited as being responsible for the opening up of public services, encouraging governments to work with third-party providers for the delivery of services, leaving them free to focus on more strategic and oversight issues (Osborne and Gaebler, 1993; Ferlie et al., 1996). It is certainly true that many public service systems have seen a reduction in the volume of services directly delivered by government and an increase in those delivered by private or not-for-profit organisations working under contract to government (Alford and O'Flynn, 2014). This pattern has created a rather complex and disaggregated public service delivery context in many cases that necessitates greater amounts of work across the multiplicity of resulting boundaries (Dickinson and Carey, 2016).

Alongside this increasingly complex service delivery context, we have also seen a rise in the number of individuals and organisations seeking a voice in the design and delivery of public services. Many governments around the world are facing lower levels of trust than they have previously seen (Sullivan, 2015). Indeed, research found that satisfaction with democracy in Australia is at its lowest level since 1996 and levels of trust in government and politicians are at their lowest level since 1993 (Evans, Stoker, and Halupka, 2016). In 2015 just 16% of those surveyed by the Scanlon Foundation considered that the system of government 'works fine as it is' and less than 10% indicated a 'lot of trust' in the federal parliament (Markus, 2015). Those who are wealthier and older are more trusting of government (Edelman Trust, 2016). Moreover, the increasingly diverse populations that exist in many different areas mean that governments are being more and more encouraged to think about the particular needs and interests of different individuals and groups (Phillimore et al., 2015) Perhaps it is therefore unsurprising that we have seen increasing numbers of interest groups, think tanks, community organisations etc., who have sought to have a greater voice in policy processes than before. Accordingly, we have seen a rise in considerations of participative governance mechanisms (Wagenaar and Cook, 2003) and a focus on the theme of co-production (Alford, 2016, Pestoff, Brandsen, and Verschuere, 2012).

As Dickinson (2014b) describes, one of the rationales of the NPM movement was that it should enhance transparency in public service design and delivery, replacing the rather opaque and exclusive networks of individuals that were perceived to sit at the heart of government. In practice these networks were not opened up and made more transparent, but arguably became even more opaque than those that they replaced. The increased diversity of organisations, agencies and individuals involved in public services delivery contexts and the new nature of specialised organisations means that networks are more apparent. Paulsen (2003) concludes that these forces mean that 'intergroup functions' (p. 16), i.e. boundary work, are even more important than ever before.

The final driver we consider here is that related to the types of problems that contemporary public service organisations face. It has been argued that these have become more complex in recent years and are often referred to as 'wicked issues.' Originally coined by Rittel and Webber (1973), this phrase is used to refer to problems that are very difficult (or even perhaps impossible) to solve because of a number of potential reasons including: incomplete or contradictory knowledge; the number of people and opinions involved; the large economic burden; and the interconnected nature of these problems with others. Examples of wicked issues include things like climate change, social injustice, nuclear disarmament, disease epidemics and poverty. Williams (2002) argues that such problems disrespect boundaries, which "bridge and permeate jurisdictional, organizational, functional, professional and generational boundaries" (p. 104). These problems are capable "of metamorphosis and of becoming entangled in a web of other problems creating a kind of dense and complicated policy swamp" (p. 104). It has therefore been argued that boundaries have come to the forefront of public policy and public management practice as governments (and academics) are increasingly looking to 'wicked' or complex issues.

By their very nature we might question the degree to which wicked problems are amenable to resolution. Moreover, as Dickinson (2014b) argues, there has often been somewhat of a tendency for governments to reconstruct wicked issues as rather more tame (and therefore manageable issues) in order to gain the political legitimacy to be able to take action around a particular area. Within this context, it is perhaps unsurprising that attempts to work across or blur boundaries have not always been successful. Yet, as we will see in more detail later in relation to the coordination of activity across boundaries, governments have not always achieved their stated goals. Even where there have been substantial investments in expansive new information technology systems, such as we saw with the reorganisation of British child protection services at the start of this century (see White, Hall, and Peckover, 2009; White et al., 2010), attempts to communicate across boundaries have not always been unqualified successes.

The three drivers outlined previously (in addition to those featured in O'Flynn, 2014), describe a situation where individuals and organisations are expected to carry out greater amounts of work across boundaries than ever before. Boundaries are therefore more visible today in the practice of public policy and public management. As Cortada et al. (2008) assert, "more connectedness and cooperation is needed than ever before: across agencies, across governments and with more constituencies" (p. 2). They describe a need for governments to develop 'perpetual collaboration' capacities to work across boundaries. Others too have argued strongly for the need for governments to work across boundaries and collaborative working has become an important function for contemporary public services (Williams, 2012; Bevir, 2013). Yet, despite the importance of working across boundaries, the literature often points to collaboration as something that is not always done well (Mayntz, 1993; Jessop, 2000; Carey, Landvogt, and Barraket, 2015). This perceived failure is all the more problematic because we have seen many examples of the blurring of seemingly immutable boundaries in other areas of public life.

Effective Boundary Blurring

In the broader literature, there are countless accounts of boundaries being 'blurred,' whereby they are rendered benign through some sort of process. These observations are of interest in a public management context where boundaries seemingly pose greater challenges than ever. As examples of this, Hernes and Paulsen (2003a) chart a recent trend towards the blurring of boundaries in arts, fashion and politics. The rise of technology and its presence in our everyday lives through smart phones and other devices have: disrupted the traditional limits of home and work (Derks et al., 2014); blurred the lines between the real and virtual worlds (Lazarević et al., 2015); changed the relationship between space and place (Mosco, 2009); and even between past and future (Hüppauf and Weingart, 2008). Of course, the suggestion that it is possible to blur boundaries implicates that these entities exist in the first place in a clear, identifiable and shared way—a position that will be challenged further later.

In Western Europe there have been a number of discussions of the idea of a 'borderless world' (Van Houtum and Strüver, 2002). The Schengen Agreement was adopted into European Union law in the late 1990s and led to the gradual abolition of common border controls. Today many European workers, and even school children, cross state borders on a daily basis no longer restricted by the need to present passports or visas. The opening of these boundaries was

> accompanied by the coming together of nations of peoples who had formerly been antagonistic towards each other. The road from perceived hatred and fear to a situation in which borderland residents commute on a daily basis to a neighbouring country, or allow their children to be educated in a different cultural milieu, was a gradual one, during which time information about, and familiarity with, the other, increased.
>
> (Newman, 2003, pp. 20–21)

In recent years the desirability of the openness of these borders has come under question given waves of mass emigration from countries such as Syria. These examples require an additional boundary navigation, as the commitments of past supranational agreements, such as *The United Nations Convention Relating to the Status of Refugees* come into conflict with the directions of newer agreements, such as the *EU Dublin*

Regulation which assigns responsibility for refugee status determination and support to the country that an asylum seeker first enters. Likewise, the decision of the UK to leave the European Union creates an evolving case study of the boundaries which need to be navigated when such an agreement dissolves. However, an important question remains regarding why we can see such profound blurring and overcoming of boundaries in technology, time, space and place and yet boundaries are still so difficult to overcome within the context of public policy and public management?

What's the Problem with Boundaries in Public Policy and Public Management?

There is growing consensus within the literature that at least part of the reason for an inability to work effectively across boundaries is an overly simplistic or inadequate understanding of what these entities actually are. The idea of stable boundaries, for example, public/private, federal/state, citizen/bureaucrat, has underpinned this type analysis for decades; however this notion of stability is no longer sufficient within the contemporary era (Hernes, 2004). Lanham (2006) argues that boundaries are a topic that is dramatically underworked and will need interpreting in new ways if the various espoused challenges for public policy and public services are to be addressed.

As Marshall (2003) argues, "although the language of boundaries regularly makes an appearance in organization theory, efforts to conceptualize them have remained by and large less than explicit" (p. 56). There are:

> surprisingly few works where boundaries are given exclusive attention. Boundaries tend to be seen as the result of organizing processes, or they are relegated to a secondary role in relation to the existing order. In either case, they are not given the status as phenomena giving rise to their own dynamics.
>
> (Hernes and Paulsen, 2003b, p. 3)

Heracleous (2004) comments that the failure to appropriately account for boundaries in theory has important implications for our understanding of these;

> in the management literature . . . there has been little serious and concerted study of the formation, properties and consequences of boundaries per se as complex, shifting, socially constructed entities. Organizational boundaries are often treated as socially and organizationally unproblematic, to be determined by considerations of economic efficiency.
>
> (p. 95)

Treating boundaries in this limited way "can arguably be seen as parsimonious to the point of reductionism, caricaturing complex phenomena in terms of propositions that are clear but perhaps not always enlightening on actual boundary decisions taken by managers" (p. 96). As a result of the failure to treat boundaries in an appropriate way, the mainstream public policy and public management literatures are not well placed to support boundary work or those carrying out these tasks.

To summarise the argument that has been set out in this part so far, boundaries are not new entities in either theory or practice but have become increasingly identified as important components of the work of governments, public policy, public services and public servants alike. Driven by a range of factors, we are seeing greater attention being paid to boundaries than ever before. Although other areas of public life have reported successes in working across and blurring boundaries, the same kinds of successes are not quite as prevalent within the public policy and public management literatures. One of the reasons offered for this is a failure to effectively conceptualise boundaries and a tendency to treat these in a rather simplified manner.

2 Classifications of Boundaries

Helen Dickinson and Catherine Smith

As the previous chapter identified, there are a range of different ways in which we can classify boundaries and these have impacts for the ways in which we view boundaries, the impact they have on ways of organising and the implications of this in terms of how we think about working across boundaries. In this chapter we move on to provide a more detailed account of the different ways in which we can classify these entities. Often a simplistic binary division is used identifying boundaries as cages or networks. However, we argue that this distinction is rarely as straightforward as this might seem. Having made this argument, we move on to set out some more nuanced ways of distinguishing between different forms of boundaries, explore what boundaries are made of and consider what it is we want to do to boundaries.

Boundaries as Cages or Networks

Reflecting the simplified way in which boundaries are often treated, they are typically viewed as within one of two contrasting groups (Halffman, 2003; Quick and Feldman, 2014b). The first treats boundaries as barriers that reinforce separations between groups of people, organisations or institutional entities—'cages.' The second sees boundaries as more porous or tenuous—'networks.'

The first group typically views boundaries as a form of 'container' and is often described as a ***Parsonian view of boundaries*** after the American sociologist Talcott Parsons, best known for his work on structural functionalism (e.g. Parsons, 1971, 1977, 2005). Parsons viewed systems (e.g. social, cultural or personalities) as having boundaries, with parts comprising the inside and outside. A system comprises a series of interconnected parts (Adams and Sydie, 2001) where the components can be structures or institutions (e.g. the legal system, religious institutions or the economy) or smaller subsystems (e.g. a family, an individual or a group). Each system has certain needs or conditions that are necessary for the system to continue operating and to survive. Systems work to maintain their boundaries and relations of the parts to the whole in an ordered way. Parsons argued that the internal components therefore work in a self-regulating way to maintain equilibrium within a system. According to such a perspective, societies are ordered into a series of 'containers' that reinforce differences between groups as these are important for the overall operation of the system. Hernes (2003) argues that a Parsonian view prevails in mainstream organisation theory, where "the idea of the organization as essentially a boundary maintaining system is widely entertained" (p. 35). In this sense an organisational boundary is essentially

> a device of internal ordering and external protection . . . boundaries work as enclosure where they constrain the flow of new opportunities and ideas. On the other hand, they also help form stability in time and space enabling individuals and groups to develop their distinctive strengths that enable them to act effectively outside themselves.
>
> (pp. 35–36)

The second category of boundaries is typically described as a *socio-cultural perspective*, viewing boundaries as constructions. The issue for Barley and Kunda (2001) is not "whether boundaries do or do not exist, but how and where people draw boundaries" (p. 78). Such a perspective starts from the view that boundaries do not pre-exist as material entities, but are constructed by actors and/or actions (Abbott, 1995). Socio-cultural readings of boundaries focus on how people create entities by linking those boundaries into units: "Social entities come into existence when social actors tie social boundaries together in certain ways" (Abbott, 1995 p. 860). The implication of this reasoning is that boundaries are in one sense the outcome of struggles between different groups in the classification of reality in terms of which are deemed most legitimate (Gieryn, 1983). Boundaries are not *a priori* entities, but are the result of work done by people—they are constructed.

Jasanoff (1987) argues this means that boundaries are constituted by language, rather than material entities (albeit that some items may hold particular meaning as boundary objects—which will be covered in more detail later) and boundary disputes largely play out in the realm of language. Similarly, Akkerman and Bakker (2011) describe boundaries as a "socio-cultural difference leading to discontinuity in action or interaction" (p. 133). According to such a perspective, boundaries are not given entities but are continually open to negotiation. Writing from an organisational studies perspective, Hernes (2004) views boundary-drawing as intrinsic to the very process of organising. Boundaries are "not by-products of organization, but rather organization (defined broadly, ranging from informal groups to formal organizations) evolves through the process of boundary setting. Like any social system, an organization emerges through the process of drawing distinctions" (p. 10). The important point Hernes is making here is that organisations are in some senses incentivised to reproduce and sediment boundaries as they are essential to their survival. It is well established in the literature that it can be difficult to drive change in organisations (Kanter, 1989). At least some of the problem here relates to the fact that organisational change involves the unsettling and re-drawing of boundaries (Balogun et al., 2005).

The two categories of boundaries described earlier treat these entities in different ways and represent the two poles of debate. In the first, boundaries are more fixed and contain a series of activities within. These boundaries are typically less porous and actors often have little influence in shaping and reshaping these, with this job falling to the broader system as it establishes equilibrium. The latter perspective views boundaries as constructed through language as part of a process of interaction between different actors and therefore more permeable and open to negotiate. One major difference between these perspectives is the room they make for structure and agency within their conceptualisation of boundaries.

In considering the major determinants of social phenomena, social theorists often distinguish between social structure and individual actions (human agency). Contest comes about in terms of the relative importance of these factors. In the Parsonian view of boundaries, social structure is seen as the crucial factor in creating boundaries within systems. In the socio-cultural perspective of boundaries, there is more room for agency—that is, the volitional and purposeful nature of human activity. This observation is important because social structures have typically been viewed as having a constraining effect on human activity, while agency is seen as a way of individuals to act independently of these constraining structures. As Dickinson (2014b) argues, the literature on public service collaboration is dominated largely by structural accounts, often making little room for agency (see also Dickinson and Sullivan, 2014). Although in more recent years, the literature has attempted to draw greater attention to issues of agency through an interpretive turn associated with decentred governance (Bevir and Rhodes, 2003). On the whole, however, considerations of boundaries largely remain situated within a structuralist paradigm.

Attempts have been made to bring together these two categories of boundaries, viewing both as simultaneously a function of the activity of the system and a product of the strategy of description involved. According to such a perspective, boundaries are not seen either as a purely 'real' or an 'imagined entity' but are both/and. Boundaries are emergent properties of the interaction of structure and agency and therefore inseparable from either. Notable contributions to this debate come from the so-called British School of Complexity (Cilliers, 1998; Byrne and Callaghan, 2014), the field of relational sociology (Donati and Archer, 2015), in discussions of structuration theory (Giddens, 1993) and even feminist quantum physics (Barad, 2007). In considering the operation and impact of boundaries in public policy and public management, it is important that consideration is given to both potential facets of boundaries and they are not seen as simply residing at either end of the structure/agency, cage/network continuum.

Classifying Boundaries

Beyond the broad distinction between boundaries as cages or networks, there are a range of different ways that we can classify boundaries. One way is in a purely descriptive sense, relating to the level these boundaries emerge at, or around which kinds of phenomena. There are a number of examples of this, such as: Miller and Rice (1967) who distinguish between task (the work objectives of an organisation) and sentient (human needs of workers) boundaries; Van Maanen and Schein (1979) who distinguish between functional, hierarchical and inclusionary boundaries; and Hirschorn and Gilmore (1992) who write about authority boundaries, political boundaries, task boundaries and identity boundaries. In a study of leadership as a form of boundary work in health organisations, Chreim et al. (2013) describe a number of different types of boundaries including those relating to role, profession, knowledge, task and hierarchy (p. 204).

In a review of different types of boundaries found in the social science literature, Lamont and Molnár (2002) identify the following areas:

- Social and collective identity
- Class, ethnic/racial, and gender/sex inequality
- Professions, knowledge, and science
- Communities, national identities and spatial boundaries.

In addition to these more descriptive categories, the authors go on to distinguish between symbolic and social categories, explaining:

> Symbolic boundaries are conceptual distinctions made by social actors to categorize objects, people, practices, and even time and space. They are tools by which individuals and groups struggle over and come to agree upon definitions of reality. . . . Symbolic boundaries also separate people into groups and generate feelings of similarity and group membership. . . . They are an essential medium through which people acquire status and monopolize resources.
>
> (Lamont and Molnár, 2002 p. 168)

Table 2.1 Hernes' (2004) Framework for Interpreting Boundaries

	Mental boundaries (relate to core ideas and concepts that are central and particular to the group or organisation)	Social boundaries (relate to identity and social bonding tying the group or organisation together)	Physical boundaries (relate to forma rules and physical structures regulating human action and interaction in the group or organisation)
Ordering The extent to which boundaries regulate internal interaction	To what extent are the main ideas and concepts decisive for what members do?	To what extent do members feel that they are socially bonded together by, for example, loyalty	To what extent do formal rules or physical structure regulate the work of members?
Distinction The extent to which boundaries constitute a clear demarcation between the external and the internal	To what extent are the core ideas and concepts distinctly different from those of other groups?	To what extent are we socially distinct from other groups?	To what extent does our formal structure set us apart from other groups or organisations?
Threshold The extent to which boundaries regulate flow or movement between the external and the internal spheres	To what extent can outsiders assimilate core ideas and concepts?	To what extent is it possible for outsiders to be considered full members of the group?	To what extent do formal structures hinder the recruitment of outsiders?

(Hernes, 2004 p. 13)

Social boundaries are the differences resulting in unequal access to resources, be they material or nonmaterial, and social opportunities: "They are also revealed in stable behavioural patterns of association, as manifested in connubiality and commensality" (p. 169). What this demonstrates is that boundaries can be intangible in nature (related to behaviour, identities or cultures), but have a significant impact on those individuals and organisations around them.

Hernes (e.g. 2003, 2004) has written extensively on boundaries within the context of organisational studies and draws heavily on the work of Henri Lefebvre in doing so. Although Lefebvre's work is principally about philosophy and sociology, Hernes argues that these distinctions are also relevant to organisation studies. Lefebvre (1991) makes the distinction between three different sorts of space; physical, social and mental. Hernes argues that Lefebvre's distinction between these three forms of space are similar to orderings of social life found in the works of other prominent sociologists such as Scott (1995) and Giddens (1984). *Physical space* relates to the material—typically those things that can be touched. However, Hernes distinguishes between three different aspects of physical boundaries as they relate to organising processes: the material (e.g. walls), access to information, and rules and regulations.

Social space encompasses the social relations that enable production and reproduction. This factor relates to identity and how groups maintain norms of behaviour. *Mental space* refers to theory and to meaning. The category of mental boundaries in Hernes' work refers to the types of ideas and symbols that enable groups to communicate, to act and to understand. Mental boundaries are therefore important in terms of how we make sense of the world. Hernes (2004) draws on these three categories of boundaries to set out a framework which can be used as a way of interpreting boundaries (set out in Table 2.1). This framework starts to develop questions that can be used to interrogate different forms of boundaries in terms of their impact and effect.

What Are Boundaries Made of and What Do They Do?

If there are different forms of boundaries, comprising various elements, it follows that it is likely these will exert different kinds of impacts. Facets of this will be recognisable to most of us as we go about negotiating different boundaries in our day-to-day life. We implicitly know that some boundaries are highly policed (e.g. crossing between two countries), but others are more porous (e.g. crossing between states or counties within a country). Transition over boundaries can be facilitated via possession of appropriate items (e.g. passport or visa—more is said about boundary objects later) and hindered by their absence. Some boundaries have significant and sustained histories that render them immutable, while others are newer and subject to revision with less resistance. Some are highly controversial (e.g. Israel/Palestine) and others viewed as 'natural' (e.g. the geographical limits associated with islands).

Even after some boundaries are formally erased or superseded, they remain virtual, with the potential to be reinstituted in the future (Shields, 2006). Traversing some boundaries can signal great changes in terms of language, culture and beliefs, although others may render little in the way of difference. These points remind us that although there may be differences in 'objective' and 'subjective' boundaries, both are powerful in their own right. Crossing physical boundaries between states can be far easier than traversing borders between cultural and religious groups (Newman, 2006). This discussion also highlights the fact that there are many different types of boundaries and the form and extent of their impact is driven by several factors, including the actors that operate in these spaces. There is no simple, stable and static story of boundary work (see later for further discussion of the idea of boundary work). As Halffman (2003) reminds us, we cannot just reduce boundaries to language. Ideas, concepts, values and beliefs all have important implications for how we go about our everyday work.

Hernes (2003) attempts to capture some of the notion of the composition and effect of boundaries through a discussion of the 'texture' of boundaries. In doing so, one of the important distinctions made relates to whether boundaries act as a constraining or enabling mechanism. Often the discussion of boundaries in the context of public policy and public management relates to the ways in which they constrain or inhibit activity. As Quick and Feldman (2014b) describe, "previous conceptualizations often presume not only that these boundaries are tangible, but also that they are barriers that must be overcome" (p. 673). The solution typically offered in this context is to remove boundaries or, at the very least, to find ways to work across these so they do not detrimentally impact on the operation of those involved. However, it is important to recognise that while boundaries can constrain, they may also enable in the sense that they allow individuals and groups to mobilise the energies and resources to act (Giddens, 1984).

As a number of authors have noted, collaboration (working across boundaries) is typically seen as being a 'good thing' and as embodying positive values (Sullivan and Skelcher, 2002; O'Flynn, 2009; Dickinson and Glasby, 2010). Boundaries, on the whole, are described more negatively. Miller et al., (2011) illustrate this in their discussion of the UK Labour government's commitment to address perceived boundaries between health and social care services, where the then Secretary of State for Health described this as the need to 'break down the Berlin Wall.' This is a powerful metaphor, where the boundaries between health and social care are likened to such a formidable barrier that could be transcended—although at the risk of death or imprisonment. In reality boundaries between public agencies are rarely quite this dramatic, although multiple reports into failings in, for example child safeguarding, do highlight that a failure to work collaboratively can result in very real implications for individuals and communities (Glasby and Dickinson, 2014).

It is important to recognise that in addition to being constraining entities, boundaries also have enabling properties in the sense that they help form stability and allow individuals and groups to develop strengths. Cilliers (2001) discusses this in the field of complex systems theory in an attempt to chart a middle ground between Parsonian and socio-cultural perspectives of boundaries, arguing that boundaries are simultaneously a function of the activity of the system itself and a product of the strategy description involved. Within the context of research into groups, Berg and Smith (1990) describe this as being a paradox, whereby boundaries limit the action of groups but also make it possible for them to take action. Hernes (2003) elaborates on the idea of boundaries being both enabling and constraining entities, setting out some of the ways in which this takes place across three classifications of boundaries (mental, social and physical). This is important because the boundary type and the effect that it has varies across the different forms. Hernes outlines examples of constraining boundaries across different forms, namely:

- Mental boundaries—indoctrination groupthink and alienation ('not-invented-here' syndrome)
- Social boundaries—conformity to norms of behaviour, exercise of power through social interactions
- Physical boundaries—internal control through segregation, or surveillance.

Examples of enabling boundaries include:

- Mental boundaries—the basis for sense making, innovation and learning
- Social boundaries—the basis for identity, belonging and interpersonal trust
- Physical boundaries—stability and resources for developing knowledge and skills.

Within the literature on borders (associated with the disciplines of International Relations and Geography), there is a different way of describing their impact on the local area than is typically set out in the public policy and public management literature. Martinez (1994) describes this in terms of the generation of different forms of borderlands. He categorises these into:

- *Alienated borderlands*—tension prevails, the border is functionally closed and there is little cross-border interaction
- *Co-existent borderlands*—stability is on and off, although there is little cross-border interaction
- *Independent borderlands*—stability is in place most of the time as is cross-border interaction and over time we might see the expansion of borderlands
- *Integrated borderlands*—stability is strong and permanent, residents perceive themselves as part of one system.

Although a different analysis to that set out in the organisational theory or management literatures, what this illustrates is that although borders can be constraining and enabling, they are not simply barriers to movement, but can "also constitute gateways" (Rumford, 2006b p. 135). What this highlights is that boundaries need to be enacted in order to produce impacts and effects—they are not given or predetermined. Barad (2007) makes a similar observation in writing about boundaries in the context of scientific inquiry, arguing that these are produced through an iterative process where the enactment of a particular boundary is what develops the nature and content of these entities.

A key point to draw from the discussion of the work of Hernes and others is that boundaries are not static, but dynamic entities that are the product of the interaction of material and ideational factors (Yuval-Davis, 2004). As an example of this, Dickinson (Dickinson, 2010, 2014b; Dickinson and Sullivan, 2014, 2016) discusses the enactment of boundaries in her work exploring the performance of collaboration and the impact of collaborative working arrangements. She argues that traditional research approaches have not managed to capture the full range of different performances that boundaries produce, arguing that they have traditionally remained restricted to techno-bureaucratic understandings of the work of collaboration. There is an 'added value' to collaboration that is missed when such an approach is taken. Drawing on the work of McKenzie (2001), Dickinson argues that performance is not a simple, coherent and stable concept, but one that is dynamic, adaptive to and reflective of, prevailing socio-cultural and discursive forces. McKenzie identifies three inter-linked performance paradigms—organisational, technological and cultural—that Dickinson uses in this work to interrogate the impact of boundaries.

Organisational performance prioritises efficiency, achieving more for less by employing tools of performance improvement such as setting targets, identifying relevant performance indicators and measures, and initiating regular reviews and assessments. These tools are employed within a culture of worker 'empowerment,' decentralising decision-making to teams and individuals in order to foster creativity and innovation. This paradigm dominates public management systems in the global north and is immediately familiar to those who work in and/or study them. Assessments of collaborative performance mimic these tools, for example devising targets for and indicators of collaborative performance. They also assume a rational basis for collaborative action—i.e. collaboration will lead to improved outcomes that are tangible and measurable (see Sullivan et al., 2013 for a discussion of this). Returning to the distinction between enabling and constraining boundaries, the workings of the organisational performance paradigm can be understood as simultaneously liberating, freeing individuals to be creative in pursuit of efficiency, and constraining, regulating how that freedom is exercised through the institutionalisation of performance regimes.

Technological performance promotes effectiveness. McKenzie focuses attention on the way in which technological advancements can enhance the performance of everyday objects as well as highlighting the creation of a niche group of 'high-performance' objects constituted by 'cutting-edge' technologies working together. For our purposes, the technological paradigm is relevant because of the contribution of machines and innovations, particularly computers, telecommunications and robotics, to improving the overall performance of other systems, including public policy and/or service delivery systems. Ironically perhaps, public policy and public service collaboration often experience technology as a barrier to enhanced collaborative activity with examples of incompatible IT systems preventing, rather than promoting, improved performance (Sullivan and Williams, 2009).

Cultural performance privileges social efficacy, the constitution of meaning and affirmation of values that is achieved via an engagement with social norms. Drawing on Performance Studies literatures, McKenzie identifies cultural performance as an expression of staged or ritualised representations or enactments of particular social and cultural traditions. Performances may be transformative or transgressive, encouraging and securing conformance to a set of traditions and values or promoting subversion of those same traditions and values in pursuit of others. Cultural performance then can offer the means of both reaffirmation and resistance. This paradigm offers an opportunity to view collaboration differently, to explore it as "a performance act, interactional in nature and involving symbolic forms and live bodies, [that] provides a way to constitute meaning and affirm individual and cultural values" (Stern and Henderson, 1993 p. 3).

A summary of the three different performance types is set out in Table 2.2. What this analysis means in the context of this discussion is that we cannot just look at the actions (and interactions) of individuals and organisations as being primarily motivated by rational motives: their meaning goes beyond this. Decisions to collaborate are likewise complex, driven by motivations that are not rational but reflective of particular values or meanings that are attached to collaboration. Dickinson argues that exploring these motivations might provide helpful insights into why actors opt for, or persist with, collaboration in the face of limited evidence of its capacity to improve outcomes. In addition, the idea of cultural performance allows us to consider collaboration as a means of transforming services in line with dominant societal values and/or subverting dominant norms or ways of doing things in pursuit of alternative values. In exploring a number of different policy areas through the lens of cultural performance (child safeguarding, urban regeneration, health and social care), rather than simply organisational efficiency or technological effectiveness, Dickinson (2014b) offers alternative explanations for why actors collaborate that are based on discursive representation and construction of social efficacy, shape and constrained by social values and individual agents' attachment to them and/or interpretation of them.

Table 2.2 The Three Dimensions of Collaborative Performance

	Efficiency	*Effectiveness*	*Efficacy*
Paradigm	Performance management	Techno-performance. No specific paradigm, although closely aligned with computer science	Performance studies
Tools and techniques	Setting targets, performance indicators and measures, pay for performance, restructuring	Computers, statistical modelling, computer-aided design	Dramaturgy, reflexive practices, storytelling, ethnography
Performance is. . .	Rational, it can be controlled for, predicted, managed, and ultimately delivered	Satisficing, different facets of performance are weighed up against one another. It is the result of a long and open series of negotiations and compromises	Always interactional in nature, it can both reaffirm existing traditions and beliefs or resist and adapt these

Source: Dickinson and Sullivan (2014 p. 165)

This analysis demonstrates that boundaries are not just impediments to practice but also do 'work' for individuals and organisations.

To summarise, the composition and texture of boundaries are highly dependent on the ways in which they are constructed. Moreover, the specific nature of boundaries are constituted through their enactment. Although there is a tendency to view boundaries as mechanisms of constraint within the mainstream literature, they also have important enabling facets. This point has significant connotations when it comes to considering what it is we wish to do to boundaries within the context of collaborative working arrangements.

What Do We Want to Do to Boundaries?

At the start of this section, it was argued that boundaries have often been viewed as inherently problematic within the public policy and public management literatures. Consequently, much has been written about the need to change boundaries to produce more effective policies and public services. The types of proposed changes to boundaries range from a desire to keep these largely intact but work across them in a more effective way, blurring boundaries (that is, at times moving across boundaries in different ways), through to an aim of removing boundaries altogether. If boundaries are an inevitable and potentially even a desirable component of organising processes, then finding ways to work across or re-draw and re-constitute boundaries are important activities of organisational practice. As Braithwaite (2010, p. 10) notes,

> the quest to bridge gaps, fill structural holes, connect groups, services and professions, and strengthen weak ties or remedy absent ties in network structures is perennial. Yet the ways to do this remain unclear, and lack a sound evidentiary basis.

Given the lack of a clear evidence base, it is perhaps not surprising that there are a variety of different approaches suggested in terms of the ways in which boundaries might be rendered more permeable or blurred in ways that enable better collaborative working. Potential techniques that might help blur boundaries include information sharing, developing a common mission, common planning, sharing joint resources, risk sharing, developing collaborative cultures, shared targets, capacity building and training at the individual and team level, restructuring performance management systems and others still (Christensen and Laegreid, 2007; Ling, 2002; Alford and O'Flynn, 2012). There is more as follows in relation to the evidence surrounding these ideas in the section on boundary work.

The idea of the *boundaryless organisation* is at one extreme of the continuum, where it is suggested that boundaries should be removed altogether. Those promoting this idea typically view boundaries as a historical relic unsuited to contemporary organisations. Such arguments typically note that we are seeing the dismantling of boundaries in other spaces, that this has a positive impact and therefore organisations would be more effective without boundaries. For example, it is argued that in Western Europe we have seen the opening up of national borders, which as noted earlier, have become more easily traversed following the Schengen Agreement. Boundaries are therefore viewed as something that are anachronistic, constraining freedom of movement and activity. Our organisations, it is argued, should mirror the types of changes that are taking place in the technological sphere where we see shifts in the nature of time/space (Braithwaite, Vining, and Lazarus, 1994). The boundaryless organisation is presented as a new and exciting possibility that will be able to overcome all of the challenges associated with these entities and their inhibitors of practice.

Discussions of boundaryless organisations often critique hierarchical organising arrangements and set out a desire to move instead to networks of practice. Traditional organisations are seen as 'self-contained and well-defined,' whereas boundaryless arrangements are 'loosely networked' and 'diffuse' (Braithwaite, Vining, and Lazarus, 1994, p. 569). These kinds of debates are redolent of the sorts of criticisms made of the organisation of governments and public services in the late 1990s, in response to the perceived negatives of New Public Management-inspired reforms and their use of market mechanisms (Dickinson, 2016). Osborne (2006, 2010), for example, sets out a theory of New Public Governance (NPG), which posits a plural state with multiple independent actors contributing to the delivery of services and a pluralist state where multiple processes inform the policy-making system. Such an approach draws strongly on network and institutional theoretical perspectives with the aim of capturing real world complexity of the design, implementation and management of public policy in the contemporary era. Other concepts that similarly placed networks centre stage, include the Third Way (Giddens, 1998) and ideas of policy networks (Marsh and Rhodes, 1992; Rhodes, 1997, 1996) amongst others. These kinds of critiques were influential in driving the joined-up government and collaborative agendas of the late 1990s that we saw play out across many different national jurisdictions (Glasby and Dickinson, 2009).

Other commentators argue against the idea of the boundaryless organisation (Hernes and Paulsen, 2003a; Llewellyn, 1998). As noted earlier, it is likely not possible to remove all boundaries; they are an inevitable component of human cognition and organising processes. Even if it were possible to remove boundaries, we should remember that they are capable of acting not just to constrain activity but as enabling and constitutive forces. Boundaries that exist, for example, around areas of specialist knowledge are important and highly productive (Carpenter and Dickinson, 2016). Removing these might not improve the ways that we work and may actually serve to make us less effective. As Chreim et al. (2013) note, the delivery of health care services is challenging because we are required to navigate divergent objectives of multiple actors linked through fluid power arrangements: "When different professions work together, they bring with them different sources of expertise and different professional cultures that must be bridged and mobilized to generate collaborative action" (p. 202). The answer is not to remove boundaries as they serve a particular purpose, it is to find different ways to work across these entities. The literature on team working has some strong evidence that generalisation can lead to reduced effectiveness as individuals become unsure of their roles and responsibilities (Jelphs, Dickinson, and Miller, 2016). It is not possible for individuals to have knowledge about all things, therefore some kinds of boundaries are necessary for the effective function of teams.

Those arguing against the removal of boundaries also point to the important functions that they perform and go as far as to argue that even the blurring of boundaries is not a good thing. Hernes and Paulsen (2003a p. 2) state that

> some important institutions do require integrity and longevity. We are well served with responsive public institutions, but they serve us poorly if they become morally malleable. We like such institutions to open their organizational boundaries in the name of efficiency, public accountability and scrutiny, but not at the expense of their integrity. For example, we want our justice system to be sensitive but not corruptible.

The durability of certain institutions and functions is seen to be of great value. Although there is somewhat of a trend right now within the management literature for organisations to change so that they can be more lean, nimble and agile (e.g. Young et al., 2004), this is an important reminder that in some cases there are very good reasons for us to have rigid boundaries. This is particularly the case in relation to certain bureaucratic functions (Du Gay, 2000, 2005) that are required to retain a strong sense of integrity and particular forms of accountability structures. Boundaries, therefore, are not simply problems that should be resolved, but provide opportunities for partners to engage with one another (Quick and Feldman, 2014b).

Llewellyn (1998, p. 25) provides an example of the importance of maintaining boundaries, in this case in the context of the caring professions, in order to protect service users from the activities associated with the costing of care; "maintaining boundaries around 'caring' prevents the conflicts engendered by the encroachment of costing information on 'care' as the core valued activity of social services." She goes on to argue that any boundary work to integrate 'costing' and 'caring' has to address the reconstitution of social relations in the social services. What this points to is the fact that boundaries are not only important in terms of the work that they do in strengthening and focusing individuals or groups on particular activities, but how we achieve change within organisations is through the dissolution and reconstitution of organisational boundaries. That is, ***boundary-blurring, boundary-crossing*** and ***boundary permeation*** are all important activities in how we drive change within organisations.

A final point to note is that if boundaries are produced by the interplay of structure and agency and are required to be enacted to have effect, then it follows that boundaries may prove to be more or less permeable for particular groups. Research into trade and partnerships in West Africa demonstrates that the formal colonially drawn borders are less relevant to collaborative working than the systems and groupings that pre-date these (older trade alliances, family/ethic groupings etc.). Although these boundaries exist in a formal sense and do some work in containing aspects of trade, alternative gateways have also been created through linguistic, ethic and familial ties (Walther, 2015).

Similarly, in a study of cross-cultural working relations between American and Israeli managers and engineers who work together in 'high-tech' companies in Silicon Valley, Shamir and Malik (2003) identified a number of types of boundaries (expressive boundaries, bureaucratic and role boundaries, time boundaries, boundaries between work and non-work roles, physical boundaries and boundaries between the individual and the collective) and explored whether these were experienced differently by the Israeli and American employees. Shamir and Malik found that:

> the Americans were characterized as relatively 'bounded,' while the Israelis were characterized as relatively 'boundary-less' in many respects. The Americans maintained more rigid boundaries between their thoughts and feelings and their overt behaviour, between different organizational positions, between their different roles and activities, and between types of relationships. The Israelis tended to disregard these boundaries or bend them. These differences were reported to have many behavioural manifestations, which created difficulties in communication and affected the level of trust and cooperation between members of the two nationalities working in the same organizations.
>
> (p. 282)

The authors are keen to point out that they do not believe that their study merely explored a stereotype of the different nationalities and instead argue that what this demonstrates is that boundaries are cultural constructs and therefore the same boundary may be experienced or understood to be more or less permeable depending on the context of the individual/group. The important point here is that we may need diverse approaches to working across boundaries as they are experienced and enacted differently across individuals and groups.

Having set out a sense of some of the different things that the literature talks about 'doing to' boundaries, the part now moves on in the next chapter to set out an overview of some of the concepts in the literature relating to changing boundaries.

3   Boundary Concepts

Helen Dickinson and Catherine Smith

As the literature relating to boundaries has expanded, we have seen a plethora of terminology emerge around these entities. This chapter explores a series of the different ideas that have proved most relevant to date and a sense of the evidence base surrounding these concepts. The aim is to set out the broad range of different boundary-related concepts, to describe these and set out research relating to these various different ideas. Some of these concepts are fairly common in terms of the literature (e.g. boundary work, boundary objects, boundary spanners), while others appear with less frequency but still offer a helpful perspective on these entities (e.g. boundary shakers).

Boundary Work

Gieryn (1983) originally coined the term boundary work to refer to the work that public managers do in negotiating boundaries. In practice, public servants do a significant and growing amount of boundary work, although we still lack good quality evidence about the best ways to navigate this (O'Leary and Bingham, 2009). The type of boundary work done will be highly dependent on how we view boundaries. As argued earlier, there has been somewhat of a tendency to view boundaries as material entities within the mainstream public policy and public management literature. What this means is that recommendations about how to conduct boundary work have tended to be restricted to formalised structures or processes such as integrated team structures, inter-departmental taskforces, co-location of different teams or the pooling of budgets, for example. Yet, much of the evidence suggests that these kinds of boundary work are not sufficient to drive effective collaboration (O'Flynn, 2014).

Technological fixes, such as electronic records or shared database, have similarly struggled to aid effective boundary work (White et al., 2010). Human resources solutions, such as recruiting individuals to formally span more than one organisation, have also not succeeded. This is, in part, because the evidence suggests that this can be challenging and lead to burnout for these actors (Dickinson and Carey, 2016). Janet Newman (2012) notes that boundary work is an incredibly taxing activity and one which draws heavily on the emotional registers of those engaged in this act.

Despite the growing literature on boundary spanners (explored later in more detail), little is agreed on in terms of the specific skills or characteristics needed (Williams, 2012). However, research examining public servants in hybrid roles, such as medical administrators (Dickinson et al., 2016; Loh et al., 2016), points to the active use of identity by agents negotiating boundaries. Although identity has been recognised as an important component of facilitating boundary work (e.g. Palma, Cunha, and Lopes, 2010), the evidence base exploring this issue remains limited to date (Maguire and Hardy, 2005). Identity is not a singular or fixed entity as it is often assumed in the public policy and public management literatures, and studies have shown that actors who conduct boundary work engage in the construction and reconstruction of certain facets of their identity to facilitate collaborative processes (Zhang and Huxham, 2009). Reshaping identities helps in negotiating boundaries and actors may draw on resources around themselves in this process. These processes are not well recognised in public policy and public management, but are well-evidenced in the geography and international relations literatures in relation to geographical borders. Rumford (2006a, p. 159), for example, describes how borders "can be appropriated for societal actors for non-state purposes; signaling an important dimension of community identity, for example." The important point here is that "the real 'meat' of this subject" is not in the "concrete exo-skeleton of gates, fences, signage or border posts" but the performative actualisation of border through "embodied behaviors and concrete objects" (Shields, 2006, p. 226). The border only operates as a boundary once it is enacted in some way.

Quick and Feldman (2014a) draw on the public management literature to identify three boundary work practices that are concerned with rendering boundaries more porous, increasing numbers of connections or flexibility. Quick and Feldman argue that finding ways to connect partners supports resilience. In doing so they acknowledge that systems will always be subject to disruption and adversity and therefore resilience is required to reorganise connections within the system: "engaging in boundary work that treats differences among, for instance, organizational entities, geographic scales, issue definitions, or kinds of knowledge as potential sites of connection rather than as barriers is a powerful way to enact resilience" (p. 680). Boundary work that seeks to separate partners by barriers, it is argued, can be helpful under some circumstances but they undermine longer term resilience. The three forms of boundary work identified by these authors are:

- *Translating across differences*—the process of adopting another language or way of expressing understandings to create a new, shared domain: "Translation can create boundaries when it is used unidirectionally to privilege one domain of understanding. Translating across difference, however, involved multidirectional translation of the collaborative production of new ways of expressing understandings that diminish the barriers created by differences" (p. 677). This approach can help to create junctures, but it usually reinforces separation because it sees one domain as more important and participation is only possible if we are to learn the specialised knowledge of that group (Yanow, 2004).

- *Aligning among differences*—this involves recognising that there are distinctions between groups and trying to find ways to enhance connections across these:

This practice involves accepting the differences and using them as a basis for pursuing new, shared interests. The differences may be considered unchangeable (i.e. public safety offices and engineers have some areas of expertise they do not share with each other) or worth sustaining (i.e. there are useful distinctions between police and water treatment departments).

(p. 678)

Quick and Feldman argue that this is the most common form of boundary work where organisations need to bring together different interests and resources in order to solve complex problems.

- *Decentring differences*—this is about finding ways to work that do not identify meaningful distinctions between parties:

This kind of boundary-work makes junctures possible by eliding boundaries that have been enacted as barriers. Public managers who decenter differences may be cognizant of potential distinctions but structure action in ways that deactivate the importance of, remove attention from, or change the meaning of differences. The differences can be rendered inconsequential by finding new ways to work together or by decentering the usual primacy of one entity over others.

(p. 679)

Many of the recent co-productive approaches (e.g. Durose et al., 2011; Pestoff, Brandsen, and Verschuere, 2012; Alford, 2016) would fall into this category of boundary-work. The active use of boundary objects (see the next section for further) as a way to ally partners would also be seen as this form of boundary-work.

What is clear from the literature is that boundary work is an important activity for individuals and/or groups to engage in and this takes many different forms. As yet we lack good evidence though about which different types of boundary work are most effective in which particular contexts, although the evidence base is starting to grow and become more differentiated in terms of the types of boundary work being reported.

Boundary Objects

Boundary objects make a significant and increasingly frequent appearance within the literature on collaborative working. Originally identified by Star and Griesemer (1989), these are artefacts that are actively used to help negotiate boundaries. Inspired by writings around the social studies of technology (e.g. Latour, 1996, 2005), it is argued that we cannot explain all social action via a focus on language. Although an important part of the communication process, symbols that we find in communication processes do not explain all of this interaction and objects are important in terms of the endurance of interaction.

Nicolini et al. (2012) argue that although the work of interactionalist sociologists (e.g. Bechky, 2006) and organisational communication studies (e.g. Taylor and Robichaud, 2004) have been helpful in exploring the practices of collaboration, they have typically foregrounded human agency in these discussions, focusing on discursive practices and interpretations. As argued earlier, much of the public policy and public management literature has remain wedded to a rather structural account of boundaries and so this is a welcome corrective in some senses. However, as Nicolini and colleagues point out, the focus has shifted to being so significantly on discursive and interpretive practices that they deny materiality of objects. This is not to say that objects derive the work that they do simply from their materiality in a predetermined sense (Star, 2010), but that objects can be powerful embodiments of particular theories or ideas. Boundaries can be trajectories in an assemblage of public (and private) relations. The boundary object therefore acts as an associate in the becoming of new possibilities. Boundary objects are those things that bridge social and cultural worlds. They are meaningful for both of these worlds, but may mean several things to different groups. They are interpretively flexible, meaning that groups do not have to have a deep sharing of ideas.

In the science and technology literatures boundary objects are also often referred to as **boundary devices**. An example of a boundary device might be a modelling process that is used to negotiate the space between theory and data or between theoretical worlds and policy worlds (van Egmond and Bal, 2011). In modelling data, interdisciplinary teams will have to define what they wish to value and the process to do important boundary work in prioritising different issues (Wehrens, Bekker, and Bal, 2011).

Boundary objects can operate in a number of different ways in the context of collaborative arrangements. Sullivan and Williams (2012) explored the meanings that individuals in health and local government organisations in Wales attach to different objects, the work that these do in influencing policy and practice, and the ways that they are shaped by power relationships. In doing so they identified objects doing many different forms of work within collaborative practice, including:

- *Objects as symbols*—where physical manifestations are overlaid with an alternative representation, they can perform a powerful symbolic role. Examples of this include the design, architecture and layout of buildings as an indicator of power structures and relationships within organisations. Sullivan and Williams observed a number of examples of this within their research, where teams were co-located as a means to drive collaborative practice. However, co-location without accompanying collaborative management arrangements was found to be insufficient and to allow some groups to continue with existing practices.

- *Objects as models and concepts*—objects help individuals to make sense of changes and to offer alternative approaches. However, we cannot assume that all individuals will understand or make sense of objects in the same way. Sullivan and Williams identify the 'locality' model that was used to promote integration between different organisations and the range of different understandings concerning what this entails. In this case it was found to be both facilitative and inhibitory in the sense that it acted to promote the virtues of integration, but its flexibility allowed different actors to pursue separate paths, inhibiting whole system change.

- *Objects as bridging mechanisms*—where these help to facilitate interactions across knowledge boundaries. In the case studies explored in Sullivan and Williams these were typically understood to be information technology systems and different ways of sharing data and information more effectively.

- *Objects as stories of practice*—stories can exert a significant influence over the views, opinions and perspectives of people about particular issues. In the Welsh research a number of stories were identified that were compelling and/or emotionally persuasive and were used time and time again to express meanings that are difficult to express in other senses. Such stories were seen as more effective in driving change than formal evidence and statistics had often been.

- *Objects as social identity formation*—creating and managing boundary objects can prove to be a resource that supports the formation of social identities between different social groups. Sullivan and Williams reflect on the creation of different forms of multi-disciplinary teams. Although again these were understood in different ways by various actors, they did succeed in bordering groups as a model of good practice for other services and also as a means of recruiting other professional stakeholders to the multi-disciplinary cause.

Sullivan and Williams conclude that the use of objects in exploring collaborative practice can be helpful in demonstrating how professionals and others may feel about integration and also reveal the types of attachments that individuals have to values, ideas and practices that might be challenged by working collaboratively.

As the discussion of boundary objects in the Welsh example illustrate, one of the challenges in defining boundary objects is that they can mean different things to different people. In fact, the idea of the boundary object has been critiqued by a number of different commentators for the tendency of some to use it to explain all the kinds of work that are done by material and symbolic objects in the context of collaborative practice (Zeiss and Groenewegen, 2009). Like most concepts, if we stretch this to use it to explain every eventuality, there is a danger that it loses its analytical capacity (Trompette and Vinck, 2009). Indeed, it has been argued that this idea has at least four distinct theoretical bases—material infrastructures, boundary objects, epistemic objects, activity objects (Nicolini, Mengis, and Swan, 2012). The differences in these approaches are set out in Table 3.1. As this table illustrates, there are a number of common basic assumptions between these different conceptualisations, although each views the way in which objects trigger collaborative activity in different ways. Nicolini et al. go on to integrate these different theoretical approaches, arguing that they explain different functions for objects in collaborative activities. For example, if we are attempting to trigger, sustain or motivate collaborative work, then the theoretical approaches of epistemic objects and activity objects are most applicable. If the aim is to facilitate work across different types of boundaries, then we might draw on boundary objects theory. If the aim is to provide a basic infrastructure support to a collaborative activity, then infrastructure theory has greatest applicability.

In a similar vein to the analysis offered by Nicolini et al. (2012), other authors have attempted to categorise different forms of boundary objects, their characteristics and the contexts in which they have greatest application. Carlile (2002), for example, studies different forms of knowledge boundaries in new product development settings and identifies different categories and characteristics of boundary objects that are most applicable to those purposes. In doing so Carlile argues that this analysis demonstrates why knowledge can be both a barrier to collaborative working and a source of innovation.

To summarise, boundary objects play an important part in the literature on collaborative working, but are far from a simple idea. Multiple forms of boundary objects can be found and these have implications for how they might be used and their impact.

Table 3.1 Differences Between Theoretical Approaches for Studying Objects in Cross-disciplinary Collaboration

	Material infrastructures	Boundary objects	Epistemic objects	Activity objects
Affordances of objects in cross-disciplinary settings	Everyday mundane objects support and shape collaboration in their conjunction (they form an ecology of supporting objects).	Objects act as translation and transformation devices across various thought worlds. They make cross-disciplinary work possible.	Objects fuel cooperation and generate mutuality and solidarity by triggering desire and attachment and creating mutual dependencies.	Objects motivate the collaboration and direct activities. They hold together different types of knowledge, and in so doing, they generate contradictions and trigger innovation.
Disciplinary, professional, and cultural boundaries	Objects became infrastructure when boundaries are uncontested and fall into the background.	Boundaries are foregrounded and potentially problematic for aligning understanding and interests: they need to be overcome.	Boundaries are only partially relevant: foregrounded is the common pursuit and collectiveness.	Boundaries between activities are only considered when they become a source of tension and contradiction.
Completeness of objects	Objects are taken for granted, or 'black-boxed,' and only became visible in case of breakdowns.	Objects are open and malleable only inasmuch as they are interpretively flexible across boundaries.	Objects are incomplete, emergent, and expansive, which gives them their performative character.	
Conflict	Objects can resolve the tension between local practices within large-scale technologies by creating assemblages of objects.	Conflict is backgrounded, yet objects can shed light on the pragmatic implications of different forms of knowing (what is at stake).	Distinction, difference and conflict are temporally suspended or backgrounded, and the union/attachment with the object of desire is stressed.	Conflict is foregrounded because the multiple nature of the object produces contradictions between elements triggering creative remedial work.

Novelty	Novelty is backgrounded: the more objects become infrastructure, the more they are considered stable.	Novelty lies outside the objects themselves and is located in the environment or task at hand.	Novelty emerges from the inner development of an existing practice.	Novelty emerges from addressing the emerging contradictions through expansive learning. The productive role of objects is emphasised.
Historical conditions	The historical context, politics and authorship are embedded and materialised in the shape of the infrastructure.	Little attention is given to the wider historical conditions.	Epistemic objects are grounded in historically developed 'knowledge cultures.'	Through individual and group motives, the object of work translates locally wider historical conditions as well as societal ideas, ideologies and discourses.

Source: Nicolini, Mengis, and Swan (2012, p. 624)

Boundary Spanners

Boundary spanning and those who engage in these practices (known by a variety of names including boundary spanners, reticulists, strategic brokers) are a key concept in terms of the collaboration literature and one that we return to a number of times throughout this book. In this section the basic ideas around this concept are established and more detail is provided in relation to these individuals and roles in later chapters. Other authors do not explicitly use the terminology of boundary spanners although they are referring to similar kinds of processes. For example, Garsten (2003) talks of *boundary breakers* and *boundary intermediaries*.

A key theme within this part of the book has been the definitional confusion surrounding many concepts and this continues in relation to the topic of boundary spanning. Williams (2012, p. 32) notes, "there is considerable degree of conceptual confusion about the terms and an absence of definitional clarity that must be addressed." The first distinction that we can make in terms of boundary spanners refers to who it is that is playing this sort of role. The public policy and management literature typically refers to boundary spanners as individuals who do some sort of bridging work as part of their job, but we can also think of boundary spanners as being teams or groups of people.

Within the literature, we find that many different types of individuals have been described as boundary spanners (see Dickinson and Carey, 2016 for an overview). Within this group, Williams (2012) argues that we find two categories of people. The first comprises individuals who have a dedicated role in working in multi-organisational/multi-sector settings. This group is small in number in the context of the overall public service workforce. The second group comprises those managers, leaders and practitioners who undertake boundary-spanning activities as a function of their role.

In defining who boundary spanners are and what work they do in collaborative settings, Williams (2012) identifies four major roles: Reticulist, Interpreter/Communicator, Coordinator and Entrepreneur (p. 58). He goes on to argue that there are particular competencies associated with these roles and there is a "high degree of connectivity and interplay between the role elements and competencies" (p. 60). An adapted version of these roles and competencies is outlined in Table 3.2 and it is important to note that some, if not all, of the characteristics identified by Williams as common to boundary spanners might also be recognised as fundamental in all organisational managers.

In his work on boundary spanners, Paul Williams (2005) sets out an account of the kinds of personal characteristics that are desirable in boundary spanners. An overview of these is provided in Table 3.3. There is a danger in this context that boundary spanners begin to be viewed as some form of modern superwoman. Indeed, gender is an interesting facet to consider in relation to the boundary spanner. Williams (2012)

Table 3.2 Roles and Competencies of Boundary Spanners

Role	Dominant Images	Main Competencies
Reticulist	Informational intermediary, gatekeeper, entrepreneur of power	Networking, political sensitivity, diplomacy, bargaining, negotiation, persuasion.
Interpreter/ communicator	Culture breaker, frame articulator	Interpersonal, listening, empathising, communication, sense making, trust-building, conflict management.
Coordinator	Liaison person, organiser	Planning, coordination, servicing, administration, information management, monitoring, communication
Entrepreneur	Initiator broker, catalyst	Brokering, innovation, while systems thinking, flexibility, lateral thinking, opportunistic
Learning and connecting	Stewardship, cultural broker, knowledge broker	Building knowledge of policy networks, bridging skill and knowledge gaps in how to work in relational environments

Source: Adapted from Williams (2002, p. 58).

Table 3.3 Desirable Personal Characteristics of Boundary Spanners

Personal attributes	Description
Respect for others and their views	Appreciating, comprehending and accommodating diversity and difference in people's perspectives and opinions. The key word here was respect, which does not mean agreement but valuing other people's right to their own views. It is considered important also to look for opportunities to demonstrate this respectfulness, and to be tolerant of others' positions on various matters. Innate curiosity about the 'bigger picture' is thought to be an invaluable personal attribute.
Honest, straight and trustworthy	Evidenced by being open in dealings with people, not being underhanded or devious, or going behind their back.
Approachable	This is about people who are accessible and not 'standoffish'; sometimes amusing, talkative and interesting.
Diplomatic	Actors with well-honed political antennae who are careful in their use of language.
Positive and enthusiastic	Constantly champion and extoll the virtues and benefits of partnership working.
Confident and calm	People who exude good judgement and are firm where necessary.

Source: Adapted from Williams (2005)

argues that women may be better placed to exhibit many of the kinds of desirable personal characteristics with greater ease than men. We should, of course, be wary of suggesting that any one gender is naturally better predisposed to particular sorts of activities.

Having set out a basic introduction to boundary spanners here, Part 2 explores this concept in more detail.

Boundary Shakers

Balogun et al. (2005) argue that boundary-spanning activities have typically been conceived as an activity that takes place between an organisation and another organisation with which it works. They suggest that little attention has been paid to internal change agency and boundary spanning to implement change initiatives across internal organisational boundaries. In addressing this gap they focus on individuals who they identify as 'boundary-shakers' who are "tasked with implementing change across existing internal organisational boundaries in ways that simultaneously alter those boundaries" (p. 262). Balogun et al. describe these change processes as boundary-shaking as it does not involve the removal of boundaries, but their reconfiguration in terms of the ways in which work and different interactions flow across these.

From research with seven different organisations that engaged in boundary-shaking activities, Balogun et al. (2005) identify a number of boundary-shaking practices (Table 3.4). What this table demonstrates is that the majority of practices associated with boundary-shaking relate to making meaning within organisations. They are about the ways that issues are framed and defined, rather than use of 'harder' levers of power. This aligns with the kinds of roles and attributes outlined by Williams (2012) in his work on boundary spanning, suggesting the difference in spanning boundaries inside or outside of organisations although this may be a qualitative, rather than a quantitative, difference in practice.

Additional Boundary Concepts

Many of the different boundary concepts discussed so far in this chapter are relatively well established within the literature and have a number of contributions that discuss these ideas. However, there are also a number of other concepts that appear that are less frequently referred to and often are less well conceptualised. In this section we provide a brief overview of some of the more interesting ideas that we have encountered and conclude by reflecting on why it is that these new linguistic devices and concepts have emerged in what is already a rather congested conceptual terrain.

In an Australian study of the treatment of gender in the Victorian Government's 2015–2016 Royal Commission into Family Violence, Yates

Table 3.4 Boundary-shaking Practices

Practice	Definition
Adjusting measurement systems	Bringing in new measurement systems (rewards, objectives, for example) or getting existing measurement systems changed to encourage individuals to support the change initiative.
Aligning agendas/selling	Using meetings (specially arranged and others opportunistically), conferences, one-to-ones, e-mails, newsletters and many types of formal and informal communications to persuade and convince people of the merit of the change initiative and to cooperate/help. Also involves selling the change initiative to others in a way that fits with their agendas/issues.
Engaging in stage management	Manipulating situations in particular ways to ensure a message is delivered more effectively. For example, setting up meetings or discussion in a particular way, such as use of experts to reinforce particular points, or deliberately creating a particular self-image or impression, or making visible the added value of their work to others. Stage management may also require recognising the different identities of the individuals they are working across when trying to bring them together.
Gathering intelligence	Finding out the agendas/issues of others—both junior and senior—to feed into managing up, stage management and aligning agendas/selling.
Managing up	Lobbying for help from more senior managers, getting support of more senior managers for intended interventions/courses of action, developing/using senior-manager sponsors, developing initiatives that tie in with/support the interests of more senior managers.
Local autonomy	The extent to which the different communities within the organisation form networks of interest associated with a strong individual identity, systems, ways of working, history of autonomy and freedom to act on their own.
Managerial priorities	Organisational and senior management preferences about where effort should be expended, e.g. short-term profitability at the expense of longer-term more strategic concerns, and the extent to which this supports or mitigates against boundary-shaking change initiatives.
Reward/performance management systems	The basis on which individuals are rewarded, assessed and promoted, and the extent to which these systems can be utilised locally to support projects of boundary-shakers and incentivise adoption.
Financial measurement/reporting systems	The emphasis in terms of the financial measurement systems, and the extent to which these systems encourage others to work with boundary-shakers on their change projects.

Source: Balogun et al. (2005, pp. 267–277)

(2017) observed a gendered approach to alcohol and other drugs (AOD) and family violence. She argues that the Commission's findings were strongly influenced by feminist advocates more than other experts as they demanded more attention be paid to alcohol-related family violence, but sought to place AOD misuse in the context of unequal power relations between men and women. In her research, Yates argues that individuals used the framing of AOD whether it has a relationship with family violence as a ***boundary marker*** to indicate broadly to which 'camp' they aligned. She explains that those from a public health background and viewpoint indicated that AOD misuse causes family violence. What this means is this has primarily an individual cause with a potentially genetic basis. A feminist reading views violence as having a primarily societal cause (through gender inequities) and therefore AOD misuse may be a factor related to family violence, but it is not the cause of it. Yates goes on to argue that expert witnesses were assessed by some in the AOD and family violence sectors in terms of how they spoke about causality between these different factors. Those that were judged to be on 'the wrong side of the boundary marker' lost credibility with particular audiences as a result. To this extent, a boundary marker plays a similar role to Sullivan and Williams' (2012) boundary object as a process of social identity formation, albeit without a material object. A boundary marker is an ideational boundary object in this case.

In a study of journalists, Singer (2015) similarly defines boundary markers as ethical practices that distinguish professional and non-professional journalists. These boundary markers and their associated practices are important in the contemporary era given the relatively open media environment we find in many developed countries, where there are few limits on who can publish new items. Professional journalists have ensured that they enact particular ethical practices (such as verification), principles (e.g. independence) and promises (e.g. accountability for the consequences of their actions) to mark themselves out as professional news workers and also demarcate professionals from non-professionals. As in the study by Yates, boundary markers are a way of identifying particular ideas or practices that separate individuals into different kinds of groups based on specified beliefs or values.

Within the geology literature the terminology of ***boundary events*** is used quite broadly to refer to particular sets of occurrences that took place on the limits of one era of time and another. For example, on the boundary of the Cretaceous period and the Paleogene period we saw a mass extinction event through the demise of non-avian dinosaurs (Renne et al., 2013). Within the business literature, the idea of boundary events is used in processes of Business Process Modelling (Jarrar and Aspinwall, 1999) to refer to particular activities or processes that have implications for other activities or processes. For example, in the insurance industry, an operational risk boundary event is defined as "an operational risk event which triggers a consequence (e.g. financial loss) in another risk category" (KPMG, 2016, p. 4). In both cases this idea is being used to encapsulate a sense of time and also of cause and effect between different identified domains.

In a study of the wildlife-utilisation industry in southern Africa, Wels (2003) studies the existence of private land set aside by animal conservancy organisations and the community who live in and around these spaces. He argues that these fences pose a formidable boundary but not simply just because of their physical presence, but also in terms of their symbolic characteristics. For many local communities in Zimbabwe the creation of public wildlife areas was started under white minority governments and many people were violently forced off their land. The resulting fences have therefore been seen as a "hated symbol of this form of white land appropriation" (p. 212). Wels refers to those imposing the fences as *boundary bullies*, where white not-for-profit agencies were perceived to have bullied local black communities. Wels studied fences in a number of locations around Zimbabwe, noting that their appearance was an indication of the degree to which communities had jointly agreed on the appropriateness and acceptance of these demarcations. Where fences were in a poor state, this was illustrative of low trust and acceptance between groups.

In concluding this part we will briefly reflect on why it is that we have seen the emergence of a range of new boundary-related terms such as those explored here. As we have illustrated, many of these terms are restricted to a small number of applications and have not been sufficiently conceptualised to merit their own section. But the existence of this plethora of terminology is of interest. Of course, we do see the emergence of new terminology or ideas within the academic literature on a frequent basis. There is much that can be gained in coining the latest academic phrase or idea in terms of generating interest (and importantly, citations) for work. The reasons for the emergence of these terms go beyond a purely cynical way of garnering interest and attention on a set of ideas.

One reason we may see the emergence of these terms is because the existing literature does not sufficiently accommodate some of the facets of boundaries or boundary work that authors are seeking to achieve. In talking about boundary markers, Yates and Singer are referring to particular ideas or practices that individuals use to infer where individuals sit in relation to particular ideas, norms and values. In these cases it appears that the existing literature does insufficient work in accommodating aspects of politics (with a small 'p') into considerations of boundaries. The use of the concept of boundary events may be a reflection on the fact that the public policy and public administration literature has not traditionally explicitly incorporated considerations of time and space in a satisfactory way (Pollit, 2013). This term further tries to encapsulate some of the causal links between one domain of activity and another in a rather straightforward way.

In referring to boundary bullies, we see not just an illumination of the boundary spanning practices of a particular set of individuals, but the ways in which the physical and symbolic registers of boundaries come together and interact in compelling ways that generate activity.

Having set out an account of the broad literature on boundaries and the ways in which they have been conceptualised in the literature through the last three chapters, the concluding chapter of this part moves on to consider where next for boundaries. In other words, what will the new frontiers of this area of study bring?

4 Where Next for Boundaries?

Helen Dickinson and Catherine Smith

This part of the book has sought to unpack the concepts and ideas around boundaries and to argue for a more sophisticated account of these entities than that which we tend to get in the mainstream public policy and public management literatures. In doing so we have argued that despite being a key concept within these literatures, boundaries have received insufficient critical attention. All too often boundaries remain undertheorised and have not garnered close scrutiny in terms of the many different potential forms that these might take. In some senses the conclusions that Paulsen and Hernes (2003) reached from the collection of chapters they curated on boundaries over a decade ago still stand. Boundaries are still a universal feature of ways of organising and yet we are left with significant numbers of questions about these entities.

The mainstream public policy and public management literatures remain dominated by structuralist accounts of boundaries, where these are predominantly viewed as material and tangible entities, rather than more dynamic considerations of the full range of boundary forms and the ways in which these are enacted by actors. In recent years some of these features have started to be acknowledged as we have seen a turn in the literature away from totalising perspectives on boundary work to more interpretive and decentred accounts that acknowledge the role that agency plays in boundary work (Bevir and Rhodes, 2010, 2006). As a result of these insights, we have seen a greater interest in issues of practice emerge in an attempt to understand precisely the types of actions and behaviours that promote particular types of boundary work (Rhodes, 2014; Dickinson, 2014a). Such accounts attempt to tread a middle ground between boundaries being the product of structure or of agency. These kinds of approaches recognise that boundaries are simultaneously a function of the activity of the system they reside within and also a product of the strategy of description involved. However, as yet, these perspectives have not coalesced around a core set of theories or concepts. If these ideas are to become more embedded within the mainstream literature, we will need to see some key concepts and ideas develop that are able to provide a more dynamic account of boundaries and boundary work than we see at present within the literature.

The mainstream public policy and public management literature is in need of the development of a set of theories and concepts that can accommodate considerations of structure and agency and the enactment of different kinds of boundaries within the context of public policy and public management settings. Greater evidence needs to be developed in relation to the most effective forms of boundary work for particular types of boundaries with different aspirations in terms of changing or working across boundaries. As this chapter has sought to demonstrate, some of these concepts and insights currently reside in broader literatures beyond public policy and management. However, if these are to be helpful in this different disciplinary context, work will need to be done to ensure that they are portable across these boundaries.

References

Abbott, A. 1995. "Things of boundaries." *Social Research* 62 (4):857–882.

Adams, B. N., and R. A. Sydie. 2001. *Sociological theory*. Thousand Oaks, CA: Pine Forge.

Akkerman, S. F., and A. Bakker. 2011. "Boundary crossing and boundary objects." *Review of Educational Research* 81 (2):132–169.

Alford, J. 2016. "Co-production, interdependence and publicness: Extending public service-dominant logic." *Public Management Review* 18 (5):673–691.

Alford, J., and J. O'Flynn. 2012. *Rethinking public services: Managing with external providers*. Basingstoke: Palgrave Macmillan.

Alford, J., and J. O'Flynn. 2014. *Rethinking public service delivery: Managing with external providers*. Basingstoke: Palgrave Macmillan.

Balogun, J., P. Gleadle, V. H. Hailey, and H. Willmott. 2005. "Managing change across boundaries: Boundary-shaking practices." *British Journal of Management* 16:261–278.

Barad, K. 2007. *Meeting the universe halfway: Quantum physics and the entanglement of matter and meaning*. London: Duke University Press.

Barley, S. R., and G. Kunda. 2001. "Bringing work back in." *Organization Science* 12 (1):76–95.

Bechky, B. A. 2006. "Talking about machines, thick description, and knowledge work." *Organization Studies* 27 (12):1757–1768.

Berg, D. N., and K. K. Smith. 1990. "Paradox and groups." In *Groups in context: A new perspective on group dynamics*, edited by J. Gillette and M. McCollom, 106–132. Reading, MA: Addison-Wesley.

Bevir, M. 2013. *A theory of governance*. Berkeley: University of California Press.

Bevir, M., and R. A. W. Rhodes. 2003. *Interpreting British governance*. London: Routledge. Reprint.

Bevir, M., and R. A. W. Rhodes. 2006. *Governance stories*. London: Routledge. Reprint.

Bevir, M., and R. A. W. Rhodes. 2010. *The state as cultural practice*. Oxford: Oxford University Press.

Bevir, M., and R. A. W. Rhodes. 2011. "The stateless state." In *The SAGE handbook of governance*, edited by Mark Bevir, 203–217. London: Sage Publications Ltd.

Bourdieu, P. 1979. *Distinction: A social critique of the judgement of taste*. Cambridge, MA: Harvard University Press.

Braithwaite, J. 2010. "Between-group behaviour in health care: Gaps, edges, boundaries, diconnections, weak ties, spaces and holes: A systematic review." *BMC Health Services Research* 330 (10):1–11.

Braithwaite, J., R. F. Vining, and L. Lazarus. 1994. "The boundaryless hospital." *Australia and New Zealand Journal of Medicine* 24:565–571.

Byrne, D., and G. Callaghan. 2014. *Complexity theory and the social sciences*. Abingdon: Routledge.

Cabrera, D., L. Cabrera, and E. Powers. 2015. "A unifying theory of systems thinking with psychosocial applications." *Systems Research and Behavioural Science* 32 (5):534–545.

Carey, G., K. Landvogt, and J. Barraket. 2015. *Creating and implementing public policy cross-sectoral debates*. London: Routledge.

Carlile, P. R. 2002. "A prgamatic view of knowledge and boundaries: Boundary objects in new product development." *Organization Science* 13 (4):442–455.

Carpenter, J., and H. Dickinson. 2016. *Interprofessional education and training*. Bristol: Policy Press.

Chreim, S., A. Langley, M. Comeau-Vallee, J. Huq, and T. Reay. 2013. "Leadership as boundary work in healthcare teams." *Leadership* 9 (2):201–228.

Christensen, T., and P. Laegreid. 2007. "The whole-of-government approach to public sector reform, public administration review." *Public Administration Review* 67 (6):1059–1066.

Cilliers, P. 1998. *Complexity and postmodernism: Understanding complex systems*. London: Routledge.

Cilliers, P. 2001. "Boundaries, hierarchies and networks in complex systems." *International Journal of Innovation Management* 5 (2):135–147.

Cortada, J. W., S. Dijkstra, G. M. Mooney, and T. Ramsey. 2008. *Government 2020 and the perpetual collaboration mandate: Six worldwide drivers demand customized strategies*. New York: IBM Institute for Business Value.

Derks, D., D. van Duin, M. Tims, and A. B. Bakker. 2014. "Smartphone use and work-home interference: The moderating role of social norms and employee work engagement." *Journal of Occupatiional and Organizational Psychology* 88 (1):155–177.

Dickinson, H. 2014a. "Making a reality of integration: Less science, more craft and graft." *Journal of Integrated Care* 22 (5–6):189–196.

Dickinson, H. 2010. "The importance of being efficacious: English health and social care partnerships and service user outcomes." *International Journal of Integrated Care* 10. http://doi.org/10.5334/ijic.646

Dickinson, H. 2014b. *Performing governance: Partnerships, culture and new labour*. Basingstoke: Palgrave Macmillan.

Dickinson, H. 2016. "From new public management to new public governance: The implications for a 'new public service'." In *The three sector solution: Delivering public policy in collaboration with no-for-profits and business*, edited by J. Butcher and D. Gilchrist, 41–60. Canberra: ANU Press.

Dickinson, H., M. Bismark, G. Phelps, and E. Loh. 2016. "Future of medical engagement." *Australian Health Review* 40:443–446.

Dickinson, H., and G. Carey. 2016. *Managing and leading in interagency settings*. Bristol: Policy Press.

Dickinson, H., and J. Glasby. 2010. "Why partnership working doesn't work." *Public Management Review* 12 (6):811–828.

Dickinson, H., and H. Sullivan. 2014. "Towards a general theiry of collaborative performance: The importance of efficacy and agency." *Public Administration* 92 (1):161–177.

Dickinson, H., and H. Sullivan. 2016. "Collaboration as cultural performance: Agency and efficacy." In *Creating and implementing public policy: Cross-sectoral debates*, edited by G. Carey, K. Landvogt and J. Barraket, 207–222. London: Routledge.

Donati, P., and M. S. Archer. 2015. *The relational subject*. Cambridge: Cambridge University Press.

Du Gay, P. 2000. *In praise of bureaucracy: Weber, organization, ethics*. London: Sage Publications Ltd.

Du Gay, P. 2005. *The values of bureaucracy*. Oxford: Oxford University Press. Reprint, In File.

Durkheim, E. 1933. *The division of labor in society*. New York: Free Press. Reprint, Not in File.

Durose, C., Y. Beebeejaun, J. Rees, J. Richardson, and L. Richardson. 2011. *Towards co-production in research with communities*. London: Arts & Humanities Research Council.

Edelman Trust. 2016. *Edelman trust barometer: 2016 Annual global survey*. Available from www.edelman.com/insights/intellectual-property/2016-edelman-trust-barometer/executive-summary/ accessed 21st October 2016.

Evans, M., G. Stoker, and M. Halupka. 2016. "Now for the big question: Who do you trust to run the country?" *The Conversation* 2nd May. Available from https://theconversation.com/now-for-the-big-question-who-do-you-trust-to-run-the-country-58723 accessed 21st October 2016.

Ferlie, E., L. Ashburner, L. Fitzgerald, and A. Pettigrew. 1996. *The new public management in action*. Oxford: Oxford University Press. Reprint, Not in File.

Garsten, C. 2003. "Colleague, competitor, or client: Social boundaries in flexible work arrangements." In *Managing boundaries in organizations: Multiple perspectives*, edited by N. Paulsen and T. Hernes. Basingstoke: Palgrave Macmillan.

Giddens, A. 1984. *The constitution of society: Outline of the theory of structuration*. Cambridge: Polity Press.

Giddens, A. 1993. "Structuration theory: Past, present and future." In *Giddens' theory of structuration*, edited by C. Bryant and D. Jary. London: Routledge.

Giddens, A. 1998. *The third way: The renewal of social democracy*. Cambridge: Polity Press.

Gieryn, T. F. 1983. "Boundary-work and the demarcation of science from non-science: Strains and interests in professional ideologies of scientists." *American Sociological Review* 48 (6):781–795.

Glasby, J., and H. Dickinson. 2009. *International perspectives on health and social care: Partnership working in action*. Oxford: Wiley-Blackwell.

Glasby, J., and H. Dickinson. 2014. *Partnership working in health and social care: What is it and how can we deliver it?* Bristol: Policy Press.

Halffman, W. 2003. "Boundaries of regulatory science: Eco/toxicology and aquatic hazards of chemicals in the US, England and the Netherlands." PhD, University of Amsterdam.

Heracleous, L. 2004. "Boundaries in the study of organization." *Human Relations* 57 (1):95–103.

Hernes, T. 2003. "Enabling and constraining properties of organizational boundaries." In *Managing boundaries in organizations: Multiple perspectives*, edited by N. Paulsen and T. Hernes, 35–54. Basingstoke: Palgrave Macmillan.

Hernes, T. 2004. "Studying composite boundaries: A framework for analysis." *Human Relations* 57 (1):9–29.

Hernes, T., and N. Paulsen. 2003a. "Introduction: Boundaries and organization." In *Managing boundaries in organizations: Multiple perspectives*, edited by N. Paulsen and T. Hernes, 1–13. Basingstoke: Palgrave Macmillan.

Hernes, T., and N. Paulsen. 2003b. "Introduction: Boundaries and organization." In *Managing boundaries in organizations: Multiple perpectives*, edited by N. Paulsen and T. Hernes. Basingstoke: Palgrave Macmillan.

Hirschorn, L., and T. Gilmore. 1992. "The new boundaries of the 'boundaryless' organization." *Harvard Business Review* May–June:104–115.

Hüppauf, B., and P. Weingart. 2008. *Science images and popular images of the sciences*. London: Routledge.

Jarrar, Y. F., and E. M. Aspinwall. 1999. "Business process re-engineering: Learning from organizational experience." *Total Quality Management* 10 (2):173–186.

Jasanoff, S. S. 1987. "Contested boundaries in policy-relevant science." *Social Studies of Science* 17:195–230.

Jelphs, K., H. Dickinson, and R. Miller. 2016. *Working in teams*. 2nd Edition. Bristol: Policy Press.

Jessop, B. 2000. "Governance failure." In *The new politics of British local governance*, edited by G. Stoker. Basingstoke: Palgrave Macmillan.

Johnson, B. K., and G. Ranzini. 2018. "Click here to look clever: Self-presentation via selective sharing of music and film on social media." *Computers in Human Behavior* 82:148–158.

Kanter, R. M. 1989. *When giants learn to dance*. New York: Simon & Schuster. Reprint, In File.

KPMG. 2016. *Defining the boundary: An industry-wide appraisal of the operational risk-insurance risk boundary*. London: KPMG.

Lamont, M., and V. Molnár. 2002. "The study of boundaries in the social sciences." *Annual Review of Sociology* 28:167–195.

Lanham, R. L. 2006. "Borders and boundaries: The ends of public administration." *Administrative Theory & Praxis* 28 (4):602–609.

Latour, B. 1996. " On interobjectivity." *Mind, Culture, Activitty* 3 (4):228–245.

Latour, B. 2005. *Reassembling the social: An introduction to actor-network-theory*. Oxford: Oxford University Press.

Lazarević, E. V., M. Vukmirović, A. Krstić-Furundžić, and A. Đukić. 2015. *Keeping up with technologies to improve places*. Newcastle Upon Tyne: Cambridge Scholars Publishing.

Lefebvre, H. 1991. *The production of space*. Oxford: Wiley-Blackwell.

Ling, T. 2002. "Delivering joined-up government in the UK: Dimensions, issues and problems." *Public Administration* 80 (4):615–642.

Llewellyn, S. 1998. "Boundary work: Costing and caring in the social services." *Accounting, Organizations and Society* 23 (1):23–47.

Loh, E., J. Morris, L. Thomas, M. Bismark, G. Phelps, and H. Dickinson. 2016. "Shining the light on the dark side of medical leadership—a qualitative study in Australia." *Leadership in Health Services* 29 (3):313–330.

Maguire, S., and C. Hardy. 2005. "Identity and collaborative strategy in Canadian HIV/AIDS treatment. strategic organization." *Strategic Organization* 3:11–45.

Markus, A. 2015. *Mapping social cohesion: The Scanlon foundation surveys 2015.* Caufield East: Monash University.

Marsh, D., and R. Rhodes. 1992. *Policy networks in British government.* Oxford: Clarendon.

Marshall, N. 2003. "Identity and difference in complex projects: Why boundaries still matter in the 'boundaryless' organization." In *Managing boundaries in organizations: Multiple perspectives*, edited by N. Paulsen and T. Hernes, 55–75. Basingstoke: Palgrave Macmillan.

Martinez, O. 1994. "The dynamics of border interaction: New approaches to border analysis." In *Global boundaries, vol. I: World boundaries*, edited by C. Schofield, 1–15. London: Routledge.

Marx, K. 1963. *The eighteenth brumaire of Louis Napoleon.* New York: International Publishers.

Mayntz, R. 1993. "Governing failures and the problems of governability: Some comments on a theoretical paradigm." In *Modern governance: New government-society interactions*, edited by J. Kooiman, 9–20. London: Sage Publications Ltd.

McKenzie, J. 2001. *Perform or else: From discipline to performance.* London: Routledge. Reprint, Not in File.

Miller, E. J., and A. K. Rice. 1967. *Systems of organization—the control of task and sentient boundaries.* London: Tavistock.

Miller, R., H. Dickinson, and J. Glasby. 2011. "The care trust pilgrims." *Journal of Integrated Care* 19 (4):14–21.

Mosco, V. 2009. *The political economy of communication.* 2nd Edition. London: Sage Publications Ltd.

Newman, D. 2003. "On borders and power: A theoretical framework." *Journal of Borderland Studies* 18 (1):13–25.

Newman, D. 2006. "Borders and bordering: Towards an interdisciplinary dialogue." *European Journal of Social Theory* 9:171–186.

Newman, J. 2012. *Working the spaces of power: Activism, neoliberalism and gendered work.* London: Bloomsbury Academic.

Nicolini, D., J. Mengis, and J. Swan. 2012. "Understanding the role of objects in cross-disciplinary collaboration." *Organization Science* 23 (3):612–629.

O'Flynn, J. 2009. "The cult of collaboration." *Australian Journal of Public Administration* 68 (1):112–116.

O'Flynn, J. 2014. "Crossing boundaries: The fundamental questions in public management and policy." In *Crossing boundaries in public management and policy: The international experience*, edited by J. O'Flynn, D. Blackman and J. Halligan. London: Routledge.

O'Flynn, J., D. Blackman, and J. Halligan. 2013. *Crossing boundaries in public management and policy: The international experience*. Abingdon: Routledge.

O'Leary, R., and L. Bingham. 2009. *The collaborative public manager*. Washington, DC: Georgetown University Press.

Osborne, D., and T. Gaebler. 1993. *Reinventing government: How the entrepreneurial spirit is transforming the public sector*. London: Penguin Books. Reprint, In File.

Osborne, S. P. 2006. "The new public governance?" *Public Management Review* 8 (3):377–387.

Osborne, S. P. 2010. *The new public governance*. New York: Routledge.

Palma, P. J., M. P. Cunha, and M. P. Lopes. 2010. "The best of two worlds: How privatisation affects the identity of a public organization." *Public Management Review* 12 (5):725–746.

Parsons, T. 1971. *The system of modern societies*. Upper Saddle River, NJ: Prentice Hall.

Parsons, T. 1977. *Social systems and the evolution of action theory*. New York: Free Press.

Parsons, T. 2005. *The social system*. Oxford: Taylor and Francis.

Paulsen, N. 2003. " 'Who are we now'? Group identity, boundaries, and the (re) organizing process." In *Managing boundaries in organizations*, edited by N. Paulsen and T. Hernes. Basingstoke: Palgrave Macmillan.

Paulsen, N., and T. Hernes. 2003. "Epilogue: A reflection and future directions." In *Managing boundaries in organizations: Multiple perspectives*, edited by N. Paulsen and T. Hernes, 302–308. Basingstoke: Palgrave Macmillan.

Perri 6. 1997. *Holistic government*. London: Demos.

Pestoff, V., T. Brandsen, and B. Verschuere. 2012. *New public governance, the third sector, and co-production*. New York: Routledge.

Phillimore, J., H. Bradby, M. Knecht, B. Padilla, T. Brand, S. Cheung, S. Pemberton, and H. Zeeb. 2015. "Understanding healthcare practice in superdiverse neighbourhoods and developing the concept of welfare bricolage: Protocol of a cross-national mixed methods study." *BMC International Health and Human Rights* 15 (16).

Pollit, C. 2013. *New perspectives on public services: Place and technology*. Oxford: Oxford University Press.

Quick, K. S., and M. S. Feldman. 2014a. "Boundaries as junctures: Collaborative boundary work for building efficient resilience." *Journal of Public Administration Research and Theory* 24:673–695.

Quick, K. S., and M. S. Feldman. 2014b. "Boundaries as junctures: Collaborative boundary work for building efficient resilience." *Journal of Public Administration Research* 24:673–695.

Renne, P. R., A. L. Deino, F. J. Hilgen, K. F. Kuiper, D. F. Mark, and W. S. Mitchell. 2013. "Time scales of critical events around the Cretaceous-Paleogene boundary." *Science* 339 (6120):684–687.

Rhodes, R. A. W. 1996. "The new governance: Governing without government." *Political Studies* 44 (4):652–667.

Rhodes, R. A. W. 1997. *Understanding governance: Policy networks, governance, reflexivity and accountability*. Buckingham: Open University Press.

Rhodes, R. A. W. 2014. *Recovering the 'craft' of public administration in network governance*. Pleanary address to the International Political Science

Association World Congress, Montreal, 19th–24th July. Available from www.ipsa.org/my-ipsa/events/montreal2014/plenary/plenary-recovering-%E2%80%98craft%E2%80%99-public-administration-network-governa accessed 22 August 2014.

Rittel, H., and M. Webber. 1973. "Dilemmas in a general theory of Planning." *Policy Sciences* 4:155–169.

Roberts, M. J. D., and P. W. Beamish. 2017. "The scaffolding activities of international returnee executives: A learning based perspective of global boundary spanning." *Journal of Management Studies* 54 (4):511–539.

Rumford, C. 2006a. "Theorizing borders." *European Journal of Social Theory* 9:155–169.

Rumford, C. 2006b. "Rethinking European spaces: Territory, borders, governance." *Comparative European Politics* 4:127–140.

Schermerhorn, J. R. 1975. "Determinants of interorganizational cooperation." *Academy of Management Journal* 18 (4):846–856.

Scott, W. R. 1995. *Institutions and organizations*. Thousand Oaks, CA: Sage Publications Ltd.

Shamir, B., and Y. Melnik. 2003. "Some organizational consequences of cultural differences in boundary permeability." In *Managing boundaries in organizations: Multiple perspectives*, edited by N. Paulsen and T. Hernes, 281–301. Basingstoke: Palgrave Macmillan.

Shields, R. 2006. "Boundary-thinking in theories of the present." *European Journal of Social Theory* 9:223–237.

Singer, J. 2015. "Out of bounds: Professional norms as boundary markers." In *Boundaries of journalism: Professionalism, practices and participation*, edited by M. Carlson and S. C. Lewis, 21–36. Oxford: Routledge.

Star, S. L. 2010. "This is not a boundary object: Reflections on the origin of a concept." *Science Technology Human Values* 35 (5):601–617.

Star, S. L., and J. R. Griesemer. 1989. "Institutional ecology, 'translations' and boundary objects: Amateurs and professionals in Berkeley's museum of verterbrate zoology." *Social Studies in Science* 19 (3):387–420.

Stern, C. S., and B. Henderson. 1993. *Performance: Texts and contexts*. London: Longman. Reprint, In File.

Sullivan, H. 2015. "What can government and leaders do when trust evaporates." *The Conversation* 9th February. Available frrm https://theconversation.com/what-can-governments-and-leaders-do-when-trust-evaporates-37333 accessed 21st October 2016.

Sullivan, H., and C. Skelcher. 2002. *Working across boundaries: Collaboration in public services*. Basingstoke: Palgrave Macmillan. Reprint, Not in File.

Sullivan, H., and P. Williams. 2009. "The limits of co-ordination: Community strategies as multi-pupose vehicles in Wales." *Local Government Studies* 35 (2):161–180.

Sullivan, H., and P. Williams. 2012. "Whose kettle? Exploring the role of boundary objects in managing and mediating the boundaries of integration in health and social care." *Journal of Health Organization and Management* 26 (6):697–712.

Sullivan, H., P. Williams, M. Marchington, and L. Knight. 2013. "Collaborative futures: Discursive realignments in austere times." *Public Money and Management* 33 (2):123–130.

Taylor, J. R., and D. Robichaud. 2004. "Finding the organization in the communication: Discourse as action and sensemaking." *Organization* 11 (3):395–413.

Trompette, P., and D. Vinck. 2009. "Revisiting the notion of boundary object." *Revue d'anthopologie des connaissances* 3 (1):3–25.

Van Egmond, S., and R. Bal. 2011. "Boundary configurations in science policy: Modeling practices in health care." *Science, Technology & Human Values* 36 (1):108–130.

Van Houtum, H., and A. Strüver. 2002. "Borders, strangers, bridges and doors." *Space and Polity* 6 (2):141–146.

Van Maanen, J., and E. H. Schein. 1979. "Toward a theory of organizational socialization." In *Research in organizational behaviour*, edited by B. Staw, 209–264. Greenwich, CT: JAI Press.

Wagenaar, H., and S. D. Noam Cook. 2003. "Understanding policy practices: Action, dialectic and deliberation in policy analysis." In *Deliberative policy analysis: Understanding governance in the network society*, edited by M. A. Hajer and H. Wagenaar, 139–171. Cambridge: Cambridge University Press.

Walther, O. J. 2015. "Business, brokers and borders: The structure of West African trade networks." *Journal of Development Studies* 51 (5):603–620.

Wehrens, R., M. Bekker, and R. Bal. 2011. "Coordination of research, policy and practice: A case study of collaboration in the field of public health." *Science & Public Policy* 38 (10):1–12.

Wels, H. 2003. "Formidable fences: Organizational cooperation and boundary bullies in Zimbabwe." In *Managing boundaries in organizations: Multiple perspectives*, edited by N. Paulsen and T. Hernes, 211–225. Basingstoke: Palgrave Macmillan.

White, S., C. Hall, and S. Peckover. 2009. "The descriptive tyranny of the common assessment framework: Technologies of categorization and professional practice in child welfare." *British Journal of Social Work* 39 (7):1197–1217.

White, S., D. Wastell, K. Boradhurst, and C. Hall. 2010. "When policy o'erleaps itself: The 'tragic tale' of the integrated children's system." *Critical Social Policy* 30 (3):405–429.

Williams, P. 2002. "The competent boundary spanner." *Public Administration* 80 (1):103–124.

Williams, P. 2005. "Collaborative capability and the management of interdependencies: the contribution of boundary spanners." Unpublished PhD thesis, University of Bristol, Bristol.

Williams, P. 2012. *Collaboration in public policy and practice: Perspectives on boundary spanners*. Bristol: Policy Press. Reprint, In File.

Yanow, D. 2004. "Translating local knowledge at organizational peripheries." *British Journal of Management* 15 (Suppl 1):S9–S25.

Yates, Sophie. 2017. *Alcohol, drugs and family violence: A question of framing and boundary markers*. Power to Persuade, 5th July. Available from www.powertopersuade.org.au/blog/4bhjmxkw1nkuxsyxhqjewkrwupfl6g/4/7/2017 accessed 22nd February 2018.

Young, T., S. Brailsford, C. Connell, R. Davies, P. Harper, and J. H. Klein. 2004. "Using industrial processes to improve patient care." *British Medical Journal* 328 (7432):162–164.

Yuval-Davis, N. 2004. *Borders, boundaries and the politics of belonging*. Cambridge: Cambridge University Press.

Zeiss, R., and P. Groenewegen. 2009. "Engaging boundary objects in OMS and STS? Exploring the subtleties of layered engagement." *Organization* 16 (1):81–100.

Zerubavel, E. 1991. *The fine line: Making distinctions in everyday life.* New York: Free Press.

Zerubavel, E. 1996. "Lumping and splitting: Notes on social classification." *Sociological Forum* 11 (3):421–433.

Zerubavel, E. 1997. *Social mindscapes: An invitation to cognitive sociology.* Cambridge, MA: Harvard University Press.

Zhang, Y., and C. Huxham. 2009. "Identity construction and trust building." *The Journal of Applied Behavioral Science* 45:186–211.

Part 2
The Practical Challenge

Introduction

This Part examines the practical challenges faced by policy makers and practitioners involved in crossing boundaries in public management and policy, and the ways in which they are approached and tackled. As Radin (1996, p. 145) reflects:

> Government in a complex society, by definition, is characterised by boundaries. Whether a result of a fragmented and segmented political system, differentiation by policy issues, or because of functional imperatives, lines have been drawn that separate organizations from one another. Although these boundaries are both understandable and sometimes appropriate, the organizations created by boundaries often seem unable to respond to the changing social, political, and economic demands that are placed on the. Adaptation or even survival appears to require that public agencies look across the boundary lines that now define them.

Consequently, the public management and policy landscape is now littered with numerous and diverse expressions of cross-boundary working designed to deliver societal goals across a wide range of policy areas (as explored in Part 1 of this text). The history of this form of working and governance varies considerably across different countries but there is a real sense that its potency is deepening and widening. It is driven by a number of analytically distinct but intricately connected discourses (Sullivan, Williams, Marchington, et al., 2012) that gain traction at different times in response to different interests coupled with frequent exhortations by politicians and policy makers to engage in this form of cross boundary policy and practice. However, despite an accumulated body of practice and experience of this form of working, underpinned by an increasing, but still limited body of evaluation and evidence, cross-boundary working continues to be highly challenging in reality with outcomes often far less impressive than the energies invested in them.

A sobering conclusion of one report suggests that: "there is very little evidence linking partnership working in the UK public services to improved outcomes" (Cook, 2015, p. 1) and similarly a Cochrane Systematic Review (2012) concluded that: "despite decades of research on the impact of enhanced collaboration between local health and local government services there is no reliable evidence that it necessarily improves health outcomes when compared to standard services" (p. 36) and

> a similar systematic review looking at the impact of multi-agency partnerships on public health outcomes, which excluded studies measuring impact on individuals, reported that evidence was partial and it was difficult to ascertain any health effects attributable to partnership working, despite the costs associated with establishing these public health partnerships.
>
> (p. 36)

This Part of the book focuses on cross-boundary work between organisations and sectors—referred to variously as collaboration, partnership, integration, joint working amongst others. In doing so, it touches on the implications of managing across other boundaries—professional, social, cultural—raised in the Part 1 of this book. It endeavours to consolidate and synthesise what we know about the determinants of effective cross-boundary working including 'what works,' and the levers and mechanisms that are most effective in fostering this form of governance. It uses evidence from different policy areas, parts of the world and stages of the policy process to explore various challenges and strategies. It also investigates whether working between different combinations of tri-sector working—public, private, third sector—present any unique challenges, particularly those that might offer the potential for inter-sectoral and inter-organisational learning.

This part of the book is organised into three major chapters. The first chapter sets out a discussion on the nature of the challenges that are faced by actors and organisations engaged in collaborative policy and practice—those that are different from other forms of management by virtue of their motivation, accountability, power relationships and difference. The second chapter sets out and examines the key lessons for policy and practice—the complicated interweaving and alchemy between structural and agential factors, and the manner in which they constrain and enable particular actions and interventions. It is interesting to reflect on why politicians and policy makers often tend to reach for structural levers (reconfiguration, statutory powers, financial incentives) to direct and influence the course of collaboration, rather than attend to agency. Is it because these are easier to manage, or are they the most instrumental in determining outcomes?

The lessons for policy and practice have been gathered and sifted from a diverse body of evidence collected primarily from practice guides and frameworks with a 'what works' emphasis but, reliably underpinned by a robust research and academic foundation. These have been assembled under a number of broad headings—purpose and strategy; governance and resources; agency which includes leadership, management and inter-professionality; learning and knowledge management; and finally, performance and evaluation. This list is not necessarily exhaustive but represents the key factors that are likely to influence the shape and trajectory of collaboration, together with the practical challenges of the cross-boundary work inherent in this form of governance and management.

The following chapter considers the training and development implications for people and organisations working in this policy arena. The discussion looks at how 'learning' about collaborative policy and practice is translated into forms that are timely and digestible for practitioners through practice guides, workshops, training, consultancy and other mechanisms; the challenges associated with working across the boundaries between academia and practice, and what practitioners want from research and how can the respective constituencies communicate effectively with each other. Further, the discussion also touches on the effectiveness of different learning and knowledge management methods and carriers, and looks at how best to convert and translate what is known for the training, education and development of boundary-spanning agents. The final chapter sets out the conclusions of this Part in which it is noted that it is important for the practice challenge to consider the question of whether leading and managing in collaboration is similar to or different from that in hierarchical forms of governance, and if it is the latter, to set out the most effective capabilities and behaviours that need to be practised by boundary spanners of different types and operating in different situations.

Overall, this part of the book aims to consolidate and highlight what we know about the cross-boundary challenges of working in collaborative environments. Undoubtedly, these have proved to be complex in practice and will continue to tax academics, policy makers and practitioners into the future.

5 The Challenges of Crossing Boundary Practice

Paul Williams

Inter-organisational and cross-sector boundary management, policy and practice are confronted by a complex tapestry of boundaries—real, manufactured and variously constructed through the lenses of key actors. The means of coordination in this mode of governance—network governance—is materially different from that in markets and hierarchies (Thompson et al., 1991), and its defining characteristics are the source of boundary challenges not encountered within intra-organisational forms of management, particularly in terms of number, diversity and fluctuation. Key distinguishing characteristics include the following:

- There can be differences in the motivation to collaborate between different actors and organisations. Efficiency, effectiveness and responsiveness discourses have been detected in the history of collaborative endeavours. They often co-exist, vary over time, are stimulated by prevailing social, economic and governmental drivers, and are closely associated with key actors and interests. In the UK for instance, the merits of collaboration as the dominant mode of governance for tackling a wide range of policy issues has resulted in a significant trend towards mandated collaboration through prescribed statutory duties and powers being placed on particular organisations. However, a strategy of endeavouring to force people and organisations to work across boundaries against their will may not always be effective. Unless that coercion is supported by efforts to help actors and organisations appreciate the possibilities of collaboration for their own self-interests, the challenges of cooperative action may be tortuous and limited. Grasping the very essence of collaboration is absolutely fundamental, a point highlighted by Manzini (2015, p. 93) in the following passage: "collaboration takes place when people encounter each other and exchange something (time, care, experiences, expertise, etc.) in order to receive a benefit; in other words, they create a shared value."
- The people assembled within collaborative arenas often have many differences relating to their professional identity, experience,

knowledge and background, and represent organisations that are different in the ways in which they are organised, governed, and managed—resulting in coherent cultural and value-based entities. Arguably, the sectoral differences that distinguish the public, private and third sectors represent major hurdles to overcome in cross-boundary policy and practice. Understandings of these sectors differ between different countries, but certainly the value base underpinning them is comparable. The private sector is consistent in its quest for 'maximising profit' and 'shareholders value'; market mechanisms mediate and coordinate behaviour; and the notion of the 'customer' is fundamental in this mode of governance. In contrast, the public sector is driven by a desire to create social value with elected representatives deliberating on the allocation of resources based on need between competing demands, invariably against a background of limited resources. The recipients of public services are conceived as 'clients,' 'service users' and 'patients,' and collectively as citizens and communities. Third-sector organisations—'not for profit,' 'social enterprises,' 'charities,' voluntary groups and others—represent additional variation primarily in terms of a specific focus on the interests of defined groups or communities.

Different sectors are the subject of appreciably different operating environments, particularly in terms of Government legislation. Public agencies are highly prescribed in their duties, legal responsibilities, decision-making structures, financial systems and accountability structures, whereas private and third sectors operate within different system of regulation, legal and financial frameworks.

- The dissimilarities between organisations and sectors are magnified through the differences in the performance management, accountability and scrutiny systems in place to oversee them. Public organisations are usually the subject of comprehensive and sometimes 'oppressive' systems of accountability and oversight. Checks and balances take many forms including independent auditing, scrutiny panels and Ombudsman arrangements. Power relationships are significantly different in collaborative arrangements. Whereas classical forms of social organisation and governance have power relationships that are single and sovereign—with power vested in positions within the hierarchy reinforced by control over resources such as people, land and budgets—power relationships in forms of collaboration are more complex, contested, negotiated, diffuse and rely on strategies that draw on an understanding of processes, meaning and politics.

Organisational goals are often unclear, ambiguous and shift over time. Individuals and organisations are the subject of multiple and sometimes conflicting accountabilities—variously to their home organisation, to the collaboration itself and to the recipients of their services—the customers, clients and citizens. The Christie Commission on the Future Direction of Public Services in Scotland (2011, p. 21) neatly sums up the problems emanating from a patchwork of public bodies created over a number of years:

this complexity is reflected in inadequate strategic coordination between public service organisations that work routinely to different objectives, with separate budgets and processes for accountability; operational duplication is rife between different services; points of authority and control are dispersed widely among varied public bodies, making joint-working and reform difficult. Collaboration often relies on the persistence and flexibility of individual front-line workers and leaders.

This is by no means an exhaustive list of the characteristics of a collaborative environment, but it does represent the key components that together present a highly complex, interrelated and dynamic set of challenges faced by policy makers and practitioners.

6   Lesson for Policy and Practice

Paul Williams

The perennial question of endeavouring to determine 'what works' or, which factors and their combinations, produce particular outcomes is particularly complex. As outlined in Part 1 of this book, one enduring debate in the social sciences that underlies this question concerns 'structure and agency.' The essence of this debate concerns the position that structuralists adopt, believing that social, political and economic outcomes can be explained by 'structure'—that is form, function, context and setting—as opposed to the behaviouralists who argue that agency is the determining factor—the ability or capacity of people to act consciously to realise particular intentions. Needless to say, there are many different views and permutations on this debate, and I will offer you one position that I believe may be helpful and that is: that while actors may manufacture outcomes, the parameters of their capacity to act—the constraint and opportunities—are set by the structured context in which they operate. So, it's a combination of both structure and agency. However, into this mix, some commentators argue that the influence of ideas also plays an important role. Ideational influences vary widely at different levels and in different policy areas—they gain traction and popularity at particular times—through narratives, stories and policy paradigms (e.g. Hay, 1995). For example, within the general area of collaboration, different notions—such as 'integration,' 'citizen-focus' and 'new public management' can be seen to shape the design and delivery of collaborative solutions.

In reality, there is a complex interweaving and interplay between structure, agency and ideas that conspire to determine the course of cross boundary governance. Although there is no 'holy grail' to ensure effective and successful outcomes in this mode of governance, the lessons from empirical research and practice suggest there are a number of key ingredients or factors that help shape effective outcomes. For instance, in a report by the United States Government Accountability Office (2012) the key considerations for managing inter-agency collaboration were judged to be those set out in Box 6.1:

Box 6.1:   Key Considerations for Managing Inter-Agency Collaboration

Outcomes and Accountability: Have short-term and long-term outcomes been clearly defined? Is there a way to track and monitor their progress?

Bridging Organisational Cultures: What are the missions and organisational cultures of the participating agencies? Have agencies agreed on common terminology and definitions?

Leadership: How will leadership be sustained over the long-term? If leadership is shared, have roles and responsibilities been clearly identified and agreed upon?

Clarity of Roles and Responsibilities: Have participating agencies clarified roles and responsibilities?

Participants: Have all relevant participants been included? Do they have the ability to commit resources for their agency?

Resources: How will the collaborative mechanism be funded and staffed? Have online collaboration tools been developed?

Written Guidance and Agreements: If appropriate, have participating agencies documented their agreement regarding how they will be collaborating? Have they developed ways to continually update and monitor these agreements?

In the specific context of integrated care, a Context and Capabilities for Integrated Care Framework has been developed (through a literature review and empirical research in Canada) to help policy makers and managers devise and implement effective practical solutions (Evans et al., 2016). O'Leary and Gerard (2012) suggest that there are five major catalysts for getting collaboration to work effectively in practice which they list in order of importance as—people and their relationships, the need to achieve results, a sense of urgency, directions from the top and organisational support. These kinds of frameworks have been encapsulated in innumerable 'good practice guides' and 'aide memoires' of variable authenticity and robustness (see Box 6.2). An interrogation of these and other relevant material indicates the importance of a number of key factors as follows—Purpose and Strategy; Governance and Resources; Agency: Leadership, Management and Inter-professionality; Learning and Knowledge Management; and Performance and Evaluation. The remainder of this chapter explores these in turn.

Purpose and Strategy

Given the often-unquestioning belief in the virtues of collaborative working, it might appear rather heretical to suggest that it is not a panacea for

Box 6.2:   Good Practice Guides and Framework Examples

ARACY (2006) *Effective Collaboration* Canberra: ARACY

Audit Commission (1998) *A fruitful partnership: Effective partnership working* London: Audit Commission

Cameron, A. and Lart, R. (1997) *"Factors promoting and obstacles hindering joint working: A systematic review of the literature"*, Journal of Integrated Care, Vol. 11, No.2, pp. 9–17

Centre for the Advancement of Collaborative Strategies in Health (2002) *Partnership self-assessment tool* New York: CACSH

DCLG (2006) *Supporting people for better health: A guide to partnership working* London: DCLG

Grieg, R. and Poxton, R. (2000) *Partnership readiness framework* London: Kings College

Halliday, J. Asthanana, S.N.M. and Richardson, S. (2004) "Evaluating partnerships: the role of formal assessment tools", *Evaluation*, Vol. 10 No. 3, pp. 285–303

Hardy, B. Hudson, B. and Waddington, E. (2000) *What makes a good partnership? A partnership assessment tool* Leeds: Nuffield Institute for Health

Huxham, C. and Vangen, S. (2005) *Managing to collaborate: The theory and practice of collaborative advantage* London: Routledge

Mattessich, P.W. and Monsey, B.R. (1994) *Collaboration: What makes it work?* St. Paul, Minnesota: Amherst H. Wilder Foundation

Scottish Executive (2004) *Partnership working* Edinburgh: Scottish Executive

The Sainsbury Centre for Mental Health (2000) *Taking your partners: Using opportunities for inter-agency partnerships in mental health* London: The Sainsbury Centre for Mental Health

Tsou, C. Haynes, E. Warner, W.D. Gray, G. and Thompson, S.C. (2015) "An exploration of inter-organizational assessment tools in the context of Australian Aboriginal-mainstream partnerships: a scoping review of the literature", BMC Public Heath, Vol. 15, p. 416

Williams, P. and Sullivan, H. (2007) *Learning to collaborate: Lessons in effective partnership working in health and social care* Cardiff: NLIAH

Williams, P. and Sullivan, H. (2007) *Getting collaboration to work in Wales: Lessons from the NHS and partners* Cardiff: NLIAH

Wilson, A. and Charleton, K. (1997) *Making partnerships work: A practical guide for the public, private and community sectors* York: York Publishing Services

Victoria Heath (2011) *The partnership analysis tool* Melbourne: Victoria Heath Promotion Foundation all forms of public service design and delivery. It is a form of governance that has both costs and benefits, and it is important to determine when it is appropriate and when more traditional forms of organising are likely to be the most effective.

There is a need to engage, at the very outset of potential cooperative action, in a hard-headed assessment of its appropriateness to particular circumstances and objectives. Whilst the benefits of collaboration seem alluring, the downside of collaboration—in terms of a potential loss of status, stability, control, autonomy and legitimacy of individual agencies; reconfigured power relationships; confused accountabilities; and conflict over goals and methods leading to tortuous and lengthy decision-making processes—can be easily overlooked. The clear message for policy makers and practitioners is to ensure that collaboration is the most appropriate response to the particular policy problems and issues being addressed.

Having made a choice in favour of collaboration, the evidence points to the importance of establishing both clarity and strength of purpose (see Case Study in Box 6.3). This involves a process that aims to secure a collective vision and values to underpin this form of working. This needs to be capable of being translated into jointly agreed aims and objectives which are sufficiently precise and unambiguous, both to drive the delivery of collective actions, and which can be used as a reference to measure outcomes and impact. There can be a tendency for vision and value exercises to be overly vague and aspirational—bland, high level and rhetorical 'motherhood and apple pie' statements that are capable of multiple interpretations by different interests. This is sometimes a reflection of the need "to enable disparate stakeholders to easily 'buy into' the collaboration, and avoid early potential conflict that may sour future progress" (Williams and Sullivan, 2007, p. 9). However, the quest for 'too much clarity,' which might involve complicated and potentially unresolvable discussions about basic values, risks paralysing the whole process. On the other hand, an absence of clarity at the outset risks problems at the implementation stage of the policy process. Arguably, the answer is to negotiate a balance at the outset that allows a sufficient consensus and clarity of purpose to mobilise joint action, whilst allowing flexibility for the strategy to emerge and be crafted rather than be predetermined. The importance of linking aims and objectives to outcomes is underscored by (Hardy et al., 2000), and of making a clear distinction between the 'non-collaboration' business of organisations and 'collaboration' business.

A report by Kindornay et al. (2014) into cross-sector partnerships highlights the fundamental importance of achieving clarity around objectives and purposes at the outset of any potential collaborative engagement. These are summarised in Box 6.4.

Box 6.3   Case Study—Common Purpose: Making the Connections

This case study exemplifies the importance of, and rationale for securing 'common purpose' for adopting a collaborative approach to a complex and interconnected problem between a number of public bodies involved in a Community Safety Partnership in South Wales. The following scenario was used by one member of the Partnership to justify the case for a collaborative Youth Engagement Programme, and he argued that too often public bodies respond independently to the symptoms and not the causes of problems and issues.

> A young man is at a bus stop—he is wearing a 'hoodie,' jogging bottoms and trainers, and is smoking a 'spliff' with mates; he fits the profile of someone who is likely to set fire to a wheelie-bin, to throw stones at a fire engine, to set an alarm off by throwing a stone through a shop window, or to commit minor criminal damage to street furniture and public landscaping. Each one of these actions has traditionally led to a fragmented approach by an individual public body—the fire service if it involves arson, the police if it involves criminal damage and anti-social behaviour, the health service if actions result in personal injury, harm or lifestyle, the probation service if he is on their books, and any affected third-sector organisation which may have dealings with this individual. The point is that there are so many different public agencies that have an interest in this 'individual,' and this demands a collaborative approach base on a shared and common purpose. Treating the individual as the starting point will be better for him, and more efficient and effective for the public services involved.

Source: This example was taken from an interview with a Senior Member of a Fire and Rescue Service in South Wales

---

There is an interesting debate about the effectiveness of different strategic management approaches in theatres of collaboration. In general, the public sector is accustomed to a planning model (Mintzberg, 1994) which is rational and comprehensive in its conceptualisation; where there is a presumption of rationality between means and ends; and where a top-down, ordered and sequential approach is encouraged to achieve a 'grand plan' (Flynn and Talbot, 1996). Experience suggests that, all too often, this approach to strategic management is inflexible and inappropriate particularly for managing in a complex, interdependent and turbulent policy environment. Predicting the future is a notoriously thankless exercise, and the separation between the formulation and implementation stages of the process is a major fallacy.

Box 6.4: A Guide to Creating Value in Cross-Sector Partnerships (Kindornay, et al., 2014)

- Policy makers and partnership practitioners should define from the outset the objectives and purposes of a partnership and outline the roles of different actors: Realising the full potential of Cross-Sector Development Partnerships largely depends on the management and maintenance of the relationship between actors, ability to develop trust and sharing of organisational values as actors move along the collaboration continuum. Consequently, overcoming differences and aligning contributions is pivotal so that all partners can co-create social and organisational value.

- The level of engagement between and among partners should depend on the objectives and purposes of the partnership: Deeper integration among public, private and non-profit actors leads to greater value creation, but the management and maintenance of these engagements is a challenging task. Policy makers and practitioners should carefully examine the benefits and costs of forming and maintaining a partnership.

- In addition to partnership objectives, the comparative advantages of different partners determine the types of value—associational, resource, interaction and synergistic—derived from the partnership: Assessment of the core competencies that each partners possesses is important. It is equally important for each partner to identify their weaknesses. Organisations should assess whether collaboration with a particular partner can strengthen organisational shortcomings and enhance complementing capabilities. Potential partners need to assess partnerships not only in terms of the combined resources and capabilities that each partner brings, but the organisational impacts that the formation and maintenance of a partnership may entail.

As an alternative, and more appropriate to the prevailing context and conditions of a cross-boundary collaboration, a more emergent approach to strategic management might be more practical—a kind of "sniff the wind, and then move in the right direction" attitude. Here, strategy is 'crafted' (Mintzberg, 1994), and more open to creativity, innovation and entrepreneurial intent. It is:

> Sensitive to the involvement of a diverse set of stakeholders in the process—both at strategic and operational levels—it encourages processes that are negotiative and interactive, acknowledges that power relationships are dispersed rather than sovereign, and accommodates bargaining and political manoeuvring within and between dominant coalitions of interests.
>
> (Williams and Sullivan, 2009, p. 18)

An emergent approach to strategic management (Mintzberg and Waters, 1998) is characterised by:

- A fusing of the formulation, implementation and evaluation stages of the process with actors primarily responsible for individual stages being involved from the outset
- Where strategies are open, flexible and responsive, inviting strategic learning rather than control
- In contrast to more planned and deliberate strategies that emphasise central direction and hierarchy, emergent forms open the way for collective action and collaboration
- A political process involving different groups and interests using multiple faces of power to achieve collective action.

An emergent approach to strategic management is particularly suitable to volatile, complex, ambiguous and interdependent situations where processes can be 'messy,' sometimes experimental, and where frontline stakeholders working from the bottom up are accepted as a legitimate part of the process. Arguably, more planned approaches are suitable for situations that are less complex and turbulent.

Governance and Resources

The design, structure and governance of collaborative relationships, and the resources that are available to manage the processes involved are key factors in effective collaboration. Emerson et al. (2011, p. 2) define collaborative governance:

> as the processes and structures of public policy decision making and management that engage people constructively across the boundaries of public agencies, levels of government, and/or the public, private and civic spheres in order to carry out a public purpose that could not otherwise be accomplished.

There are a host of different mechanisms to facilitate collaboration as identified in the GAO report (2012) on American Federal Government including, structures (taskforces, commissions, working groups); strategies and initiatives; inter-agency groups; leadership arrangements (lead agency, shared leadership roles); co-located facilities; positions (liaison, inter-agency); agreements; joint programmes and collaboration technologies. Critically however, in any democratic government setting, the arrangements for open, transparent and accountable governance are very important. However, the experience of collaborative ventures in many policy areas suggests that structural and governance factors are problematic, and sometimes not accorded the priority they demand.

Collaborative working brings together organisations that are often very different in their own constitutions—this is acutely the case when different sectors—public, private and third—attempt to work together. Legal and statutory duties, decision-making frameworks, financial probity, scrutiny, accountability and other rules and operating systems make up a heady and complicated mixture of ingredients to take into account. But, the need to exercise appropriate control and accountability in collaboration is no less than that in individual organisations. It is, however, probably more difficult because the levers present in hierarchical relationships through command and control and authority and accepted rules of behaviour are not usually available or appropriate in collaborative settings. Control, nevertheless, is critical to provide the clarity of joint purpose, the direction and regulation of collaborative actions, and the delivery of shared outcomes.

In a private sector context, Hughes and Weiss (2004) compile a set of 'simple' rules for making alliances work in practice involving placing less emphasis on establishing formal alliance management systems, structures and business arrangements, and more emphasis on developing the right collaborative behaviours; placing less emphasis on eliminating differences but more on embracing differences; less emphasis on managing external relationships, and more on managing internal stakeholders; and finally, less emphasis on creating ends metrics and more emphasis on fashioning means metrics.

Donahue (2004) suggests that the design of a collaborative governance arrangement needs to take account of a number of factors and these are detailed in Box 6.5.

Ansell and Gash (2007) have undertaken a meta-analytical study of the literature on collaborative governance across a range of policy sectors to arrive at a number of critical variables that influence the success or otherwise of this mode of governance. A model is constructed consisting of four broad variables—preconditions, institutional design, leadership and the collaborative process. Within each of these variables is a series of more fine-grained variables as follows:

- *Starting conditions*: these relate to power/resource/knowledge asymmetries, incentives for and constraints on participation and prehistory of cooperation of conflict
- *Leadership*: refers essentially to notions of facilitative leadership
- *Institutional design*: participatory inclusiveness, clear ground rules and transparency of the process
- *Collaborative process*: the essential ingredients here are seen to be trust-building, commitment to the process and shared ownership, face-to-face dialogues, shared understanding expressed through common problem identification, value systems and missions, and demonstrating intermediate outcomes via small wins and strategic plans

Box 6.5: Dimensions for the Design of Collaborative Governance (Donahue, 2004, p. 3)

- **Formality:** this relates to the level of institutionalisation that is required—either through formal contracts or alternately informal agreements or tacit understandings. The latter are difficult to recognise or analyse and a degree of formalism at least sufficient to permit objective descriptions of participants, procedures and goals is necessary to distinguish collaborative governance from other forms of organising.
- **Duration:** these range from permanent arrangements to ad hoc collaborations that are dissolved when a crisis or problem is resolved.
- **Focus:** whether the collaboration is narrowly structured to meet a single shared challenge or issue, or more broadly designed to meet a range of challenges whether simultaneously or sequentially.
- **Institutional Diversity:** these vary widely to embrace agencies from different sectors, tiers of government and policy areas.
- **Valence:** concerns the number of distinct players linked together in a collaboration and the number of links between them.
- **Stability versus Volatility:** a collaboration is stable to the extent its members share a normative view of successful governance, and volatile to the extent members' norms or interests diverge. The less stable is the collaboration, the larger the share of its energies must be devoted to maintaining the collaboration itself.
- **Initiative:** which collaborating institution(s) instigated the joint effort, and what is the allocation of initiative among the parties for defining goals, assessing results and triggering adjustments? Who is leveraging whom?
- **Problem-driven versus Opportunity-driven:** this refers to whether the collaboration is 'defensive' in the sense that it is devoted to solving or ameliorating a joint threat, or primarily 'offensive' in terms or pursuing a shared opportunity. In other words, maintaining or improving the status quo.

The three core contingencies the authors extract are—time, trust and interdependence and counsel that: "practitioners ought to consider each of these general contingencies before embarking on a collaborative strategy" (Ansell and Gash, 2007, p. 562). In a similar vein, Emerson et al. (2011) develop a 'collaborative governance regime' (CGR) that provides an integrative framework for situating and explaining diverse cross-boundary governance systems. Their model posits that CGRs are the product of four key drivers—leadership, consequential incentives, interdependence and uncertainty. Once established, such a system is shaped dynamically along a path through an interplay of principled engagement, shared motivations and capacity for joint action. The authors argue that such a framework offers public managers and policy makers: "a conceptual map by which to navigate the various dimensions, components, and elements of collaborative governance" (2011, p. 23). It can help with deciding whether a collaborative approach is indeed the most appropriate way forward, can assist with the co-design of the governance arrangements and might enable the development of learning systems and reflective practices.

Irrespective of the many manifestations and forms that collaborative working takes, there are important issues to address in relation to corporate governance to ensure that transparency, probity and public accountability are protected and enhanced. There has been some research (Audit Commission, 2005) that concludes that collaborative working can be somewhat risky particularly in relation to financial and performance accountability. The challenge is to strike the right balance between setting out the appropriate decision making, scrutiny and other management systems, with a culture and framework that does not become overly bureaucratic, inflexible and ultimately inhibits creativity and innovation. Corporate governance in collaboration is not the same as that within single organisations and needs to be predicated on considerations relating to purpose, membership, rules of engagement, accountability, scrutiny, delivery and ways of working.

An additional challenge in many collaborations concerns their relationship with service users and citizens and this can vary hugely depending on the models of public participation involved. Clarity and resolution need to be secured on key questions including who should be involved; at what level and stage should the involvement take place; how should marginalised and disenfranchised groups be engaged; how can the inequality and differential power relationships between different stakeholders be managed; and how can the respective legitimies of formally elected politicians be balanced with those of the more informal community leaders? This last point concerns the extent to which representative or participatory models of government are practised in a particular area.

Policy makers and practitioners engaged in collaborative working ignore resource issues at their peril. Again, these vary depending upon the type of collaboration. For instance, they are likely to be clearer when a defined amount of finance is injected into a particular community or service, but even so, clarity is essential on how this money is used and accounted for. More problematic is where collaborating agencies might be aiming to re-align or re-focus existing spending patterns and priorities on the basis of a new strategy. Delivery issues often bedevil unfocused strategic intent. Research studies often report that participants complain of a condition they refer to as *'partnership fatigue'*—a reference to the time demands and efforts involved in building and sustaining effective personal and professional relationships with a wide network of actors, attending and servicing various meetings and other machinery of collaborative governance—often considered as additional to the normal duties and demands of working within a home organisation.

An important lesson for all forms of collaboration is to acknowledge that the process of this form of governance is demanding and requires effective resourcing particularly in relation to leadership and management—building and sustaining effective relationships, servicing joint decision making structures, communication, networking and all the bureaucracy that is involved in the collaborative machinery and infrastructure. This may require dedicated personnel to coordinate and administer any joint arrangements, and/or adjustments to the mainstream jobs of managers and leaders involved. A related point is judging when to call time on collaborations that are clearly not working and/or have achieved their purpose(s). Some collaborations are perpetuated for cosmetic rather than productive purposes—actors not wanting to signal failure or damage potential future collaborations.

Agency: Leadership, Management and Inter-Professionality

There is little doubt that the role and nature of agency has a significant influence on the course and outcomes of boundary-crossing practices in collaboration across all policy areas. A critical review of the literature on this subject can be summarised and presented in relation to three main forms of agency—leadership, management and inter-professionality. Each three of these are discussed in turn as follows.

Leadership

Bryson and Crosby (1992, p. 323) consider that:

> In today's shared-power, no-one-in-charge, interdependent world, public problems and issues spill over organizational and institutional boundaries . . . but no one person, group or organization has the necessary power or authority to solve these problems. Instead, organizations and institutions must share objectives, resources, activities, power or some of their authority in order to achieve collective gains or minimise losses.

This observation has a huge bearing on the demands of leaders and leadership approaches in this context, which arguably are different to those within organisations where the forms of organising are traditionally more structured and controlled. Wading through the literature on leadership is no easy task because of its magnitude, diversity, inter-disciplinarity, theoretical variety and contestation. Parry and Bryman (2006) offer a useful framework that summarises the main types of leadership theories, including

- trait theories (Van Wart, 2003) that highlight the personal qualities and characteristics of leaders
- style theories that forefront observable leadership behaviours
- contingency theories where situational and contextual factors are seen to influence leadership approaches
- new leadership theories where leaders are considered to be managers of meaning and reflected in transformational, transactional, charismatic and visionary approaches
- shared (Fletcher and Kaufer, 2003), dispersed (Pearce and Conger, 2003) or distributed (Brown and Gioia, 2002) theories that reject the notions of leaders being 'heroic' in favour of developing followers to embrace leadership processes and skills.

Crevani et al. (2007, p. 48) have an excellent summary and comparison of the main aspects of traditional heroic leadership and postheroic leadership approaches.

It may well be that some of these theories resonate to various degrees with the requirements of cross-boundary settings. Contingency and style approaches might reflect the need to be responsive, flexible and adaptive to the variety of situations and contexts found in collaborative settings; the different life cycle stages of collaborative endeavours; the mixture of different policy areas; and the multiplicity of inter-organisational forms devised to govern them. New leadership theories with their emphasis on 'managing meaning' has a great deal of resonance in arenas that value the catalytic effect of visioning and value articulation, and the importance of communicating shared meanings and purposes between different interests. However, these leadership approaches can be criticised because of their preoccupation with 'heroic' leaders at the top of organisations, and influencing in a predominantly downward and hierarchical direction to groups of 'followers.'

In contrast, shared, dispersed or distributed theories have an immediate attraction for cross-boundary milieus, particularly in response to the non-hierarchical and complex interweaving of power relationships between assembled parties, where accountabilities are multiple and various, and where knowledge and expertise are widely distributed. However, the inherent tensions of such approaches particularly around balancing control with autonomy (Child and Heavens, 2003) and handing control over to others, ensures that putting it into practice is inevitably problematic and risky.

In the last decade or so, the leadership literature has been joined by a body of studies that can be described as 'collaborative leadership' specifically to reflect the perceived interdependencies in public management detected in Bryson and Crosby's quotation at the outset of this section. This tradition is reflected in the theorising of Lipman-Blumen's 'connective leadership' (1996); Allen et al.'s (1998) 'collaborative/reciprocal leadership'; Denis et al.'s (2001) 'collective leadership; and Marion and Uhl-Bien's (2011) 'complex leadership'. Interestingly, these theories can apply to both intra and inter-organisational frameworks.

Ansell and Gash (2007) note that collaborative governance requires specific types of 'facilitative' leadership which is reflected in the work of Ryan (2001), who identifies three components of effective collaborative leadership as: management of the process, maintaining technical credibility and ensuring that the collaborative is empowered to make credible and convincing decisions that are acceptable to all; and Lasker and Weiss (2001), who refer to the importance of leaders having the skills to promote broad and active participation, broad-based influence and control, facilitate productive group dynamics and extend the scope of the process. In the context of integrated health and social care, Klinga et al. (2016) advance the practice of 'co-leadership' to enable "robust management by providing broader competence, continuous learning and joint responsibility for services" (p. 7). This is dependent upon having certain contextual preconditions, namely an organisation-wide model that supports such management as well as co-location of services. Also, "on the personal and interpersonal level, the prerequisites are perception of the management role as a collective activity, continuous communication and lack of prestige" (p. 7).

It is now possible to discern an emerging and growing body of literature on leadership for collaboration models that are specifically contextualised to inter-organisational and cross-sector arenas. The work of Chrislip and Larson (1994), Crosby and Bryson (2010), Luke (1998), Linden (2002), Kanter (1997), Alexander et al. (2001), Huxham and Vangen (2005), and Sullivan, Williams, Jeffares, et al. (2012) fall into this category. This work emphasises the importance of leaders having a number of key skills and competencies to be effective as follows:

- Being able to deploy a set of interpersonal skills including diplomacy, empathy, communication and trust, to build and sustain relationships between diverse stakeholders, and to promote inclusive processes particularly in groups and networks
- Being able to appreciate complexity and connectivity between interdependent policy systems and environments over time, space and function. Moss Kanter (1997) emphasises that working in collaboration is a job for 'clever people' and 'deep thinkers.' The skill rests not so much in having an in-depth knowledge and expertise of relevant policy areas, but in knowing what pieces need to go into the jigsaw and how to fit it together. For instance, an understanding of

the configuration of the prevailing organisational and governance landscape; statutory duties and responsibilities; funding regimes and possibilities.

- Have an ability to perform as translators by understanding the diverse meanings and aspirations of disparate constituencies and interests assembled—the agencies, professions, cultures and sectors involved in collaborative action. This involves being able to help partners understand the potential of collective action and how this might marry with individual and organisational self-interests.
- Collaborative endeavours are often stimulated by a need to tackle complex tasks and challenges that have been resistant to conventional solutions. Hence, there is a high premium placed on leaders being able to promote creativity through innovation, experimentation and a cross fertilisation of ideas and practices available from the assembled partners.
- Collaborative leaders need to be able to facilitate the creation of a learning environment to reflect the emergent and complex nature of the prevailing setting, and to promote reflection, conceptualisation and thinking amongst the participants. A coherent and planned learning and knowledge management strategy (see discussion which follows) is an important ingredient of an effective collaboration.
- Lastly, although certain circumstances and pressures may demand more directive approaches to leadership, the default position for collaborative leaders requires a commitment to dispersed, shared and distributed forms of leadership, realised through empowerment strategies and decision-making processes that encourage accountability and responsibility amongst the varied interests represented in a collaboration.

Palus et al. (2014) refer to their notion of 'boundary-spanning leadership' as the capability of enacting a number of leadership practices across different types of boundaries to achieve collective outcomes. The boundaries are vertical, horizontal, stakeholder, demographic and geographic, and the leadership practices are buffering, reflecting, connecting, mobilising, weaving and transforming. This is developed into a diagnostic tool to help practitioners foster effective boundary-spanning leadership.

One important point to make about leadership is its relevance at different levels in the organisational hierarchy. In a report by the Government of South Australia (2016, p. 9) it refers to leadership as:

having champion leaders/intrapreneurs at each level who nurture the right skills and attributes among staff, undertake creative problem-solving, craft 'workarounds' and harness collaborative opportunities. Craftmanship can often require people to stretch outside of formal structures or boundaries in order to facilitate joined-up working.

Of course, whilst there is a tendency to sometimes conflate leadership and management, they are different, and it is to management that this discussion now turns.

Management

It can be argued that, for broadly similar contextual reasons that leadership needs to be different for collaboration, so does management and the behaviour of managers. Network management, policy network and collaborative public management perspectives (Kickert et al., 1997; Agranoff, 2007; Goldsmith and Eggers, 2004; O'Leary and Bingham, 2009) reflect the need to adapt to the demands and peculiarities of this highly interdependent environment where crossing boundaries becomes the mainstream. This requires a particular skill set, although there is a school of thought that argues that these are equally applicable within organisations, particularly those that are highly fragmented by professional, division, department and geography. This view is well set out by Fountain (2013, p. 18) in the following extended extract:

> The structures and processes that constitute management capacity are themselves similar whether a manager is working within or across agencies. For example, many cross-agency collaborations are hierarchical in their design and of necessity use formal roles and structures, coordination mechanisms, and other design elements of traditional hierarchical organizations. . . . What is different? Indirect management—using persuasion, negotiation, conflict resolution, and similar tools of horizontal management—is typically highlighted as key to collaboration. It is necessary but not sufficient. In addition to collaborative management skills and cohesive cross-boundary teams, interagency projects require rigorous, systematic management systems and processes. Ultimately, government executives and managers working across boundaries have to develop and sustain authority, legitimacy, and credibility across jurisdictions and often across cultures. What holds the actors together in a network are perceptions that joint gains will be produced that will exceed the costs of forgoing some measure of agency autonomy.
>
> Working across agencies is demanding, takes extra communication and persuasion, and extracts high transaction costs. Size, complexity, and interdependence of collaborative arrangements make the job much more challenging than most within-agency management as well. Lack of regularized flows of resources, expertise, and authority has to be negotiated and the legitimacy of the enterprise sustained. Managers have to exert additional effort to build processes across formal organizations, to establish and maintain communications in a

network, to secure legitimacy for the project, and to secure and share resources in a sustainable way. To build and sustain cross-agency collaborative management, managers need three sets of skills: First, understand and work strategically within the institutional environment; Second, develop and use interpersonal skills to build strong professional relationships and teams; Third, build capacity across boundaries through rigorous structures and processes with the extra commitment and coordination required to work across agency boundaries.

Research by Williams (2017) involving middle managers concluded that it was not possible to reach any definitive consensus on whether managing internally was different to that in collaboration. Various positions were taken on this matter along a continuum from there being a: "discernible difference between the two because internally you have the choice of being directive or collaborative, but in collaboration, you have no option but to adopt a collaborative approach." to those who, whilst recognising that there were different challenges posed by working in collaborative arenas, did not consider that they demanded management approaches and skills that were in any way different to their normal within-organisation practices. One middle manager asserted that: "management styles between the respective modes does not materially differ—it is contingent on the context and issue," and in a broadly similar vein, another manager concluded that: "the same skills were necessary for both but needed to be used in a slightly different way." For instance, collaboration brought to the forefront the need for particular skills such negotiation, consensus seeking and networking. At the other end of the spectrum, some middle managers agreed that collaboration demanded a distinct set of management approaches and skills.

Notwithstanding this argument, Williams (2002, 2012) refers to the importance of boundary spanners and boundary-spanning behaviours in collaborative arenas where activities, processes and tasks permeate, bridge and cut across conventional boundaries of organisation, profession, sector and policy. Noble and Jones (2006) observe similar actors in the context of Public/Private Partnerships. Williams (2012) argues that boundary spanners discharge a number of key roles—reticulist, interpreter/communicator, coordinator and entrepreneur—with a high degree of interplay and connectivity between them, and each demanding a particular set of skills and competencies:

- The reticulist role focuses on the management of relationships and interdependencies highlighting the skills of diplomacy, negotiation, network management and influencing without formal power— they are sometimes referred to as 'informational intermediaries' or 'gatekeepers.'

- The interpreter/communicator function centres on an appreciation of the diversity of actors and their backgrounds, and an ability to liaise and connect with different and changing interests. At the heart of this role is the ability to build and sustain effective interpersonal relationships using the skills of communication, listening, empathy, conflict management and consensus seeking. Cultivating trusting behaviours is paramount in these processes.
- The coordinator role majors on the planning, servicing and coordination of the collaborative process, and the entrepreneurial function focuses on the importance of developing new solutions to complex problems evidencing creativity, opportunism and innovation.
- This entrepreneurial role is not just a technical one relating to ideas and resources, but also a personal and political one involving building coalitions and brokering deals amongst disparate interests.

Carey (2017) develops a typology of boundary spanners based on motivation and ways of operating. Four different types are advanced and referred to as: 'traditional,' 'looking for an edge,' 'moving on up' and 'pushing the ideas.' From their research in New Zealand, Ryan et al. (2008) consider that a trio of roles (not necessarily a single individual)—the public entrepreneur, their guardian angel(s) and their fellow travellers—are necessary to form the core of collaborative management—working in an innovative, learning-orientated and networked fashion. The value of attempting to provide a more nuanced understanding of the different types of boundary spanners and the roles that they play lies in its potential to influence collaborative policy design and practice, and in the training and development of boundary spanners.

Donahue and Zeckhauser (2008) argue that orchestrating collaborative arrangements demands particular skills, the foremost of which are analytical and these "have relatively little to do with classic public administration and a great deal to do with economics, institutional analysis, game theory, decision analysis, and other relatively advanced tools for predicting and influencing outcomes" (Donahue and Zeckhauser, 2008, p. 522). In more detail, Donahue (2004) suggests that a collaborative governance pedagogy might usefully centre around six categories of professional skills illustrated in Box 6.6.

From the evidence of O'Leary and Gerard's (2012) research on US federal senior executives, the skill set of the successful collaborator is considered to consist of *individual* attributes including having an open mind, patience and self-confidence; *interpersonal* skills of being a good communicator, an excellent listener and working well with people; *group process skills* including facilitation, negotiation and collaborative problem-solving; *strategic leadership skills* including big-picture thinking, strategic thinking and facilitative leadership; and finally, *substantive/technical expertise* including technical knowledge of the subject area, project

---

Box 6.6: Professional Skills for Collaborative Governance (Donahue, 2004)

Appraisal: calibrating the dimensions of a governance challenge and the defects of the *status quo* in the absence of collaborative efforts to address it

Analysis: appreciating, in a sophisticated way, the forces at work in the policy area; identifying the incentives and predicting the behaviour of the actors within it

Assignment: selecting the institutional players to be recruited into or tasked with a particular responsibility within a collaborative system (to the extent the organisational constellation is malleable)

Architecture: designing a structure of information flows, financial relationships, and accountability arrangements with the best odds of focusing the collaboration's energies on real sources of public value

Assessment: evaluating the collaboration, to whatever level of precision permitted by the available data and the degree of normative clarity and consensus that exists

Adjustment: deploying formal or informal authority, guided by analysis and assessment, to fine-tune the structure, targeting or operations of the collaboration

---

management and organisational skills. Agranoff (2012) offers a wealth of operational advice/tips to network practitioners based on his engagement with actors over a long career—this ranges widely to include being patient; confronting power; building trust; developing multiple communication vehicles; being a decision broker to build consensus; looking to achieve small wins; sharing the network administrative burden; being creative, to name but a few. He takes the view that:

> the network effort will only be as good as the skills, experience, and knowledge of the persons sent by an organization to be at the table" and reinforces his view that: "public service in formal networks requires considerable knowledge and commitment to a process that is different from that of hierarchical management. Yet it is nevertheless management, across the boundaries of organizations.
>
> (2012, p. 58)

In a guide for managers working in collaborative networks, Milward and Provan (2006) highlight the central tasks as managing accountability, legitimacy, conflict, design and commitment.

Fountain (2013, p. 5), in a guide to help managers in the US federal government sustain effective collaboration, concludes that collaboration is only sustainable if managers develop two types of practice as follows:

- *Collaboration through people*: Relationship skills must be developed for effective managers and teams. Team-building skills are those used by managers willing and able to work across jurisdictional boundaries to develop effective professional relationships and cohesive working groups. Skills needed by effective managers include active listening, fairness and respect—qualities that produce trust in a cross-agency collaborative initiative. In cross-boundary teams, managers build informal relationships outside regular hierarchical channels. Teams function well when productive communities based on trust and professional experience form around a problem, project or practice.
- *Collaboration through processes*: In addition to effective managers and effective teams, cross-agency collaborative initiatives need effective organisational processes which include a focus on strategy, operations, systems and their management. Effective organisational processes demand an organisational skill set that emphasises rigour and clarity in setting goals, designing systems, building in milestones, attracting resources and framing an organization that lies across agency boundaries.

The implications of this discussion for policy and practice in cross-boundary work centres on the need to ensure that actors involved in this activity are suitably trained and developed to discharge this form of management. There is a tendency to assume that a proven ability to manage intra-organisationally is a sufficient passport to gain entry to cross-boundary management. There is compelling evidence to suggest that this is false and counterproductive to effective cooperative behaviours.

Inter-Professionality

Actors from diverse professional backgrounds populate theatres of collaboration, and the trajectory and success of collective endeavours are significantly influenced by the ability of these people to work together. Evidence over many years suggests that professional boundaries constitute a major hurdle to negotiate and overcome in the search for common purpose and practice (GAO, 2005). The notion of professionalism is firmly embedded into public policy and practice, and the gatekeepers—individual professional bodies—are sources of considerable power and influence. They are invariably highly protective of their areas of knowledge and expertise, and control their member's behaviours through education, training, qualifications and standards. Tensions exist at the interface of inter-professional engagement that stem from organisational factors such as differences in employment practices and governance arrangements; operational factors that are entrenched in roles, duties, jurisdictions and accountabilities; and deep-rooted cultural influences stemming from different models of practice. These problems can be compounded in some situations where the perceptions of a 'hierarchy of professions' based on notions of full and semi-professional status and different views on the legitimacy of length of training, legal registration and rights to practice, are used to exert influence over others.

D'Amour and Oandasan (2005, p. 9) define the notion of 'interprofessionality' as:

> The process by which professionals reflect on and develop ways of practicing that provides an integrated and cohesive answer to the needsof the client/family/population. . . . [I]t involves continuous interaction and knowledge sharing between professionals, organized to solve or explore a variety of education and care issues all while seeking to optimize the patient's participation. . . . Interprofessionality requires a paradigm shift, since interprofessional practice has unique characteristics in terms of values, codes of conduct, and ways of working. These characteristics must be elucidated.

Barrett and Keeping (2005) compile a checklist of factors that are likely to enable professionals to work together in the field of health and social care including the following:

- Clarity and knowledge of professional roles: this helps in particular to delineate respective boundaries, and may even lead to opportunities for generic practices and role re-definitions.
- Willing participation, confidence, open communication, trust and mutual respect: a fundamental belief in the value of user-centred models of service design and delivery is an important lubricant of inter-professional working, and personal and professional confidence enables professionals to project their own viewpoints, but also to accept the legitimacy of other perspectives. Open and honest communication is key to effective relationship building between professionals based on mutual respect and the cultivation of trust is fundamental to the creation of social capital.
- Managing power and conflict: power relationships—both real and perceived—bedevil inter-professional practices. Conflicts arise over claims to areas of knowledge and expertise and the pre-eminence and status of particular professional groups—ceding professional power is not easy for many actors, and sharing power in arenas of non-hierarchical relationships is difficult to secure and sustain. Sources of conflict stem from individual differences in age, gender, social status through to professional differences relating to values, leadership and

competition for resources. These differences can offer a rich source of learning and innovation in dealing with complex public policy problems, but negatively they can lead to paralysis and inefficient outcomes. Van Rensburg et al. (2016, p. 7) argue that: "grasping the ways in which power is present in the relations that constitute integrated care and its governance is key to comprehending the reasons why integrated care is often such a challenging ideal to achieve." In addition, they argue that this might be helped by understanding power, not through mainstream conceptions but via more subtle and relational notions such as governmentality.

- Creating a collaborative culture: individual professions are associated with particular cultures—ways of viewing the world, values, beliefs and dominant practices. Working in collaboration often challenges these assumptions and can result in a new culture based on an emerging and collaborative footprint. This can challenge the loyalties of some professionals who have to manage in both cultures.

Faced with the challenges of inter-professional working, Barrett and Keeping (2005) advocate a number of strategies to address these problems including; reflection and supervision, managing expectations, evaluating impact and outcomes, and ensuring there is top level support. Arguably, the most important strategies lie in education and training—interprofessional training integrated into individual professional education, and continuous professional development within collaborative settings. Integration of health and social care offer a rich source of evidence about the experiences of inter-professional practice with key messages being highlighted around the importance of incremental as opposed to whole-system changes. Carpenter and Dickinson (2016) supply a comprehensive overview and critique of inter-professional education and training including the issue of involving service users, the problems associated with mainstreaming and the perennial difficulties of evaluating the impact of such initiatives.

A number of collaborative competency tools have been developed to help practitioners assess and develop their inter-professional practices and behaviours. Schroder et al. (2011) refer to a Collaborative Competency Practice Tool which is based on a framework of nine domains—mission and goals; relationships; leadership; role responsibilities and autonomy; communication; decision making and conflict management; community linkages and coordination; perceived effectiveness; and patient involvement. In a similar vein, Archibald et al. (2014) advance a similar self-reporting tool based on six domains that they refer to as the Interprofessional Collaborative Competencies Attainment Survey. The domains are communication; collaboration; roles and responsibilities; collaborative patient-family centred approach; conflict resolution/resolution; and team functioning.

A comprehensive report of a panel of US experts has developed an inter-professional competency practice tool centred on four major domains—values and ethics; teams and teamwork; communication; and roles and responsibilities—each comprising a battery of specific competencies (Interprofessional Education Collaborative, 2011, 2016). Finally, the Canadian Interprofessional Health Collaborative (2010, p. 11) has developed a competency framework with the stated goal of securing inter-professional collaboration which it defines as a "partnership between a team of health providers and a client in a participatory, collaborative and coordinated approach to decision-making around health and social issues." It consists of six competency domains that highlight the knowledge, skills, attributes and values that shape judgements essential for inter-professional collaborative practice—four central domains concerning role clarification, team functioning, inter-professional conflict resolution and collaborative leadership; and two supporting domains of communication and patient/client/family/community-centred care. The key point here is that the different domains and their associated competencies are highly interrelated and are deployed in various permutations in response to different practice challenges.

A case study of enacting effective agency for collaborative practice is illustrated in Box 6.7. It is set within the context of young people in Australia and presents the kind of behaviours that are considered appropriate to manage across the boundaries of different stakeholders, and which acknowledge the need to tackle the convoluted tensions of politics, power and complexity.

Box 6.7: Case Study—Briefing Paper for Community for Children's Programme Managers

This is an extract from a briefing paper commissioned by the Australian Research Alliance for Children and Youth (ARACY), which focuses on the well-being of Australian young people. It is designed to offer guidance for managers and other stakeholders attempting to navigate the tensions of politics, power and complexity inherent in collaborative working. These are based on overcoming, rather than avoiding, the structural tensions. It is based on the Working Alliance Theory Model and stresses the importance of the following behaviours:

1. Investing time in developing trust by getting to know each partner, their expertise, resources and limits.
2. Openly discussing relative responsibilities, liabilities, perceived benefits, good communication and participatory decision-making.
3. Engaging any non-traditional partners through innovative and strategic approaches, assuming strength-based contributions and capacities.

4. Discussing ways of minimising or avoiding the tensions of competitive relations that can undermine local alliances or collaborations.
5. Limiting onerous reporting but maintain accountability.
6. Developing performance measures that reflect local definitions of good services and minimise constraints of upward reporting.
7. Recognising that there may be competing professional priorities and local ones, which need to be discussed and integrated.
8. Avoiding unrealistic expectations and ensure that differing priorities and obligations do not lead to competing interpretations of primary goals.

This case study is taken from: ARACY (2007)

Strategies for Boundary Management

Leaders and managers are faced with devising and implementing strategies, tactics and behaviours to deal with the plethora of boundary challenges discussed previously. Broadly, these fall into a number of categories:

- Structural solutions that aim to re-position, reconfigure or remove boundaries. Politicians often see these as the antidote to system failures in many policy areas. Those familiar with the history of health services in the UK will freely testify to the challenges presented by the constant reconfiguration and structural upheavals that have taken place over many years. Whilst some may improve the efficiency and effectiveness of service provision and delivery, others are less successful because they fail to address root causes of a particular boundary configuration. The processes of reconfiguration in themselves can also be protracted and highly destabilising—often compromising personal and professional relationships developed between people in different organisations over many years. The notion of 'coterminosity' is also popular in some areas to ensure coherent geographical links between different organisations delivering services in a similar area. This is more efficient in terms of organisation and administration, and in terms of having resonated with a common user/community base. Sharing the same user/community base can facilitate notions of 'common purpose'; assist users in understanding who is responsible for what; and more generally encourage organisations to work collaboratively.
- Strategies that attempt to build bridges across boundaries and link collaborating interests. Integration of health and social care is a notoriously difficult issue to resolve in many countries, and it is the subject of numerous models of design and delivery. Some embrace

both aspects within a single organisation, whereas others attempt closer working along a broad continuum from sharing information/ co-location to coordination to complete merger of services. Scotland has recently introduced Health and Social Care Partnerships across the country but the governance is still divided between Health Boards and local authorities. Apart from two senior joint appointments, there remains an immense task of coordinating budgets, staff and resources.

- Strategies that utilise boundary objects and people to cement collaborative actions (see Chapter 3 for detailed discussion of what boundary objects are). Boundary object theory offers interesting insights and potential practical ways of conceptualising and tackling boundary management problems. Star and Griesemer (1989) suggest that boundary objects inhabit several intersecting social worlds, satisfying the informational requirements of each; they are both plastic enough to adapt to local needs and the constraints of the different parties employing them, but robust enough to maintain a common identity; they can be either abstract or concrete; and have different meanings in different social worlds, but in structure are common enough to more than one world to make them recognisable. The creation and management of boundary objects is a key process in maintaining coherence across intersecting but interdependent worlds such as collaboration. Boundary objects can take a variety of forms—tangible e.g. buildings, uniforms, reports, systems, occupational positions or non-tangible e.g. concepts, theories, narratives, stories, discourses. They can occur singly or within a constellation of boundary infrastructure of multiple objects (Bowker and Star, 1999) and be 'nested' across different levels of artefacts, interactions and forms of governance (Thomas and Hardy, 2007); they can function as 'anchors/ bridges' (Star and Griesemer, 1989) or negatively as 'barricades/ mazes' (Oswick and Robertson, 2009); the role and use of a boundary object may change over time—sometimes providing coherence, but at others, conflict (Barrett and Oborn, 2010). Boundary objects are not apolitical in the sense that they have no meaning independent of human subjectivity (Bennett, 2004), but rather, function in a mediating and performative fashion (Fong et al., 2007; Gal et al., 2004). Finally, there is a strong connection between interests/actors and the objects themselves (Kimble et al., 2010), a feature that underscores the importance of dynamic and interdependent patterns of power relationships (Thomas and Hardy, 2007).

Integrated health and social care settings are littered with examples of boundary objects—tangible such as co-located offices; common assessment and performance management frameworks; pooled budgets; common IT systems; multi-disciplinary teams; and joint appointments—and intangible ones relating to notions of 'health' and conceptions of 'service users.' Sullivan and Williams (2012) explore how some of these objects perform in a variety of health and social care settings in South Wales. Another research study (Williams, 2013) into the application of a locality model of health and social care identifies a range of interrelated objects of different types as illustrated in Table 6.1.

The adoption of a boundary object perspective—although still emergent and exploratory in nature—offers a fruitful avenue for future research and practice in understanding how best to tackle the boundary challenges faced by actors and organisations working together on joint endeavours. Such an analysis would be framed within a consideration of types, rationale, role and purpose, interests and outcomes. Hence, it would provide a coherent and integrated conceptual and practical framework; it would be multilevel in the sense that it focuses both on individual objects but also their role within a constellation of objects; it would attempt to analyse different types of objects and their relationship to interests and actors; it would be grounded in the social constructions of different actors; and lastly, would be linked to outcomes—an attribute that is highly valued by hard-pressed politicians and policy makers attempting to make collaboration work in practice.

- Strategies that aim to reframe or reconceptualise boundaries. Some boundaries are deeply rooted in social, personal, cultural and professional influences. For example, clinician practitioners are driven by medicalised versions of 'health' whereas social workers embrace a broader approach based on wider social, economic and

Table 6.1 Boundary Objects in the Locality Model of Integration of Health and Social Care

	BOUNDARY OBJECT	TYPE
Co-location of Services	Buildings	Physical artefact
Integrated Leadership and Management	Individual leader/manager	Agent/actor
Shared or Pooled Budgets	Statutory Instrument	Policy tool
Common Approach and Assessment Frameworks	Policy instrument	Professional practice
Integrated Governance and Accountability	Governance system	Management structure
Multi-Disciplinary Teams	Team	Group Structure
Common Performance Management Frameworks	Policy instrument	Professional practice
Unified IT and Information sharing systems and protocols	Operational support system	Physical Structure and system

environmental factors, and these often grate in relationships between the two constituencies. Differential framing processes influence the way in which different actors understand problems, their causes and potential solutions. Teenage pregnancy for instance—is this a problem in the first place, and if so, is this because of the lack of effective sex education strategies, wider cultural norms, traditions in local families and communities or what? Sustainable development—is this mainly concerned with the protection of the physical environment or a more broader notion of pursuing an economic model that is fair and equal for current society, but balances this with the natural environment and future generations? One mechanism for bridging these types of boundaries is through attempts to gain consensus on notions of 'common purpose' or 'the greater good' frequently mentioned in one research study (Williams, 2017). Also, using the 'user' or 'recipient of services' as the common starting point for the design and delivery of services is seen as a useful construct to work through some boundary issues. The sites of integrated health and social care are populated by numerous and diverse health and social practitioners whose contributions are essential to the well-being of people. One approach to this challenge is to ensure that the respective roles of each professional are clearly defined and coordinated in terms of designing and delivering appropriate care solutions. Another is to accept some blurring at the boundaries to facilitate the potential of generic forms of working—this might be more efficient in terms of resource use, make more sense to service users in terms of their contact with the service, and offer individual practitioners, learning and development opportunities. Blurring, of course, is not without its risks particularly in terms of professional accountability, loss of control and performance.

Learning and Knowledge Management

One of the most neglected but critically important features of cross-boundary work concerns the need to appreciate and manage learning and knowledge management (KM) strategies. The sites of cross-boundary practice—collaborations, integrated arrangements, strategic alliances or more modest forms of cooperative working—involve people, groups, organisations coming together to achieve some form of collective purpose. Typically, they involve managing knowledge in some form—sharing what they know and perhaps generating new forms of knowledge to underpin some kind of joint action. It involves learning together to help with problem definition in complex areas of societal policy; to unravel causal effects of policy; and to help design future interventions to achieve shared outcomes. However, effective learning and KM processes are notoriously difficult to design and manage in practice. There is one school of thought that suggests that emergent and spontaneous strategies may be appropriate, but another that favours a more planned and explicit learning and KM strategy.

Particularly in the case of planned strategies, an understanding of the theory and practice of learning and KM is an essential ingredient of effective cross-boundary practice. Although there is a clear case for promoting integration between these two phenomena (Vera and Crossan, 2005), the very extensive, interdisciplinary and contested literature on these subjects tends to be treated separately from one another, and grounded and theorised predominantly in a private sector context (LaPalombara, 2003; Rashman et al., 2009), which raises issues about the transferability of prevailing theories, concepts and models in a public sector domain.

There is little doubt that both phenomena are highly complex. Williams (2012, p. 2) summarises learning as:

> Conceptualised in different dimensions: levels (Crossan et al., 1999, Child et al., 2005); modes (Pawlowsky et al., 2001); types, for instance, single and double loop (Argyris and Schon, 1996), operational and conceptual (Lane, 2003) and exploratory and exploitative (Jansen et al., 2009); and stages or phases (Kolb, 1984). The determinants of learning (Child, 2003) include partner intentions and learning capacity which, in turn, are conditional on the transferability of knowledge, receptivity (time, resources, attitudes), competence (absorptive capacity and skills) and previous experience.

and knowledge as being:

> Divided into two types—explicit knowledge that is easily codified and communicated, and tacit knowledge which is not easy to capture, translate or transfer between different cultures, professions and agencies.
>
> (Schein, 2004; De Long and Fahey, 2000)

In both literatures, a number of key themes can be discerned as follows:

- Approaches tend to be polarised between structural and interpretive lenses. Structural interpretations of learning emphasise interventions affecting organisational structures, communication, absorptive capacity, resource frameworks and strategic planning. Alternatively, interpretive methodologies focus on meaning, culture and sense making. Processes of socialisation are considered to be important, both as a medium for sharing and exchanging knowledge, and as a mechanism for building social capital (Inkpen, 2000). Socialisation can be seen as an important means of transferring tacit knowledge, and building trusting relationships to lubricate cross-boundary learning.

However, Nooteboom (2008) considers that a fine balance needs to be struck in terms of the degree of 'social distance' between groups, on the one hand promoting cognitive proximity to engender mutual understanding and collaboration, and on the other fostering cognitive distance to encourage innovation and creativity.

- The structure-agency debate is a persistent theme in the literature (see Part 1 and earlier in this chapter for definitions of these terms). For instance, there are disputes about whether learning is an individual or collective experience. Child et al. (2005) take the view that only agents can create knowledge, with organisations providing the necessary support and supportive contexts. On the other hand, Huysman (2000) argues that structural factors such as culture, power, rules and norms mediate that process. Knowledge champions or brokers are considered by some (Salk and Simonin, 2011 Child and Heavens, 2003) to have an important role to play in learning and KM processes, whereas others highlight the cultural and political dimensions of knowledge sharing in practice (Currie and Suhomlinova, 2006). In the context of the factors influencing intra- and inter-knowledge transfer and organisational learning, Rashman et al. (2009) highlight the importance of power, politics and leadership with leaders inhibiting or facilitating learning, and influential individuals having a valuable role as 'learning champions.'
- Strategies for learning and KM tend to be differentiated between explicit and planned approaches, e.g. learning organisations (Senge, 1992), and those that are more instinctive, impulsive and unplanned. Nicolini et al. (2008) point to the importance of networks and communities of practice in the spread of hitherto fragmented and widely distributed knowledge between individuals and organisations, and Hartley and Benington (2006) recommend 'grafting and transplanting' as the most effective strategy for knowledge transfer.

A number of analytical frameworks have been created to provide practitioners with advice on developing learning and KM strategies. Nonaka's (1994) model for the conversion of tacit and explicit knowledge highlights the structures, processes and carriers that facilitate different forms of knowledge conversion and management, and Carlile's (2004) model spotlights the management of knowledge across different types of boundary—syntactic, semantic and pragmatic. Zhao and Anand (2013) offer an interesting perspective on the effectiveness of different methods for transferring types of knowledge between organisations. They argue that:

> given the cognitive and motivational limitations of boundary spanners in transferring highly complex knowledge, we propose an alternative interunit knowledge transfer structure, *a collective bridge*, which is a set of direct interunit ties connecting the members of the source and

the recipient units, with the configuration of the ties matching the complexity of collective knowledge intended for transfer.

(p. 1514)

The value of such a unit lies in its decentralised nature as opposed to the centralised intermediary nature of boundary spanners, but the ultimate choice lies in the complexity of knowledge itself. Williams (2012) offers a practical template to assist in the development of a learning and KM strategy and this is set out in Box 6.8.

Box 6.8:   Template for Learning and Knowledge Management Strategies

Purpose: What are the purposes of learning and KM? Clarity of role and purpose is important to link learning and KM objectives with the particular model and stage of integration.

Level: At which levels does learning take place? Individual, group, organisational and network? Are particular approaches needed at different levels? What barriers and facilitators exist at each level? How does learning transfer between different levels?

Type: What type of learning and knowledge is involved? What form of knowledge is involved—tacit or explicit? What form of learning is involved? Operational learning that requires single-loop perspectives resulting in incremental improvements in existing skills, knowledge and systems, or conceptual, double-loop or exploitative learning which requires reflection and innovation, and challenges the assumptions and substance of current policy and practice, producing new knowledge and insights?

Processes and Modes: What are the mechanisms for sharing and transferring knowledge? Nonaka's (1994) framework for knowledge conversion is a helpful 'aide memoir' for identifying potential structures, carriers and processes. What are the learning modes involved—cognitive, cultural or behavioural?

Context: What structural and organisational factors are necessary? Are management arrangements networked or hierarchical? What role does teamwork play? What levels of absorptive capacity exist amongst the different professional agencies? Are there effective and integrated information systems in place to support learning cultures and knowledge exchange? What mechanisms exist to measure interventions and strategies? Are pilot projects formally evaluated before attempts are made to mainstream lessons?

Leadership and Agency: What role do leaders and other actors perform? What style of leadership is necessary to support learning and KM strategies? Do managers and practitioners possess the skills and competencies to promote learning and KM? Are there specific catalysts and champions of learning and KM? Are there mechanisms to incentivise learning and KM? Are communities of practice encouraged and is there cross-fertilisation between them? Are there schemes that encourage learning from integration elsewhere in the UK, and from other policy areas or sectors?

Culture: Is there a collaborative learning culture? Is there a collaborative culture in place to support and promote collaborative learning and knowledge exchange? What are the key principles of a collaborative learning culture?

Resources: Are there resources available to support learning and KM activities? Is there sufficient time and financial resources available to underpin learning and KM initiatives over the lifetime progression of an integrated service?

Performance and Evaluation

Williams and Sullivan (2007, p. 89) observe that:

> Evaluation occupies an uncomfortable place in policy makers' hearts. For some, it is a 'necessary evil' unloved but required, for others it is a largely 'academic' activity with little relevance to the real world of politics, policy making and practice, while for some it is a vital but overlooked and underused part of the policy making process itself.

However, perhaps because of the need for governments to demonstrate effectiveness and efficiency particularly in time of austerity through 'evidence-based policy making' and 'what works' frameworks, and in the case of collaborative working, to counter the often uncritical acceptance of the virtues of this mode of governance, measuring performance and evaluation have assumed a greater importance and role in the policy-making process. This commitment is not without its considerable challenges especially in relation to the practical and methodological difficulties of undertaking evaluation in the context of complex, multi-party collaborations where even agreeing what constitutes success can be contested. Some of the key messages to emerge on how to embrace evaluation in the course of collaborative working include:

- Ensuring that there is a sustained investment in both time and resources to the design and implement evaluation tools and techniques
- Integrating evaluation into the policy-making process from the outset—not treating it as an 'add on' to be considered some way down the line
- Involving a full range of users and interests in the methodology, utilisation and timing of any evaluation

- Ensuring that the necessary skills for evaluation have been imparted to those involved in this activity—not only dedicated researchers but practitioners and policy makers
- Ensuring that those involved in commissioning research understand what is involved, and those that may be the recipients of research and evaluation have the skills to interpret the findings. For instance, research based on qualitative methodologies is frequently criticised by people on the basis of small samples—ignoring completely the respective and legitimate differences between sampling methodologies underpinning qualitative and quantitative approaches! This does raise the broader issue of the acceptability of research evaluation in influencing the design, course and outcomes of public policy and practice. Various commentators (Coote et al., 2004; Weiss, 1998; Percy-Smith et al., 2003) are pessimistic about its influence, concluding that its value is often limited to non-controversial, small-scale changes in stable environments. Percy-Smith et al. (2003) offer some practical suggestions for increasing the chances of evaluation being taken seriously (Box 6.9), and Serafin et al. (2008) offer further advice to partnership practitioners on the practice of evaluation (Box 6.10).

Box 6.9:   Lessons for Encouraging the Acceptability of Research

- Policy makers and practitioners understand and believe in the benefits of using evidence
- Users of research are partners in the process of evidence generation
- Research is timely and addresses an issue that is relevant and with a methodology that is relatively uncontested
- That the results support existing political ideologies, are convenient and uncontentious
- That the results are reported with low degrees of uncertainty, are robust in implementation and can be delivered without incurring high costs if the decision needs to be reversed
- That researchers and key users seek implementation with skilful advocacy and stamina

---

Any evaluation needs to consider four basic elements:

- The organisation of the partnership that is assembled to undertake it—its quality and effectiveness, including the health and quality of the relationships between the partners
- The impact or progress towards achieving anticipated sustainable outcomes

- A judgement as to the added value of using the partnership approach as compared to alternative approaches
- The likely benefits accruing to partners in line with stated expectations.

Box 6.10:   Evaluation Advice for Partnership Practitioners

- Advocate carrying out formal evaluations of cross-sector partnerships as interventions aimed at improving their performance and helping those involved in them realise their promise and potential.
- Build in evaluation into activities undertaken in all stages of the partnership cycle, ensuring where possible that a provision is made for evaluation in the early formative stages of a cross-sector partnership.
- Distinguish between evaluations undertaken from the perspective of a single partner or funder from those seeking to assess the performance, benefits and impact of the cross-sector partnership as a whole.
- Focus evaluations of cross-sector partnerships not just on their impacts or results, but also on their design and operation, benefits to partners, unexpected consequences and value-added and appropriateness or relevance in a particular situation as compared to other non-partnering approaches.
- Select tools and approaches for evaluating cross-sector partnerships, which take into account the needs, circumstances, organisational culture and context of all the partners involved.

Innes and Booher (1999) have constructed a useful framework for evaluating the effects of collaboration. They refer to first-, second- and third-order effects which aim to capture the consequences of collaboration over time. First-order effects relate to building social capital through trust and relationships; developing intellectual capital by mutual understanding, shared problem frames and sharing data; developing political capital through an ability to work together on agreed ends—second-order effects include the development of new partnerships; coordination and joint action; implementation of agreements and changes to practices and perceptions—and finally third-order effects are those of a more whole-systems change such as coevolution, new institutions, new discourses and new norms and heuristics.

Approaches to evaluation in collaborative settings vary between positivist, social constructionalist and theory-based. Positivist approaches underpin the still popular preoccupation with focusing on numbers, and measuring effects in an objective way; realist evaluation in contrast utilises qualitative methodologies to determine outcomes; and theory-based evaluation recognises context and the often-conflicting views of different stakeholders. The 'Theories of Change' model, for instance, has been used in a number of evaluation studies in areas of complex public policy interventions. The Theories of Change model is defined as "a systematic and cumulative study of the links between activities, outcomes and contexts of the initiative" (Cornell and Kubisch, 1998, p. 35) and is undertaken with the evaluator working with key stakeholders to discover their theories of why, and under what set of contextual circumstances, a particular initiative is anticipated to result in a desired outcome. It assumes that any affected stakeholders will be involved in developing relevant theory for the proposed intervention, and the assumption is that involvement will increase ownership of the intervention and support for the final evaluation. What is often quite clear is that 'evaluation' is often seen as the 'cinderella' of the policy-making process. It is very challenging to undertake both methodologically and practically, and is invariably open to challenge. However, the acid test is always going to be proving that working in collaboration brings added value.

A highly instructive case study reflects on efforts by New Zealand government over a 5-year period to measure its efforts to address societal problems that span traditional agency boundaries (Scott and Boyd, 2017). Initially, a framework referred to as 'Managing for Outcomes' involving clusters of agencies measuring their collective impact was introduced, and this was shortly followed by a sectoral approach with different sectors responsible for developing overlapping outcomes. Both regimes were eventually replaced by a system of inter-agency performance targets, and following an evaluation of the design and use of this system, insights for policy makers and practitioners have been established as indicated in Box 6.11.

Box 6.11:   Practice Insights on Addressing Cross-Cutting Problems Using Inter-Agency Performance Targets (Scott and Boyd, 2017)

Selecting Results

- Focus on a few problems
- Involve other agencies in selecting problems to be addressed
- Build on existing relationships when selecting results to pursue
- Measure intermediate outcomes
- Align results, targets and measures
- Commit publicly

Developing Accountability

- Hold leaders collectively responsible
- Get started and learn by doing

Measuring Collaboration

- Start simply
- Limit group size
- Signal shared responsibility

Reporting on Progress

- Report on trends
- Share success stories

7 Training and Development

Paul Williams

On the assumption that management and governance in collaboration—with all the attendant boundary challenges—is materially different from that in other forms of governance—it follows logically that training and development capabilities are likely to be different than those designed and delivered in conventional public management programmes. However, whilst there is no questioning the need to deliver extensive and bespoke training programmes to get people to fly to the moon, why is it so often the case that managers and practitioners are expected to perform and manage in collaborative situations without any particular preparation or training? The default position adopted in many cases is that actors need to develop their proficiency in cross-boundary work through experience. Whilst there is no doubt that experiential learning is valuable, the earlier discussion in this chapter suggests that particular skills and competencies are a crucial component of effective working in this area of public management.

There are a number of considerations to take account of in the design of education, training and development programmes for effective cross-boundary work. These revolve around a number of linked questions:

- What is the substance and content of the programmes—skills, competencies?
- At what level do they need to be delivered—individual, group?
- Who should deliver the programmes—academic, professional, experiential?
- How should the different providers be linked to the practitioners—academic, professional bodies, consultants, and Government?

A number of considerations are raised about the question of where training and development capabilities and skills should be pitched. At the level of the individual, there are three broad categories—leaders, managers and frontline practitioners—and the needs of each category need to be thought through. Also, the question of whether the intension is to build into mainstream job roles boundary-spanning competencies, and/or to develop a specific cadre of boundary-spanning actors who perform exclusively in collaborative arenas? The development of dedicated actors who possess the capabilities of managing in collaborative settings is clearly the solution for particular projects or initiatives—coordinating, lubricating, planning and servicing—on behalf of a number of different agencies. Likewise, reflecting the increasingly cross-boundary nature of many contemporary job roles and the perennial exhortations of politicians and policy makers made to individuals and organisations to work together, it seems sensible to work towards building boundary-spanning capabilities into mainstream management positions in all policy areas.

Whilst a focus on the development of individual competencies and capabilities is critical, capacity-building programmes aimed at groups involved in the design and delivery of collaborative action is also a valuable investment. Collaborative action assembles people and organisations from different backgrounds, cultures, experiences and objectives, and the challenges of working together effectively are significant—instances of conflict, overly prolonged decision making, professional and organisational jealousies, power imbalances and clashes of culture often make this form of working tortuous and unrewarding. The management of the collaborative process is then important in creating a highly performing group—developing social capital is a valuable by-product that can be released in future opportunities. The advantage of this model is that it is the actors who are responsible for the success of the particular venture who learn together and are likely to own the process if they share the same journey. Therefore, capacity-building programmes or process facilitation of collaborative groups is likely to pay dividends in the long run.

Partnership health checks are one mechanism of tracking the course of a partnership in terms of its capabilities and performance. Options exist as to whether facilitation is provided externally or handled by a group from within. Also, there are cases where individual training programmes are made available to partners in other organisations that are more cost effective and may encourage a transfer of learning between organisations. One far-sighted training and development programme is being undertaken by the Government of South Australia in support of its initiative on 'joined-up' government. It involves the identification of "change agents who are able to act as conduits between agencies and policy areas" (Government of South Australia, 2016), building their capabilities and capacities, organising and resourcing a community of practice, and setting up a reward system to encourage and share best practice.

The delivery of education, training and development opportunities and programmes centre broadly on academic, professional and experiential sources. In addition, assorted consultants and government-related bodies can offer various types of support, advice and assistance. In terms of the role of academic training, there are no programmes dedicated to the development of cross-boundary public managers—in the same way as social workers, town planners or civil engineers. However, at a post-graduate or master's level, a number of university programmes involving public policy and management and policy studies offer module options on this topic. There is a fundamental issue that needs to be explored in relation to the relationship between academia and public policy and practice. Questions relate to the extent to which academia is sensitive to the needs of practitioners in the contributions that it provides either formally through accredited programmes, or more informally through facilitation, consultancy and research.

The research relationship between academia and policy makers/practitioners needs careful consideration given the role of 'evidence based-policy making' and the focus on 'what works.' Menzies (2017) suggests that government and academic cultures rub up against each other as a consequence of different value systems and performance incentive frameworks. Areas of tension include timeliness with academics being driven by a desire to engage in robust, longer term contributions which might yield theoretical insights, whilst practitioners crave solutions and feedback that can be rapidly inserted into the policy-making machine; politics with traditional academic values do not always sit easily with government and political policy making processes; and certainty and bias for action with policy makers tend to require prescriptions and simplifications as opposed to academics who are more comfortable around ambiguity, analysis and theorising. Whilst these hurdles are problematic, they are not insurmountable, and Menzies (2017) advocates the role of public policy intermediary organisations with 'knowledge brokers' and 'boundary spanners' working to span the boundaries of the two worlds of government and academia. The key attributes for such people include being able to understand research methodology; having a broad understanding of the relevant literature; experience of academia and public policy practice; sound interpersonal skills; and an ability to translate complex information into meaningful material for users (Shucksmith, 2016)

The content of professional training programmes in general does little to reflect the collaborative working challenge in contemporary public management, but the nature of continuous professional development opportunities might be a fertile area to explore going forward. Models of experiential learning and development include coaching, mentoring and secondments—all in practice require careful design in order to be of value to the individuals and organisations concerned. UK Public Health (2016) has recognised the value of setting out a framework to map the functional areas where individuals, teams and organisations operate to deliver public health outcomes. One of the key themes of this framework is geared towards 'joint working and holistic approaches' and these are linked to functions and sub-functions that facilitate links to individual self-assessment, job roles and descriptions and learning curricula.

The Christie Commission on the Future Delivery of Public Services in Scotland (2011, p. 39) was alert to the need to promote a systematic, coordinated and inter-agency approach "to reduce silo mentalities, drive forward service integration and build a common public sector ethos" (2011, p. ix) to workforce development across all public service agencies, and recommended that Scottish Government:

- Consider how the educational and development infrastructure across the different elements of the public service could be better coordinated
- Bring together leadership and management development into a single cross public service development programme
- Develop a competency framework to apply to all public service workers which focusses on the skills required for delivering outcomes in collaboration with delivery partners and service users
- Ensure interdisciplinary training and development modules are included in all professional training for public service.

These would represent a comprehensive commitment to the improvement of the future capabilities and capacities of all actors in the spheres of collaboration in public services.

8 Conclusions

Paul Williams

It can be argued that the current and future task of effective public management rests heavily on its ability to understand and tackle the diverse challenges presented by the many, diverse and changing boundaries clearly identified in the opening chapters of this book. The boundary challenges are ever-present in the working lives of all actors and stakeholders involved in public management, but their range, intensity and complexity increases significantly within collaborative forms of governance—settings where agencies work together across organisations and sectors but also, adding to the complexity, across policy areas and levels of governance. It is unlikely that the main drivers of this form of working—efficiency, effectiveness and responsiveness—will continue to shape the discourse in a similar direction, and the appetite by politicians, policy makers and practitioners for guidance and assistance on how to make this form of public management work will continue unabated. In the face of the constant pressures on public managers to design and deliver effective public services, this community generally expresses a need for prescriptions—what works in practice? What are the key ingredients for an effective collaboration? Which leadership and management competencies are needed to work in this environment? How can success be demonstrated? The case study illustrated in Box 8.1 offers the kind of reflections that aim to synthesise the essence of effective collaboration and highlight the future of good practice.

Box 8.1: Case Study—Pathways to Work: Condition Management Programme

This was a multi-sector collaboration involving a local Council, local Health Board, the Council for Voluntary Service and the Job Centre Plus agency. The Pathways to Work was a national welfare programme aiming to provide a single gateway for people claiming incapacity benefits to financial, employment and health services. It was considered to be effective by local stakeholders for a number of main reasons:

- The initiative had a very clear focus with a defined client group in a particular geographical area and involving an appealing vision of making a difference for vulnerable people. In the words of one stakeholder: "we know we are helping people on the ground—preventing them from getting in a rut—and to hear the people who have been on the programme, lifts my heart"
- The location of the Programme was located within a prevailing organisational and institutional structure that had a previous history of collaboration and had established a fertile culture of working together at individual, organisational and sectoral levels.
- The programme was adequately managed with a dedicated project manager and assistant, and new resources guaranteed over a 3-year timescale
- The Programme was governed by an effective steering group consisting of the right people at the right level from the participating organisations; the membership was consistent and attendance good; communication and servicing arrangements for the group were efficient.
- There was evidence of connected and dispersed leadership at strategic, project, clinical and governance levels
- There was policy integration between the formulation and delivery stages with implementation managed by a delivery team.
- Quick-Wins demonstrated the immediate value of the Programme and a clear outcome framework (linked to a national framework) embraced both quantitative and qualitative measures.

This case study was summarised from NLIAH (2008).

Unfortunately, researchers and academics are unlikely to be able to provide the levels of certainty and prescription that this community craves. This is borne out in research by Ryan et al. (2008, p. 15) in a New Zealand context with their conclusion that: "the problem of working together effectively to achieve results is a complex one: it defies attempts to produce a simple cookbook of key steps." However, as this chapter has attempted to argue, there is material available that can assist with the practical challenges of managing within this galaxy of boundaries. Frequently, this has been converted into 'good practice guides' and 'policy advice' of varying authenticity and robustness. However, key themes can certainly be detected—factors and determinants that are critical in shaping the course of collaboration and boundary management. These are a combination of structure and agency, weaving together in a complex interplay of dynamic interactions. Whilst the primacy of structure or agency is a matter of keen debate, views from practitioners in some research studies (Williams, 2017) appear to favour the latter as is illustrated in the following: "we can resolve anything because of relationships," another that: "you can get around structures if you have the right people." But, a more balanced view was that: "we will make it work despite the structure, but it would work better if we had supportive structures." In other words, structures, with their attendant boundaries, can enable or hinder collaborative practices.

The growth of collaborative governance and management has been accompanied by a steady output of research—both theoretical and more practical and policy based. These should not be considered as separate and distinct endeavours as each is dependent upon the other. The quest for theory generation and explanation will ultimately be beneficial for the policy community in tackling their everyday management challenges. In terms of the direction of future research and the approaches to methodology it might embrace, there are a number of potential areas that could usefully be pursued:

- A 'Cochrane-style' systematic review of the literature to produce a guide for evidence-based practice
- Ethnographic studies that enable researchers to be grounded in the realties and challenges of the working lives of key actors in collaboration—understanding and tacking their sense-making strategies, management behaviours and tactics
- The establishment of a repository for case studies on collaborative working—perhaps on the model of the 'Case Centre'
- The promotion of 'action-research' studies that can influence and evaluate cross-boundary activity and management in practice
- Evaluation studies that examine the effectiveness and impact of different boundary management strategies.

Fountain (2013, p. 6) emphasises the enormity of the challenge of working across boundaries to design and delivery effective collaboration in the following way:

> Management advice and research on collaborative governance, networked governance, joined-up governance, and more abound. Some advice emphasizes individual leadership skills in developing collaboration. Other studies emphasize building networks for innovation. Still others focus on social media and technologies that should somehow make self-organization possible. And others stress performance management with an emphasis on clear goals, measures, and accountability. Cross-agency collaboration demands all of these skills and more.

Perhaps most of all, and reflecting Sullivan's (2014) assertion that collaboration is the new normal, is that government, politicians and policy makers create the right authorizing environment for collaboration. This reflects the view promoted by research in New Zealand that there needs to be more sustained support and learning for actors involved in collaboration and that Government: "needs not just to 'give permission' for these ways of acting but to actively encourage and enable them—to act, in other words, as the 'guardian angel of collaboration'" (Ryan et al., 2008, p. 21).

References

Agranoff, R. (2007) *Managing within networks* Washington, DC: Georgetown University Press

Agranoff, R. (2012) *Collaborating to manage: A primer for the public sector* Washington, DC: Georgetown University Press

Alexander, J.A. Comfort, M.E. Weiner, B.J., and Bogue, R. (2001) "Leadership in collaborative community health partnerships", *Nonprofit Management and Leadership*, Vol. 12. No. 2, pp. 159–175

Allen, K.E., Bordas, J., Hickman, G.R., Matusak, L.R., Soresson, G.J., and Whitmire, K.J. (1998) "Leadership in the 21st century", in Hickman, G.R. (ed) *Leading organizations: Perspectives for a new era* London: Sage Publications Ltd, pp. 572–580

Ansell, C., and Gash, A. (2007) "Collaborative governance in theory and practice", *Journal of Public Administration, Research and Theory*, Vol. 18, pp. 543–571

ARACY. (2007) *The impact of power and politics in a complex environment* West Perth, SA: ARACY

Archibald, D., Trumpower, D., and MacDonald, C.J. (2014) "Validation of interprofessional collaborative competency attainment survey (ICCAS)", *Journal of Interprofessional Care*, Vol. 28, No. 6, pp. 553–558

Audit Commission. (2005) *Governing partnerships: Bridging the accountability gap* (pp. 2–6) London: Audit Commission

Barrett, G., and Keeping, C. (2005) "The processes required for effective interprofessional working", in Barrett, G., Sellman, D., and Thomas, J. (eds) *Interprofessional working in health and social care: Professional perspectives* Basingstoke: Palgrave Macmillan

Barrett, M., and Oborn, E. (2010) "Boundary object use in cross-cultural software development teams", *Human Relations*, Vol. 63, No. 8, pp. 1199–1221.

Bennett, J. (2004) "The force of things: Steps towards an ecology of matter", *Political Theory*, Vol. 32, No. 3, pp. 348–372

Bowker, G., and Star, S.L. (1999) *Sorting things out: Classification and its consequences* Cambridge, MA: MIT Press

Brown, M.E., and Gioia, D.A. (2002) "Making things click: Distributive leadership in an online division of an offline organization", *Leadership Quarterly*, Vol. 13, pp. 397–419

Bryson, J.M., and Crosby, B.C. (1992) *Leadership for the common good: Tackling public problem in a shared-power world* San Francisco, CA: Jossey Bass

Canadian Interprofessional Health Collaboration (2010) *A national interprofessional competency framework* Vancouver, BC: CIHC

Carey, G. (2017) "Boundary spanners and wicked policy problems: Towards a theory of practice", Paper to the IRSPM Conference, Budapest

Carlile, P.R. (2002) "A pragmatic view of knowledge and boundaries: Boundary objects in new product development". *Organization Science*, Vol. 13, No. 4, pp. 442–455

Carpenter, J., and Dickinson, H. (2016) *Interprofessional education and training* Bristol: Policy Press

Child, J., and Heavens, S.J. (2003) "The social construction of organizations and its implications for organizational learning", in Dierkes, M., Berthoin Antal, A., Child, J., and Nonaka, I. (eds) *Handbook of organizational learning and knowledge* Oxford: Oxford University Press

Child, J., Faulkner, D., and Tallman, S. (2005) *Cooperative strategy—Managing alliances, networks, and joint ventures* Oxford: Oxford University Press

Chrislip, D.D., and Larson, C.E. (1994) *Collaborative leadership* San Francisco, CA: Jossey Bass

Cook, A. (2015) *Partnership working across UK public services* Edinburgh: What Works Scotland

Coote, A., Allen, J., and Woodhead, D. (2004) *Finding out what works* London: Kings Fund

Cornell, J.P., and Kubisch, A.C. (1998) "Applying a theory of change approach to the evaluation of comprehensive community initiatives: Progress, prospects and problems", in Fulbright-Anderson, K. et al (eds) *New approaches to evaluating community initiatives, vol. 2: Theory, measurement and analysis* Washington, DC: Aspen Institute

Crevani, L., Lindgren, M., and Packendorff, J. (2007) "Shared leadership: A postheroic perspective on leadership as a collective construction", *International Journal of Leadership Studies* Vol. 3, No. 1, pp. 40–67

Crosby, B.C., and Bryson, J.M. (2010) "Integrative leadership and the creation of cross-sector collaboration", *The Leadership Quarterly*, Vol. 21, No. 2, pp. 211–230

Currie, G., and Suhomlinova, O. (2006) "The impact of institutional forces upon knowledge sharing in the UK NHS: The triumph of professional power and the inconsistency of policy", *Public Administration* Vol. 84, No. 1, pp. 1–30

D'Amour, D., and Oandasan, I. (2005) "Interprofessionality as the field of interprofessional practice and interprofessional education: An emerging concept", *Journal of Interprofessional Care*, Supplement 1, pp. 8–20

De Long, D.W., and Fahey, L. (2000) "Diagnosing cultural barriers to knowledge management", *Academy of Management Perspectives* Vol. 14, No. 14, pp. 113–127

Denis, J-L., Lamothe, L., and Langley, A. (2001) "The dynamics of collective leadership and strategic change in organizations", *Academy of Management*, Vol 44, No. 4, pp. 809–837

Dickinson, H., and Carey, G. (2016) *Managing and leading in inter-agency settings* Bristol: Policy Press

Donahue, J.D. (2004) "On collaborative governance", in *Corporate social responsibility initiative working paper no. 2* Cambridge, MA: John F. Kennedy School of Government, Harvard University Press

Donahue, J.D., and Zeckhauser, R.J. (2008) "Public—private collaboration", in Moran, M., Rein, M., and Goodin, R.E. (eds) *The Oxford handbook of public policy* Oxford: Oxford University Press

Emerson, K., Nabatchi, T., and Balogh, S. (2011) "An integrative framework for collaborative governance", *Journal of Public Administration Research and Theory*, Vol. 22, pp. 1–29

Evans, G.R., Grudniewicz, A., Baker, G.R., and Wodchis, W.P. (2016) "Organizational context and capabilities for integrating care: A framework for improvement", *Journal of Integrated Care*, Vol. 16, No. 3, pp. 1–14

Fletcher, J.K., and Kaufer, K. (2003) "Shared leadership paradox and possibility", in Pearce, C.L., and Conger, J.A. (eds) *Shared leadership: Reframing the hows and whys of leadership* London: Sage Publications Ltd

Flynn, N., and Talbot, C. (1996) "Strategy and strategists in UK local government", *Journal of Management Development*, Vol. 15, No. 2, pp. 24–37

Fong, A., Valerdi, R., and Srinivasan, J. (2007) "Boundary objects as a framework to understand the role of systems integrators", *Systems Research Forum*, Vol. 2, pp. 11–18

Fountain, J. (2013) *Implementing cross-agency collaboration: A guide for federal managers* Washington, DC: IBM Centre for Business of Government

Gal, U., Yoo, Y., and Boland, R.J. (2004) "The dynamics of boundary objects, social infrastructures and social identities", Case Western Reserve University, USA, *Sprouts: Working Papers on Information Systems*, Vol. 4, No. 11, http://sprouts.aisnet.org/4-11

GAO. (2005) *Results-orientated government: Practices that can help enhance and sustain collaboration among federal agencies* Washington, DC: US Government Accountability Office

Goldsmith, S., and Eggers, W.D. (2005) *Governing by network: The new shape of the public sector* Washington, DC: Brookings Institution Press

Government of South Australia. (2016) *Working together for joined-up policy delivery report: Creating better outcomes for South Australians through joined-up policy delivery* Adelaide: Government of South Australia

Hardy, B., Hudson, B., and Waddington, E. (2000) *What makes a good partnership? A partnership assessment tool* Leeds: Nuffield Institute for Health

Hartley, J., and Benington, J. (2006) "Copy and paste, or graft and transplant? Knowledge sharing through inter-organizational networks", *Public Money and Management*, Vol. 26, No. 2, pp. 101–108

Hay, C. (1995) "Structure and agency", in Stoker, G., and Marsh, D. (eds) *Theory and methods in political science* London: Palgrave Macmillan, pp. 189–206

Hayes, S.L., Mann, M.K., Morgan, F.M., Kelly, M.J., and Weightman, A.L. (2012) "Collaboration between local health and local government agencies for health improvement", *Cochrane Database of Systematic Reviews*, No. 10

Hughes, J., and Weiss, J. (2004) "Simple rules for making alliances work", *Harvard Business Review*, Vol. 85, No. 11, p. 122

Huxham, C., and Vangen, S. (2005) *Managing to collaborate: The theory and practice of collaborative advantage* London: Sage Publications Ltd

Huysman, M. (2000). "Organizational learning or learning organization", *European Journal of Work and Organizational Psychology*, Vol. 9, No. 2, pp. 133–145

Inkpen, A.C. (2000) "Learning through joint ventures: A framework of knowledge acquisition", *Journal of Management Studies*, Vol. 37, No. 7, pp. 1019–1044

Innes, J., and Booher, D. (1999) "Consensus building and complex adaptive systems: A framework for evaluating collaborative planning", *Journal of American Planning Association*, Vol. 65, No. 4, pp. 412–423

Interprofessional Education Collaborative Expert Panel. (2011) *Core competencies for interprofessional collaborative practice: Report of an expert panel.* Washington, DC: Interprofessional Education Collaborative

Interprofessional Education Collaborative Expert Panel. (2016) *Core competencies for interprofessional collaborative practice: 2016 update.* Washington, DC: Interprofessional Education Collaborative

Kanter, R.M. (1997) "World- class leaders", in Hesselbein, F., Goldsmith, M., and Beckhard, R. (eds) *The leader of the future* San Francisco, CA: Jossey Bass

Kickert, W.J.M., Klijn, E.H., and Koppenjam, J.F.M. (1997) "Managing networks in the public sector: Findings and reflections", in Kickert, W.J.M., Klijn, E.H., and Koppenjam, J.F.M. (eds) *Managing complex networks: Strategies for the public sector* Thousand Oaks, CA: Sage Publications, pp. 116–191

Kimble, D.L., Grenier, C., and Goglio-Primard, K. (2010) "Innovation and knowledge sharing across professional boundaries: Political interplay between boundary objects and brokers", *International Journal of Information Management*, Vol. 30, pp. 437–444

Kindornay, S., Tissot, S., and Sheiban, N. (2014) *The value of cross sector partnerships* Ottawa: The North-South Institute

Klinga, C., Hansson, J., Hansson, H., and Sachs, M.A. (2016) "Co-leadership—a management solution for integrated health and social care", *Journal of Integrated Care*, Vol. 16, No. 2, pp. 1–9

LaPalombara, J. (2003) "Power and politics in organizations: public and private sector comparisons", in Dierkes, M., Berthoin Antal, A., Child, J., and Nonaka, I. (eds) *Handbook of organizational learning and knowledge* Oxford: Oxford University Press, pp. 137–161

Lasker, R.D., and Weiss, E.S. (2001) "Broadening participation in community problem-solving: A multidisciplinary model to support collaborative practice and research", *Journal of Urban Health: Bulletin of the New York Academy of Medicine*, Vol. 80. pp. 14–60

Linden, R.M. (2002) *Working across boundaries: Making collaboration work in government and non-profit organizations* San Francisco, CA: Jossey Bass

Lipman-Blumen, J. (1996) *The connective edge: Leading in an interdependent world* San Francisco, CA: Jossey Bass

Luke, J.S. (1998) *Catalytic leadership: Strategies for an interconnected world* San Francisco, CA: Jossey Bass

Manzini, E. (2015) *Design, when everybody designs: An introduction to design for social innovation* Cambridge, MA: MIT Press

Marion, R., and Uhl-Bien, M. (2001) "Leadership in complex organizations", *Leadership Quarterly*, Vol. 12, pp. 389–418

Menzies, J. (2017) "Meeting in the middle: Building a knowledge partnership between academia and government", Paper to the IRSPM Conference, Budapest

Mihm, J. (2012) Managing for results: Key considerations for implementing interagency collaborative mechanisms. GAO-12–1022). Washington, DC: US Government Accountability Office.

Milward, H.B., and Provan K.G. (2006) *A manager's guide to choosing and using collaborative networks* Washington, DC: IBM Centre for the Business of Government

Mintzberg, H. (1994) *The rise and fall of strategic planning* New York: Prentice Hall

Mintzberg, H., and Waters, J. (1998) "Of strategies, deliberate and emergent", in Segal-Horn, S. (ed) *The strategy reader* Oxford: Wiley-Blackwell

Nicolini, D., Powell, J., Conville, P., and Martinez-Solano, L. (2008) "Managing knowledge in the healthcare sector. A review", *International Journal of Management Reviews*, Vol. 10, No. 3, pp. 245–263

NLIAH. (2008) *Getting collaboration to work in Wales: Lessons from the NHS and partners* Cardiff: NLIAH

Noble, G., and Jones, R., (2006) "The role of boundary spanning managers in the establishment of partnerships", *Public Adminstration*, Vol. 84, No. 4, pp. 891–917

Nonaka, I. (1994) "A dynamic theory of organizational knowledge creation", *Organization Science*, Vol. 5, No. 1, pp. 14–37

Nooteboom, B. (2008). "Learning and innovation in inter-organizational relationships", in S. Cropper, M. Ebers, C. Husham, and P. Smith Ring (eds.) *The Oxford handbook of inter-organizational relations* New York: Oxford University Press, 607–634

O'Leary, R. and Bingham, L.B. (eds). (2009) *The collaborative public manager: New ideas for the twenty-first century* Washington, DC: Georgetown University Press

O'Leary, R., and Gerard, C. (2012) *Collaboration across boundaries: Insights and tips from federal senior executives* Washington, DC: IBM Centre for the Business of Government

Oswick, C., and Robertson, M. (2009) "Boundary objects reconsidered", *Journal of Change Management*, Vol. 9, No. 2, pp. 179–193

Palus, C.J., Chrobot-Mason, D.L., and Cullen, K.L. (2014) "Boundary spanning leadership in an interdependent world", in Langan-Fox, J., and Cooper, C.L. (eds) *Boundary-spanning in organizations: Network, influence, and conflict* London: Routledge

Parry, K. W., and Bryman, A. (2006) "Leadership in organization", in Clegg, S. T., Harry, C., Lawrence, T. B. and Nord, W. R. (eds) *The Sage handbook of organization studies*. London: Sage, pp. 447–468

Pearce, C.L., and Conger, J.A. (2003) *Shared leadership: Reframing the hows and whys of leadership* London: Sage Publications Ltd

Percy-Smith, J., Burden, T., Darlow, A., Dawson, L., Hawtin, M., and Ladi, S. (2003) *Promoting change through research: The impact of research in local government*. York: YPS

Public Health England (PHE). (2016) *Public health skills and knowledge framework (PHSKF)*. http://www.thehealthwell.info/node/1019324

Radin, B.A. (1996) "Managing across boundaries", in Kettle, D.F., and Milward, H.B. (eds) *The state of public management* Baltimore: John Hopkins University Press.

Rashman, L., Withers, E., and Hartley, J. (2009) "Organizational learning and knowledge in public service organizations: A systematic review of the literature", *International Journal of Management Reviews*, Vol. 11, No. 14, pp. 463–494

Ryan, B., Gill, D., Eppel, E., and Lips, M. (2008) "Managing for joint outcomes: Connecting up the horizontal and the vertical", *Policy Quarterly*, Vol. 4, No. 3, pp. 14–21

Ryan, C. (2001) "Leadership in collaborative policy-making: An analysis of agency roles in regulatory negotiations", *Policy Sciences*, Vol. 34, pp. 221–245

Salk, J., and Simonin, B. (2011). "Collaboration, learning and leverage across borders: A meta-theory of learning", in Easterby-Smith, M., and Lyles M. (eds.) *Handbook of organizational learning and knowledge management* (2nd Edition) Hoboken, NJ: John Wiley & Sons

Schein, E.H. (2004). *Organizational culture and leadership* (3rd edn.) San Francisco, CA: Jossey-Bass

Schroder, C., Medves, J., Paterson, P., Byrnes, V., Chapman, C., O'Riodan, A., Pichora, D., and Kelly, C. (2011) "Development and pilot testing of the collaborative practice assessment tool", *Journal of Interprofessional Care*, Vol. 25, pp. 189–195

Scott, R., and Boyd, R. (2017) *Interagency performance targets: A case study of New Zealand's results programme* Washington, DC: IBM Centre for the Business of Government

Senge, P. (1992) *The fifth discipline: The art and practice of the learning organisation* New York: Doubleday

Serafin, R., Stibbe, D., Bustamante, C., and Schramm, C. (2008) "Current practice in the evaluation of cross-sector partnerships for sustainable development", TPI Working Paper No. 1/2008 London: The Partnering Initiative

Shucksmith, M. (2016) *Interaction: How academics and the third sector work together to influence policy and practice* Dunfermline: Carnegie UK Trust

Star, S.L., and Griesemer, J.R. (1989) "Institutional ecology, 'translations' and boundary objects: Amateurs and professionals in Berkeley's museum of vertebrate zoology, 1907–39", *Social Studies in Science*, Vol. 19, No. 3, pp. 387–420

Sullivan, H. (2014) "Collaboration as the new normal? Global trends, public policy and everyday practice", Keynote speech delivered at the Policy and Politics Conference, September, Bristol

Sullivan, H., Williams, P.M., and Jeffares, S. (2012) "Leadership for collaboration: Situated agency", *Public Management Review*, Vol. 14, No. 1, pp. 41–66

Sullivan, H., Williams, P.M., Marchington, M., and Knight, L. (2012) "Collaborative futures: Discursive realignments in Austere times", *Public Money and Management*, Vol. 33, No. 2, pp. 123–130

Sullivan, H., and Williams, P. (2012) "Whose kettle? Exploring the role of objects in managing and mediating the boundaries of integration in health and social care", *Journal of Health Organization and Management*, Vol. 26, No. 6, pp. 697–712

Thomas, R., Hardy, C., and Sargent, L. (2007) "Artifacts in interactions: The production and politics of boundary objects", AIM Research Working Paper Series, ISSN 1744–0009

Thompson, G., Francis, J., Levacic, R., and Mitchell, J. (1991) *Markets, hierarchies and networks: The co-ordination of social life* London: Sage Publications Ltd

United States Government Accountability Office. (2012) *Managing for results: Key considerations for implementing interagency collaboration* Washington, DC: GAO

Van Rensburg, A.J., Rau, A., Fourie, P., and Bracke, P. (2016) "Power and integrated care: Shifting from governance to governmentality", *International Journal of Integrated Care*, Vol. 16(3), No. 17, pp. 1–11

Van Wart, M. (2003) "Public-sector leadership theory: An assessment", *Public Administration Review*, Vol. 63, No. 2, pp. 214–228

Vera, D., and Crossan, M. (2005) "Improvisation and innovative performance in teams", *Organization Science*, Vol. 16, No. 3, pp. 203–224

Weiss, C. H. (1998) "Have we learned anything new about the use of evaluation?", *American Journal of Evaluation*, Vol. 19, No. 1, pp. 21–33

Williams, P. (2002) "The competent boundary spanner", *Public Administration*, Vol. 80, No. 1, pp. 103–124

Williams, P., and Sullivan, H. (2007) *Learning to collaborate: Lessons in effective partnership working in health and social care* Cardiff: NLIAH

Williams, P., and Sullivan, H. (2009) *Getting collaboration to work in Wales: Lessons from the NHS and partners* Cardiff: NLIAH

Williams, P. (2012) *Collaboration in public policy and practice: Perspectives on boundary spanners* Bristol: Policy Press

Williams, P. (2013) *Research study on the use of the locality model in the design and delivery of mental health services in a Welsh Valley* Abercynon: Cwm Taf Local Health Board

Williams, P. (2017) "Managing sans frontieres", Paper to the IRSPM Conference, Budapest

Zhao, Z.J., and Anand, J. (2013) "Beyond boundary spanners: The 'collective bridge' as an efficient interunit structure for transferring collective knowledge", *Strategic Management Journal*, Vol. 34, pp. 1513–1530

Part 3

The Craft Challenge

Introduction

Drawing on the current research literature and current practitioner experience in the space of boundary spanning and collaboration, this Part explores the craft challenge of cross boundary facilitation. The Part is made up of contributions from a number of authors. The first chapter has been contributed by a group of authors with an academic focus. It argues that in order to understand boundaries and how they are being traversed requires a still deeper understanding of the 'practice' of boundary spanning. Building from this foundation, it outlines a new theoretical and conceptual approach to exploring different types of boundary-spanning individuals based on their motivations and ways of operating, drawing on a range of social theories of the relationship between structure and agency. In doing so, it develops a theoretical typology of boundary-spanning individuals, which theorises why and how different boundary spanners operate and the likelihood that they produce institutional gains.

The second two chapters are contributed by Flynn, and help extend our understanding of the practical implications of this typology by providing a background to the thinking and practice of a boundary-spanning practitioner. It offers models for collaboration design and complex facilitation practice in co-creation spaces as a guide to leaders, stakeholders and facilitators as they think about how to design and deliver a successful co-creation exercise. It is necessary to draw on collaboration, boundary spanning, complexity and leadership literatures in order to explore transdisciplinary knowledge processes. In practice, all such discussions are anchored in a contextual and situational perspective—in this instance, it is the perspective of experienced cross-boundary facilitation within a public management executive context.

These two chapters argue that boundary-spanning practice is as much about design which is emergent and responsive to the direction of the collaboration and being open to new spaces as it is about facilitation in the moment. This is where the sophisticated capability of the cross-boundary facilitator to identify and draw out possibilities and nuances from the collaboration members is critical. It suggests that the most successful facilitator will have developed personal mastery of their own emotional, practice and energy states. This required them to rapidly recognise these states and their drivers and the ability to re-design, re-energise or reframe as required. They constantly seek feedback from participants and clients to guide them to refine their practice. They observe others working in this space and look for new ways to work which aligns with their individual styles. What works for one facilitator may not work for another.

The two chapters build on Flynn's experience as a cross-boundary facilitator in the public management space. In contributing to the discussion about the practice of facilitating collaboration, Flynn has drawn on the experience and reflections of many colleagues as well as her own, which are explored through examples and case studies. These colleagues come from universities, public sector agencies, NGOs and private consulting firms. The commonalities between these perspectives show that there is agreement on the breadth and depth of complexity that is opened up when we decide to participate in collaboration and the challenges which are evident in facilitating across the boundaries.

Taken together, the Part presents *both* the 'big picture' of the varied boundary spanning 'types' which describes the practice of boundary spanning and a detailed reflection from a person that practices the craft of boundary spanning as a profession. The aim of presenting the chapters this way is to assist readers in understanding the nuanced connections between the theory and practice of boundary spanning, and to demonstrate how the conceptual and theoretical work of the book is reflected in many of the challenges faced by boundary-spanning practitioners.

9 Boundary Spanners

Toward a Theory of Practice

Gemma Carey, Kerry Jacobs,
Ellie Malbon, Fiona Buick, Anna Li,
and Paul Williams

Introduction

The examination of boundaries—whether they be cultural, symbolic or structural—is of central interest, and importance, to the field of public administration (O'Flynn, 2014). The current literature on boundary spanners has consistently shown that they are important players in public policy and administration, which is primarily characterised by plurality of processes, organisations and actors (Osborne, 2010). For example, boundary spanners have been shown to enable better cross-sectoral and cross-departmental working (Head, 2014; Parston and Timmins, 1998) and are central for overcoming sub-cultural boundaries within government departments (Carey et al., in press). We also know that 'competent' boundary spanners possess particular skills, such as the ability to manage through influence and negotiation, build sustainable relationships and networks, and operate across multiple contexts with a degree of legitimacy (Williams, 2002).

As Dickinson (2018) highlighted in her earlier part on the 'concept challenge' in boundary work, despite the central role of boundary crossing in public administration there is often a lack of critical consideration about what we mean when we talk about boundaries, what forms they take and how we might work across these. Dickinson's part explored the many ways to conceptualise boundaries and boundary spanners, concluding that conceptual advances should come through interpretive rather than totalising perspectives, and through the exploration of how structure and agency interact around the construction and reconstruction of boundaries. We aim to meet Dickinson's outline for the future of boundary-spanning research by exploring what sociologist Bourdieu's theory of fields and elements of Giddens' structuration theory, both theories that deal with structure-agency dualism, can contribute to current understandings of boundary spanners in practice. We take the perspective that the way that boundary spanners change, shift or progress their fields of influence (i.e.: government agencies, academic disciplines, third-sector networks) reveals the sorts of boundary spanners that they are, and their motivations for engaging with boundary spanning at an activity.

While previous work shows that boundary spanners are important, examination of how boundary spanners work across and within different contexts or domains is in its infancy. Williams (2013, 2010) has offered important theorising in this area suggesting that all individuals, from leaders to managers to street level bureaucrats, engage in boundary-crossing work. Others (see Buick, 2014a; Carey et al., in press) have explored the 'how' question through empirical research in particular settings. This work has demonstrated that working across boundaries is a significant, challenging and complex exercise that requires people to operate at the margins. Both theoretical and empirical research has concentrated on the positive aspects of boundary spanners to the exclusion of the potential negative roles such individuals might play.

To better understand boundaries and how they are being traversed requires a still deeper understanding of the 'practice' of boundary spanning (Williams, 2013). In this chapter rather than examining different boundary spanning roles, such as Williams's typology (2010), we take a theoretical and conceptual approach to exploring different types of boundary-spanning individuals based on their motivations and ways of operating. We draw on Bourdieu's (1977, 1984, 1991, 1996) work on social fields which provides a generalisable theory of the structure of 'fields,' including their boundaries, supplemented by Giddens' (1979) work on structure and agency. In doing so, we develop a theoretical typology of boundary-spanning individuals which theorises why and how different boundary spanners operate and the likelihood that they produce institutional gains. Critically, in taking this approach we hypothesise that not all boundary spanners have altruistic motives, as suggested by previous work. For example, Williams (2013) has argued that the boundary spanner's role is to ensure the effective coupling of problems, policies and politics—focusing on the development of new solutions to complex problems. In exploring motivations through individuals who illustrate boundary-spanning 'types,' we hypothesise that boundary spanners can have both positive and negative institutional effects. This is in contrast to the current literature, which focuses on the positive ways in which boundary spanners can create institutional change.

Background

To examine individual types of boundary spanners, we draw on Bourdieu's theory of fields and elements of Giddens' structuration theory. We have chosen these theorists for their focus on how individuals operate across different social settings in addition to their expositions of social practice provided by exploring the interplay of structure and agency.

Bourdieu's intertwined concepts of habitus and fields are central to this work (Hilgers and Mangez, 2014). Habitus refers to the ingrained habits, skills and dispositions we possess through our cumulative life experience

(Bourdieu, 1977). Habitus is created by an interplay of structure and agency over time; it is shaped by past events, social contexts or structures and individual's perceptions of these (Bourdieu, 1984). Hence, while habitus is partly made up of structure, it is also the source of agency. Fields are constructed by people enacting their habitus, making it a cyclical relationship between structure and action (Bourdieu, 1984).

The concept of social fields draws attention to the relational nature of social reality and, simultaneously, that this reality is made up of distinct 'sub-spaces' what Giddens (1979) calls subsystems, as we outline later). A field, for example, could be as large as the entire academic profession, or as small as an organisational unit. An individual's habitus can be well aligned or poorly aligned with different fields. Individuals can also correspond to different positions in the field depending upon their habitus (Bourdieu, 1977).

Most famously, Bourdieu studied large fields such as art (Bourdieu, 1996) politics (Bourdieu et al., 1994), culture (Bourdieu, 1984) and religion (Bourdieu, 1991)—building towards a generalisable theory of social fields. Regardless of size, fields reflect struggles for recognition (Bourdieu, 1998), and the behaviours of those who occupy them are codified, as each field has specific rules. This may pertain to symbolic structures (i.e. how people think or how they order their worlds mentally) or social structures (i.e. classifications based on objective resources, positions and so forth) (Hilgers and Mangez, 2014). These rules are legitimised by elites, who are able to create expectations and norms or the 'rules of the game' within a particular field (otherwise referred to as 'doxa' (Bourdieu, 1998). Bourdieu (1977) contends that elites reflect the specific competencies required to act with and retain legitimacy within a field. In doing so, they maintain hierarchy and exclude other actors from joining or excelling within a field (Bourdieu, 1991). Hence, individuals with more symbolic capital within a field can exert power or control over individuals with less capital (Bourdieu, 1998; Thompson, 1984).

This draws attention to a second interconnected concept of Bourdieu's— that of capital. Bourdieu famously theorised multiple forms of capital, including social, cultural, symbolic and economic capital. He argues that the ability for individuals to exert influence within a field is largely dependent on the form, quantity and strength of their capital: "a field is a structure of relative positions within which the actors and groups think, act and take positions. These relative positions are defined by the volume and structure of their capital" (Hilgers and Mangez, 2014, p. 10). Capital (social, cultural, economic and so forth) can be accumulated within a field and converted into symbolic capital, with elites holding the greatest amounts (Bourdieu, 1998, 1977). This provides individuals with status in a field. This enables the elite within the field to dictate norms, activities and what is considered legitimate practice (i.e. doxa) (Bourdieu, 1977). In doing so, embedded ways of thinking and operating are reinforced and reproduced.

It is important to note, however, that while social field theory empha- sises the reproduction of social contexts, it does not eliminate the pos- sibility of change (Hilgers and Mangez, 2014). Change can emerge as different forms of capital become valued, thereby leading to the re-organ- isation and re-definition of a field. This change results from struggles over the rules of the game within a given field. It is this possibility of change, we will argue, that enables boundary spanners to operate effec- tively across multiple fields.

Bourdieu and Giddens have a shared goal—to elucidate and explain the relationship between structure and agency—but each places a dif- ferent emphasis on how to articulate this which is helpful for this chap- ter. Both theorists see power as culturally and symbolically created and legitimised between the interplay between structure and agency. Hence, they also have a shared epistemological starting point: that social real- ity is fundamentally relational. This means that it is "the relationship among the elements, and not the elements themselves, that must be at the heart of analysis" (Hilgers and Mangez, 2014, p. 2). However, Giddens' structuration theory (including later adaptations to his work) places a particular emphasis on how social systems (or fields) can overlap and interact and the transformative capacity of social actors (Giddens, 1984).

Giddens' (1979) structuration theory is similar to Bourdieu's ambi- tions, in that it is an attempt to draw together the diverse theorising on the structure-agency dualism into a coherent theory of social practice. At the core of structuration theory is the concept of the 'duality of struc- ture.' The duality of structure refers to the processes by which structures are produced by human activity, but are also the medium of this activ- ity—much like the cyclical relationship between individuals and fields articulated for Bourdieu.

Importantly, structuration theory extends elements of Bourdieu's the- ory of social fields by emphasising that agents must be understood as existing within plural social systems. From a structurationist perspective, social systems are organised hierarchically and laterally. The practices of individuals in any given context are embedded in wider institutionalised practices (Giddens, 1984). In constructing their social practice, agents draw upon the rules and resources (i.e. structures) available in their imme- diate context and the rules and resources available more broadly in other social systems (Giddens, 1984). Taking an organisation as an example, workers produce (and reproduce) their own organisational culture—or the norms and practices specific to that group of individuals. However, they also draw on broader social norms and values in terms of the ways in which organisations are structured, for example standardised managerial hierarchies and workplace practices. Thus, a structurationist perspective considers the practices of individuals not only in the context of their own organisational structures, but also in terms of their position within and relationship to external structures that stretch beyond the organisation

(Giddens, 1984; Whittington, 1992). Hence, Giddens' emphasis is how individuals function across multiple fields at the same time, while Bourdieu concentrated on mapping power within fields. For Giddens, the actor is not merely an expression of the field but actively creating and has the potential to change the field (or multiple fields). While this is present in Bourdieu, it is underemphasised. When taken together, it provides the opportunity for theorising on boundary spanners more fruitfully.

While fields may be defined by certain activities, structuration theory enables us to see that they still exist in relation to other fields—enabling possibilities for change through access to more diverse or alternate forms of capital (referred to as resources in structuration theory). In highlighting the strengths of structuration theory for the study of institutions, Whittington (1992, p. 703) argues that both managers and the managed are "full members of society who [operate] in a diversity of systems and are therefore able to draw upon and respond to a multiplicity of rules and resources" (i.e. an individual is not just employee but also mother, activist, artist and so forth). This enables us to see how boundary spanners are able to gain different forms of capital from different fields (or social systems) and deploy them to their or their organisation's advantage in alternate contexts. When we place these two theories together, we can see that boundary spanners act in two important ways which make them different from other actors—they break the rules of a field (i.e. challenge doxa) and they bring different forms of capital.

Theorising the Practice of Boundary Spanners

Drawing on empirical research on boundary spanning in the published literature, and using concepts from Bourdieu and Giddens, we theorise a typology of boundary spanners (see Table 9.1). As follows, we explore each of these ideal types in turn—the 'traditional' boundary spanner, the 'looking for an edge' boundary spanner, the 'moving on up' boundary spanner and the 'pushing the ideas' boundary spanner—accompanied by a fictional illustrative example. Boundary spanners are delineated primarily on the basis of operation and motivation: that is, the interconnected questions of how and why they practice boundary spanning. As with all typologies, these categories represent ideal types. An ideal type sets out the defining, or essential, characteristics of a given phenomenon (Rogers, 1969; Weber, 1922). It does not extend to any one particular case, or to all cases within a given category; they are not designed or intended to accurately represent social reality. We think that these categories are important but exceptions to these categories will exist; indeed, if no exceptions or deviations existed, then an ideal type would not be necessary (Rogers, 1969).

The first category, 'the traditional boundary spanner' is where current public administration literature has focused. As a result, this category is well developed. Categories 2–4 draw less directly on the existing literature and are hypothesised based on the theory outlined earlier. We note that each category (apart from the first) has the potential for positive and negative institutional effects. Indeed, we have created categories 2–4 in order to illustrate that simply because a boundary spanner is in existence does not automatically translate to positive institutional or problem-solving effects.

1. The 'Traditional' Boundary Spanner

Our first category of boundary spanner (Box 9.1) describes that which we might typically associate with the 'positive boundary spanner' described in the literature (and as a consequence is more developed than later categories) (Aldrich and Herker, 1977; Carey et al., in press; O'Flynn, 2014; Williams, 2002). They are motivated (at least in part) by altruistic desires for more effective institutions. This type of boundary spanner has what we would call a multi-field habitus. That is, their perspectives and actions are informed by experience and capital from diverse fields (e.g. different parts of government and the non-government sector). This multi-field habitus enables them to have a reflexive form of practice (or praxis)— aware of their position across boundaries and within specific fields. In doing so, they are able to use the capital associated with one field to gain legitimacy in other fields (Bourdieu, 1998). For example, public servants who use their knowledge from the fields of education, psychology, sociology, economics, stakeholder engagement, public policy and business to address deeply entrenched Indigenous disadvantage (Buick, 2014b).

It is unlikely that these boundary spanners are considered 'elite' in multiple fields. This is because to be elite within a field requires specialist capital (Bourdieu, 1977) and accumulating enough capital to be elite across a range of fields is unlikely to be achievable (Hilgers and Mangez, 2014). Hence, we assume that these boundary spanners have a primary field in which they operate and have a high degree of legitimacy and legitimised forms of capital within that field. From this, they cross over into one or more secondary fields. In doing so, they draw on the capital of their primary field to gain access and legitimacy to other fields. For example, an academic can engage (to varying degrees) in the field of policy based on cultural and symbolic capital they hold in their academic sphere. Here, capital has been obtained through the attainment of a high standard of education and excellence in their primary field through research and publications. Both Bourdieu and Giddens stress that resources from one field (or social system) can be transferred to others when conditions are acceptable (Bourdieu, 1998, 1977; Giddens, 1984; Whittington, 1992, p. 703).

Using their multi-field habitus and capital (or the multiplicity of rules and resources available to them), this category of boundary spanner is most likely to possess the key capabilities set out by Williams (2002) (e.g.

building networks, brokering trust and solutions and managing through influence and negotiation). Boundary spanners are particularly adept at exploiting tensions between divergent fields and/or capitalising on opportunities presented by traversing different fields in order to develop alternate forms of practice that does not sit neatly within the defined activities (or the norms and rules) of one particular field. At times this may mean actively defying the rules by seeing alternate ways of being and doing, and they can mobilise various forms of capital drawn from their primary field. In doing so, they can navigate fields differently to those who are not boundary spanners. By exploiting the overlapping nature of social fields, boundary spanners can broker solutions, build networks, trust and influence because they can engage with some rules of the field, but not all. That is, they have greater mobility within secondary social fields because of their outsider status, coupled with novel capital, which appeals to elites within secondary fields. Reflexivity is key to this process. Mental reflexivity is the ability to question what might otherwise remain taken for granted (Bourdieu, 1977). Without reflexivity, we are likely to misrecognise the socialised and taken for granted (doxa) as inherently true and real (Bourdieu, 1998). Hence, reflexivity enables the boundary spanner to see the rules of different fields and their own movement through them.

Hence, traversing these different fields is also likely to mean that boundary spanners are highly attuned to their very existence and the rules that govern behaviour within them; they achieve this through engaging in reflexive practice. This is supported by the finding that effective boundary spanners have the ability to empathise with different perspectives and communicate effectively (Carey et al., in press). That is, they have a great sense of the 'whole'—the fields or systems and the ways in which they overlap. In doing so, they can create real institutional advantages. However, left to their own devices, fields have a tendency to become autonomous.

Bourdieu argues that key cultural fields such as art are losing autonomy and distinctiveness (Bourdieu, 1996). Therefore, from this perspective boundary spanners should be becoming more powerful. However, even within fields that are losing distinctiveness you would expect the specialist capital of the elite would remain dominant. Therefore, we would expect the boundary spanners to not be mobilised by the elite, but those who wish to challenge the elite or the rules of a field.

Using the skills outlined by Williams (2002), this category of boundary spanner helps to prevent fields becoming highly autonomous, thereby facilitating action on wicked policy problems. Given we are working within a context of plurality (Osborne, 2010), this role is critical to the functioning of policy networks efforts to create joined-up working (Klijn, 1997) and helps to explain why boundary spanners appear to be key to the functioning of policy networks.

While there are many positives associated with this category of boundary spanner, it is important to note that their marginal status in secondary fields means they are unlikely to be able to change the rules of the field (or rules of 'the game'). That is, while they may strive for widespread or sustainable institutional change, they do not possess enough capital within secondary fields to obtain this. This is likely to leave these boundary spanners vulnerable to burnout due to continually working against deeply embedded rules and norms. Moreover, they may not be appreciated within their primary field although their value contribution at a broader level may be significant, as illustrated by the literature.

Box 9.1:   Example: The 'Traditional' Boundary Spanner

Sharon is a public servant who works in Indigenous Affairs at the local level (i.e. street level). She has a wide range of experiences, having worked in teaching, social worker and community development roles for many years. Through her experience in these positions she has come to see Indigenous disadvantage as a complex and interwoven set of issues across health, education, employment and broader social and economic structures. This view is not shared by her superiors, who view Indigenous disadvantage as a separate or 'siloed' issue that does not require coordination and integration across different departments.

Sharon uses her experience and 'soft skills' developed in previous roles to find ways to work around governmental systems, engaging in subversive activities to meet the demands of her superiors while also achieving tangible outcomes for the communities with whom she worked. To do this, she regularly engages informally with people across different departments and areas, bringing them into meetings within her own department.

Sharon wants broader institutional change, where an integrated approach is the norm. She finds it frustrating that she does not seem able to achieve this, even though she is improving things at the local level. Yet, because her energy is focused on working with individuals at the local level and within communities, so therefore is both geographically and practically separate from the political centre of the public sector, her superiors (i.e. elites) do not perceive her as a threat. Her efforts to both change things in the communities she serves, while also pushing for institutional change without effect, mean she is often over-stretched and frustrated.

---

2. *'Looking for an Edge'*

This form of boundary spanner (Box 9.2) engages across fields in order to gain an edge in their primary field through the accumulation of novel capital from other fields (Bourdieu, 1996). For example, they may seek novel methodologies or practices from another sector or organisation. By bringing these into their primary field, they are perceived to be innovative, thereby accumulating more symbolic capital. They operate within a habitus that aligns to a single field—branching out occasionally for strategic purposes (e.g. to acquire enough capital to shift into a new 'position-practice') (Stones, 2005). Therefore, they are primarily interested in the symbolic aspects of the capital they can acquire without necessarily having or embodying the underlying habitus.

This type of boundary spanner may seek to change the rules and norms within their primary field (i.e. to reshape doxa). However, they do so with the aim of re-positioning themselves as dominant in that field by changing what is valued (Hilgers and Mangez, 2014). The act of boundary spanning is done for the purpose of opening future personal opportunities rather than with the goals of creating change in the doxa of a field. Their ultimate goal is to displace current elites, and accrue more symbolic capital rather than create true institutional change. Nonetheless, by introducing new ideas these boundary spanners offer some institutional advantages, both in the sense of generating innovation but also inadvertently connecting fields (e.g. by way of a shared methodology). They may also inadvertently create space for 'traditional' boundary spanners (or even evolve into traditional boundary spanners, if they invest the time) by changing what forms of capital are valued within a particular field. For example, a senior public servant may turn to practices in the private sector to gain an edge through the introduction of new, and seemingly better (i.e. higher in symbolic capital) approaches. The rapid rise of social impact bonds (where cross fertilisation has occurred between the private and public sector) is likely to have resulted from this type of boundary-spanning activity (Roth, 2011).

Box 9.2: Looking for an Edge: Example

Hillary is an experienced senior manager of a regional Federal government office. With recognition of the systemic and wicked nature of Indigenous disadvantage, and the challenges government had faced in attempting to address it, she adopted an 'asset-based approach' to community development to work with communities. We can consider this 'looking for an edge' because asset-based approaches have emerged from an alternate field—aid and community development. As such, they are fundamentally different, and novel, ways of working for government departments (Blackman et al., 2016). Rather than adopting top-down approaches where government assumed what Indigenous communities required, the asset-based approach works from within the communities themselves. It engages community members to identify, and work with, existing strengths and assets within the community, with community members identifying their remaining areas of need and then working with government to address them. Through introducing a new methodology to governmental practice, Hillary was able to break through some of the barriers between government and Indigenous communities, leading to improved outcomes for Indigenous communities (Blackman et al., 2016).

By looking for an edge, Hillary can make space for team (traditional boundary spanners) to engage in novel ways of thinking and operating. Although her team report to line management in other departments, her senior status, ability to play the politics and sell the benefits of working in different ways, means that the boundary-spanning efforts of her team are nurtured and supported, rather than stifled.

Hillary's boundary spanning was motivated by an altruistic desire to better serve the community. However, this category of boundary spanners may also be motivated by self-interest. In this instance, an asset-based approach may not have offered genuine benefits to Indigenous communities, but enables Hillary to advance her own position within her primary field through demonstrating her ability to adopt seemingly novel approaches from other fields.

3. Moving On Up

To understand our third type of boundary spanner (Box 9.3), we need to consider the social weight or value of different fields. The autonomy of fields is relative and some are more socially dominant than others; as Giddens (1984) suggests, social systems have a degree of hierarchy. Bourdieu attempts to capture this with the concept of the field of power; some fields are more valued by society than others on the basis of cultural and/ or economic capital (Bourdieu, 1984). Boundary spanners in the 'Moving on up' category seek to move from field to field on the basis of perceived value and/or power of each field. For example, a public servant may feel that having become elite within their current field, they can obtain greater cultural capital by moving to a more dominant field.

These boundary spanners will tend to have a habitus more closely aligned to one field (informed by their experience within a singular field) and work primarily within one field at a time. Due to their elite status and considerable capital (accumulated by shifting to more and more dominant fields), these actors have the potential to change the rules of a field. These individuals are most likely to be primarily driven by ambition, but could also be driven by a sense of service (or some combination of the two); they can exercise power to serve either in the interests of themselves or the greater good. Yet, because the rules of the field serve their purpose, they are unlikely to be interested in challenging or changing the rules—seeking the accumulation of capital rather than the transformation of institutions.

Box 9.3: Moving On Up: Example

George is chief of staff within a State government. The government he was appointed under loses power and, being closely aligned to their agenda, George risks losing his standing in the public sector. Before the government loses the election, George uses his connections (and various forms of capital) to establish a new think tank and research centre. In this new position, he uses his experience in the public sector, and ongoing networks, to gain credibility within the world of academia. From this new position, he reaches out to the incoming government—positioning himself as someone ideally placed to bridge the divide between the public sector and academia. While George has the opportunity to reshape this relationship, he focuses instead on his own standing and advancement within the field of academia by capitalising on his ongoing links with government.

---

4. Pushing the Ideas

'Pushing the ideas' boundary spanners (Box 9.4) are primarily concerned with the advancement of a set of ideas or principles. They are an ideologue who seeks institutional change (i.e. changes to doxa); these boundary spanners are always change agents. This category of boundary spanner can be driven by instrumentalism—seeking to carry forward a set of ideas and gather resources to do so by moving between fields. They occupy one field at a time, but 'span' or move between different fields in an attempt to progress their ideas (i.e. they have a multi-field habitus), using the capital gained from previously occupied fields to support their cause. These boundary spanners may shift back and forth between fields, but normally only occupy one field at a time. To move between fields, they work in partnership. That is, they are often 'hosted' by the avant-garde within a field who seek to disturb the dominant doxa or set of institutional rules (Bourdieu, 1977). Hosts may hope to create institutional change or introduce new ideas by introducing ideas of focused individuals who can carry novel capital due to their success in another field. This use by the avant-garde may mean that the 'pushing the ideas' boundary spanners may be vulnerable to exploitation, or to rejection once the ideas succeed or fail to take hold. Conversely, the 'pushing the ideas' boundary spanner maybe content with passing on their ideas into a more fruitful space then leaving the field.

Like other categories, they can be driven by a desire for service or to progress a personal set of beliefs. An example of the 'Pushing the ideas' boundary spanner is an academic who wishes to change a particular aspect of government policy, such as fundamental welfare reform. They may move between the fields of academia, government or even politics in an attempt to change the doxa of the field they view as most dominant or influential. This boundary spanner moves between fields in an attempt to secure enough capital for the uptake of their ideas. That is, while they may strive for widespread or sustainable institutional change, they do not possess enough capital within secondary fields to obtain this. This is likely to leave these boundary spanners vulnerable to burnout due to continually working against deeply embedded rules and norms (Mahoney and Thelan, 2010).

Box 9.4: Pushing the Ideas: Example

Nick has worked as a public servant for several years. He develops a particular interest in the area of welfare reform, but lacks the time and space in his job to explore his ideas about this issue. Nick decides to take up the opportunity to do a PhD, using it as a chance to flesh out his thinking for how the welfare system could be reformed to perform more effectively and efficiently and publishes this in academic journals.

Once Nick finishes his PhD, he is offered a position in a think tank. He uses this position to build momentum around his ideas—producing reports aimed at government. While Nick is working at the think tank, there is a change in federal government. The new government has a mandate for welfare reform, but its agenda is not fully formed. Nick uses his academic credibility and public profile (established during his time in the think tank) to secure a position within a new group established within the public service to develop and implement a welfare reform agenda. Nick is able to effect change in this position but is sometimes seen as an outsider by his colleagues.

When the government changes, Nick may move back into academia or a think tank to develop his work further based on his experience of attempting to implement welfare reform.

Ideal Type Boundary Spanners

The ideal type boundary spanners described earlier are not an exclusive list, but they give an idea of the possible boundary-spanning strategies that exist beyond the traditional boundary spanner that typically strengthens institutional arrangements. Table 9.1 summarises the key characteristics of this typology of boundary spanners, including the theoretical category, strategy and relationship to rules for each.

Conclusion

In this chapter we have sought to understand the practice of boundary spanners through the lens of Bourdieu's theory of social fields and Giddens' structuration theory. In doing so, we have delineated four ideal types of boundary spanners that illustrate different motivations and

Table 9.1 Typology of Boundary Spanners

Boundary Spanner Types & Motivations	Theoretical Category	Strategy	Relationship to Rules	Example
'Traditional' boundary spanner Use habitus (and associated capital) to function across multiple fields. Reflects a degree of altruism. Creates real institutional advantages.	Multi-field habitus from multi-field background. Basis for reflexivity. Aware of own position (potentially linked to marginal status).	Deploy symbolic capital advantage for legitimacy across fields. No threat to the elite (i.e. are likely to be marginal).	Seek to change the rules within fields, but lack power to do so due to their marginal status. Risk frustration and burnout.	Public servants who use their knowledge from the fields of education, psychology, sociology, economics, stakeholder engagement, public policy and business to work across silos and address wicked problems.
'Looking for an edge' Seeking advantage by engaging with an outside field. Acquires capital from other fields and converts it within primary field in order to get ahead. Acquisition or transformation of habitus is irrelevant. Some institutional advantages via the introduction of novel ideas.	Habitus aligned to a single field.	Acquire foreign capital in an 'avant-garde strategy.' Will look for capital that can easily be converted into symbolic capital (legitimised in the field).	Look to acquire exotic capital and change which capitals are valued—displacing the existing elites. May seek to change rules of the game or simply accrue more field-specific capital. Goal is to displace elites and grow individual capital.	A senior public servant who adopts a methodology or approach from another field (e.g. private sector) in order to work differently.
'Moving on up' Seeking capital to move from current field to a more dominant field.	Habitus aligned to a single field and awareness of the field of power.	Shifts from one field to another, using the capital accrued in the former field.	Likely to have the ability to change the rules but unlikely to be interested in doing so.	Public servant who shifts into academia because they view it as a more dominant field.
'Pushing the ideas' Primarily concerned with the advancement of a set of ideas of principles. Seeks genuine institutional change, but is located within one field at a time.	Multiple-field habitus but single field of operation. Multi-field habitus can be the basis for reflexivity.	Move between fields to progress ideas and take learnings from one field to another field.	Cannot change the rules but may seek to do so.	Academic who moves into politics or the public service to implement ideas.

strategy for spanning boundaries. Significantly, this theorising opens up the possibility that boundary spanners may act in ways that are not directly constructive for the solutions to wicked problems, as previous literature to date suggests that boundary spanners have a positive role in creating institutional change and institutional responsiveness to problems (Carey et al., in press; O'Flynn, 2014; Williams, 2013, 2002). In particular, we argue that recognising the varying motivations of boundary spanners may be key to understanding how different boundary spanners act.

This typology allows us to "critically consider what it is that we mean by boundaries, what form they take and how we might work across these" (Dickinson, 2018) by highlighting that the exchange of capital and symbolic capital by boundary spanners can be motivated by focus on the mobilisation of cultural ideas or the mobilisation of individuals for personal capital gain. That is, the boundary spanners may have constructive, neutral and deconstructive effects on institutional structure and responsiveness. The traditional boundary spanner, which has been the focus of research to date, is likely to produce institutional gains as a result of their altruistic motives. In contrast, the lack of altruism associated with the 'moving on up' category means that these boundary spanners are less likely to reshape the rules of particular fields. This is important because, as O'Flynn (2009) argues, the 'cult of collaboration' in public management research has too strongly emphasised the need for collaboration and boundary-spanning activities when theorising about addressing wicked policy problems. It depicts boundary spanning in normative terms, portraying boundary spanners as altruistic practitioners who make sacrifices for the collective good. Our typology highlights the potential for boundary spanners to play negative, or self-interested, roles that do little for institutional change. Based on our theorising, we hope that ourselves and other researchers will be enabled to identify new categories of boundary spanners based on those we have identified: 'Looking for an edge,' 'Moving on up,' and 'Pushing the ideas.' This also has practical application for the management of change, particularly in the context of joined-up working.

10 The Theory Underpinning Crossing-Boundary Facilitation

Christine Flynn

Introduction

This remainder of this Part draws on collaboration, boundary spanning, complexity and leadership literatures in order to explore collaborative boundary spanning, boundary objects and transdisciplinary knowledge processes. In practice, all such discussions are anchored in a contextual and situational perspective—in this instance, it is the perspective of experienced cross-boundary facilitation within a public sector executive management context. It explores the practice and capabilities that underpin engagement with critical actors in the collaboration space, e.g. academics, citizens, community bodies and others. It highlights the responsibility of practitioners, in this case cross-boundary facilitators, to access the current research literature, both research and strategic, on a broad range of public management challenges and themes, and to translate the implications for practice. While the earlier section explored the 'big picture' of the varied boundary-spanning 'types' to describe the practice of boundary spanning, the aim of these next two chapters is to present detailed reflection from a person that practices the craft of boundary spanning as a profession.

This chapter, which focuses on the theory underpinning cross-boundary facilitation, is structured in two parts:

- the theory of the craft of facilitation in collaboration, which includes a discussion of what is important, what is not and of what to be aware; research, models, behaviours and practice frameworks
- two recent Australian case studies which explore how the practice worked, or did not work.

Working across collaborative boundaries requires that we explore the key dimensions of boundary spanning and cross-boundary facilitation capability as a craft required to achieve positive outcomes by working across boundaries and creating safe spaces. This search for shared understanding extends to how many organisations can productively work together in the collaborative space to achieve collective outcomes (Flynn and Thompson, 2012).

A commonly used process to establish and build collaboration is for the government, lead agency or project team in the public sector to invite a broad mix of stakeholders into a shared space, with the intent of establishing a collaborative network. The aspiration is that the network can continue to come together in various ways to build mutuality, reciprocity and trust in order to influence policy thinking and service implementation. Building collaborative capacity can be attempted through large and small group processes such as conferences, workshops, forums and meetings, as well as multiple communication channels.

There is a broad understanding of the nature of collaboration and its lifespan depending on the view of those seeking to engage in collaborative work. It may be a way in which institutions agree that they are embarking together on a long-term exercise where relationships are built and maintained, and the final goal may never be reached (or even clear) and the value proposition lies in addressing critical issues along the way. It may also be seen as a procedural instrument to work together to deliver a defined objective in a specified timeframe.

One critical element of collaboration is that it is strengthened by a platform of physical presence: face-to-face connection and communication.

Mandell and Keast (2009) describe the role of leadership in collaborative processes where they describe the need to establish mechanisms for monitoring and protecting the collaborative process including the introduction of process or climate checkers. These are external facilitators who monitor the interactions and relationships in the collaborative network and provide feedback and reflection on attention to collaborative principles.

Theory and Dialogue

For some time there has been a call for increased dialogue between academics and practitioners, who tend to inhabit separate organisational and cultural worlds. Such dialogue is needed to share knowledge and tackle difficult issues more effectively. For example, Jocelyn Bourgon in Canada has argued that collaborative approaches across the divide between public servants and scholars can bring enhanced benefits after some decades of public sector reform initiatives (e.g. Bourgon, 2011). The use of community and governance forums with mixed groups of stakeholders to build and inform public policy, and to co-create, co-design, co-produce and deliver service outcomes has grown, and with it the need to recognise the value of the skilled cross-boundary facilitator in the complex process. The growth of interest in collaboration has been driven by several forces, including tight budgets, downsizing of public service employment and a more educated and informed community.

Problems In Building Shared Perspectives

There is detailed literature on the success factors for building shared perspectives as a basis for problem-solving (Gray, 1989; Huxham and Vangen, 2003; Ring and Van de Ven, 1994). There is general agreement that the following are involved: an interpersonal orientation (trust, reciprocity, respect, reputation), interdependency (shared reliance on each other for results), mutuality (common visions, values, communication) and the undertaking of joint programmes which span boundaries. The literature also makes some useful distinctions between three perspectives on leadership roles in networks: manipulating and influencing activities, empowerment or facilitating access to agendas for all members and opening up agendas in new ways to think creatively and create mindsets (Mandell and Keast, 2009).

While much depends on the intent of the leaders, this section focuses on broader issues of who does this work of influencing, facilitating and opening up, and how they do it. This section focuses on the literature informing the role of cross-boundary facilitators who help to shape the collaboration and transdisciplinary processes when groups of stakeholders are brought together in one place for a common purpose.

Effective boundary spanners understand that these group processes and capabilities, centred on mutuality, are fundamental to building a successful collaboration. Behaving in ways contrary to these, such as seeking to control or close down differing thinking or voices, erodes the chance of success. In practice, not all facilitators working with other members from the collaborative network have appropriate experience of how to behave in the collaborative space or have developed the capability to do so. In many situations it is useful for the experienced facilitator with boundary-spanning capabilities to be knowledgeable about the network but not 'of' the network entities, in order to guide the processes and manage the interpersonal dynamics.

The question about what collaboration is intended (hoped) to achieve has many answers. The outcome which leads to greatest societal shifts often arises from

> A transformative event, (which) . . . can be defined as something that happens in real life, whether for an individual, a group, or an entire civilization, that suddenly questions and even cancels previously taken-for-granted certainties, thus forcing people . . . to reflect upon their experiences . . . potentially changing not only their conduct of life but their identity.
>
> (Szakolczai, 2009, p. 158)

Collaborative events offer the opportunity to design such an event; the transformation is created by those present at the event, including the boundary spanners, who lift themselves, first as individuals and then as a whole, above the limiting factors of role, organisation and boundaries.

Public management agencies have become increasingly aware that achieving successful outcomes requires specialised processes for building shared understandings and commitments. As demand has grown by agencies, universities and community groups for successful collaborative processes, practitioners and consultants have developed a wide range of advice (Adams and Tovey, 2010) on the best available approaches, tools and processes to assist in building connections. In the struggle for attention, many approaches have been touted as the best. Most processes and mixes of tools have some credibility, provided that they are well facilitated.

A powerful element of any collaborative network is the presence of sub-cultures. Based on the adage 'this is how we do things around here,' the multiple sub-cultures present in a collaborative forum present a challenge to the cross-boundary facilitator. Outside the collaborative network these multiple sub-cultures may be competing with each other for clients, resources, funding or profile. Head (2008) describes the complex, uncertain or turbulent conditions around which a collaboration often forms and operates. Actors and their systems have history.

In the extreme case, they may be competing for survival if they are dependent on cyclical funding. Again, there is a need to respect and acknowledge the organisational sub-cultures present. They also need to know how to enable the sub-cultures to work together in the collaborative space. This can be done by surfacing and making visible the points of connection and difference.

'The space between,' 'new space,' 'grey space,' 'the space between' are all examples of the search for a descriptor of the new space that emerges when several entities are brought together to collaborate. These entities do not instantly form a new cohesive entity but enter a shared space which allows interaction and movement, both towards and away from others in safe behaviours and dialogue. Boundary spanning links the old individual spaces to the new space where novel opportunities emerge and members of the collaboration are sensitised to the possibilities of new and different ways of thinking, being and doing things together. New relationships develop and aspects of a new culture and ways of being together emerge. More challenging is the emergence of new individual identities which reflect the complexity and value of working in a new space in different ways. The individual experience of finding a new identity and sense of value and purpose through collaboration may lead to a sense of displacement from the home organisation and even a sense of disloyalty (or accusations by others) to the core organisation.

Acknowledging boundaries as real and powerful elements of public sector organisations and their environments, cross-boundary facilitators are often from public sector backgrounds themselves. Their professional experience provides some insights into what boundaries are (or are not) and how to use boundaries. These varying and often contradictory uses reflect systems responding to political, community or social drivers where public policy itself may be viewed as a boundary object. These perspectives may range from boundary as a weapon or threat, boundary as an excuse against innovation or change, an enabler of positive risk, or the creation of new boundaries as a safety perimeter in which to engage in mutual learning and creation of something new.

As with all new thinking, the public sector is quick to assimilate the language of collaboration, but is not quite as prepared to invest in the time, money, people and capability needed to achieve true collaboration.

Context of Collaboration

Collaborative networks are sectoral, community and governance forums with mixed groups of stakeholders brought together to build and inform public policy, and to co-create, co-design, co-produce and collaborate to deliver service outcomes. Collaborative network members know they are dependent on each other in such a way that for the actions of one to be effective they must rely on the actions of another (Mandell and Keast, 2009). They understand that "they cannot meet their interests working alone and that they share with others a common problem" (Innes and Booher, 2000, p. 7). But these arrangements take a variety of shapes. Keast (2015) has described five different inter-organisational relationships with their linking mechanisms in the process of stakeholders working together (see Figure 10.1).

The transitions between competition and ultimately consolidation reflect a shift in the thinking and practice of those seeking to work together. Keast (2015), in her Five C's, has introduced the concept of 'the blue box' as the emergence of a consolidated organisation, where the collaboration has worked well to the extent that a merging of entities follows as a logical next step.

Dickinson (2014) states that much of the literature agrees that context is an important factor, and, furthermore, that many of the mechanisms that facilitate integration might be challenged in an unreceptive context. Often a positive and apparently successful collaboration is hindered on return to individual member organisations where the support and follow through is limited by red tape, culture or bureaucratic frameworks. Where a representative does not have sufficient authority or permission to commit on behalf of their organisation, this will also limit success. The role of the ministerial portfolio and its boundaries and boundary keepers (e.g. ministerial advisers) is often cited as the reason for not 'being able to go ahead with (it).' Another often cited experience is that of the social policy collaboration which is working well and delivering measurable positive results for both government, public sector and community,

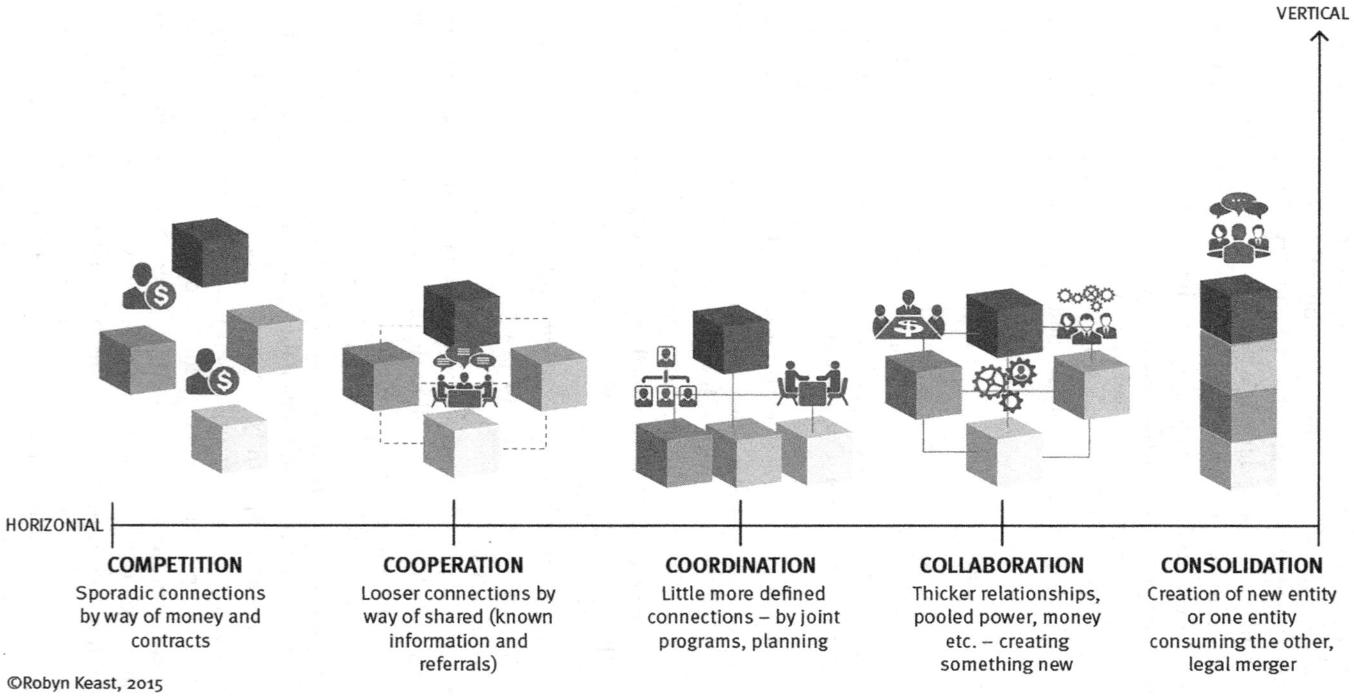

COMPETITION
Sporadic connections by way of money and contracts

COOPERATION
Looser connections by way of shared (known information and referrals)

COORDINATION
Little more defined connections – by joint programs, planning

COLLABORATION
Thicker relationships, pooled power, money etc. – creating something new

CONSOLIDATION
Creation of new entity or one entity consuming the other, legal merger

HORIZONTAL

VERTICAL

©Robyn Keast, 2015

Figure 10.1 Continuum of Inter-Organisational Relationships (from Keast 2015)

which is denied funding in the next round of submissions and is forced to cease the work.

The current preference in public sector agencies for working in the style of private sector project management or using current popular methods such as Agile predicates against the social dynamic model intrinsic in collaboration.

Much of this critical work between public service workers and community stakeholders happens in and around the boundaries that define, either formally or intuitively, the spaces that each of these groups believe they 'own.' These boundaries may be visible, enshrined in legislation, policy or organisational constitutions; or invisible, captured within the culture, values and relationships of organisations. There is growing recognition of the dependencies and interdependencies between people and the various contributions they make. What boundaries actually are and how to work across them is the challenge facing the boundary-spanning facilitator who combines the roles of strategist, process catalyst and deliberate actor. It becomes evident this goes beyond 'basic' facilitation.

The cross-boundary facilitators, working across boundaries, come from diverse backgrounds and fields. They have a wide variety of academic and other qualifications, though those from organisational psychology, social policy, education, management and organisational development backgrounds are often drawn to this space. They work in different fields, e.g. research, community service, lobbyists, public sector, consultancy. They have built their own capability in facilitation, usually as an adjunct to their professional role. They have built a reputation for working well with large and disparate groups, for managing difficult or challenging engagements and personalities.

These cross-boundary facilitators have combinations of refined capabilities essential to successful collaboration and boundary spanning. They have been labelled many things:

- Process disturber
- Process catalyst
- Provocateur
- Spanner in the works
- Bolting it all together
- Master of ceremonies

Some use metaphors for what they do when working with a group; 'weaving random threads together' or 'orchestrating multiple players' are examples of these. Their focus is to open up the group to reciprocity, relationships, learning and creativity. The concept of 'liminality' has been used to describe processes where organisational roles and status are temporarily suspended, allowing the flexibility required to explore new goals and practices (Szakolczai, 2009). Organisations and roles may have strongly marked boundaries, but an exploration of relationships can generate new ideas about boundaries, roles and shared values. Further research attention could explore the notion of the cross-boundary facilitator as a liminal personality, moving through and around the collaborative process, verging on invisible, yet collecting information, guiding processes and managing relationships.

Some Ways of Thinking About Boundaries and Collaboration

Quick and Feldman (2014) identify two contrasting ways of doing boundary work: one oriented to treating boundaries as barriers that promote separation and the other to treating them as junctures that enable connecting. They go on to describe three general practices for creating junctures: translating across, aligning among, and decentring differences. This description encapsulates much of what a cross-boundary facilitator is doing simultaneously when working in collaborative spaces.

Boundary objects are useful in enabling people from multiple and contested backgrounds to create shared meaning (Star and Griesemer, 1989). Barraket, Keast and Furneaux (2015) describe how boundary objects create space to see things from new perspectives even though that may surface conflict or controversy while leading to new insights or ways of thinking about issues.

Mandell and Keast (2009) describe collaboration as a process that enables individuals and organisations to combine their human and material resources to accomplish objectives that they are unable to bring about alone. The synergy that partners seek to achieve through collaboration creates something new—a whole rather that is greater than the sum of its individual parts. Successful collaboration often occurs in the spaces, the liminal space, between the boundaries.

A powerful element of any collaborative network is the presence of sub-cultures. Based on the adage 'this is how we do things around here,' the multiple sub-cultures present in a collaborative forum present a challenge to the cross-boundary facilitator. Outside the collaborative network they can be competing with each other for clients, resources, funding or profile. In the extreme case, the organisations they represent may be competing for survival if they are dependent on cyclical funding. Again, there is a need to respect and acknowledge the organisational sub-cultures present. They also need to know how to enable the sub-cultures to work together in the collaborative space. This can be done by surfacing and making visible the points of connection and difference.

One risk the boundary spanner faces is that of being 'filtered' about organisations or people who are present in the collaborative process. It is one of seeking to influence at the boundaries. Filtering is the term given to the experience of being told, or shown positive or negative things, about an individual or an organisation in order to sway the thinking of the boundary spanner or facilitator, such as 'they are nothing but trouble.' The facilitator must be neutral in the process and be able to respond to and manage this behaviour.

There is a significant research body exploring each of these and further discussion of the many meanings is not the subject of this section. However, what is important is how the boundary spanner seeks the shared meanings within the collaborative space.

Flynn (2011, p. 4) argues that "The differences in language, in meaning-making and in relationships, influence the outcomes of academic, policy and practitioner engagement." Public policy is a complex field with many roles:

- Governments and politicians decide the policy
- Academics influence the policy
- Policy leaders in public administration develop the policy
- Public administration practitioners administer or implement the policy
- Stakeholders and community engagement demand inclusion and a voice in policy implementation, as well are being the receptors of the service and/or products of policy.

Research across several sectors suggests that over 50% of collaborations fail to achieve their purpose (Keast, 2015). That so many fail is indicative of the challenge and complexity involved in having them succeed.

While various distillations have been attempted concerning the key elements of effective collaboration (Gray 1989; Ring and Van De Ven 1994; Huxham and Vangen 2003), there is a consensus that the following dimensions are involved: an interpersonal orientation (trust, reciprocity, respect, reputation), interdependency (shared reliance on each other for results), mutuality (common vision, values and communication), and the undertaking of joint programmes that meet both individual and collective goals (the collaborators dilemma) (Keast, 2015).

The question of the ethics of 'influencing with integrity' to achieve a specified outcome has been raised in the current literature of behaviour change where whole communities are 'nudged' to change behaviour for improved outcomes for all. The same questions may be applied to the collaborative space and emphasises the need for ethical facilitation in working with multiple groups in collaboration. There is a fine line between facilitation as influence, persuasion or manipulation. What is the trigger point at which facilitation runs the risk of becoming manipulation? Practical experience points to an intuitive 'this feels wrong' response from the facilitator who is then able to test for the ethical trigger point.

The term 'facilitator' may carry positive or negative filters. If done well, complex facilitation appears seamless. As one public service facilitator says, "we make it look easy." Expert facilitators are victims of their refined capability and expertise. Because it *looks* easy, many people think it is easy and try to do it themselves. Nothing could be farther from the truth. By creating the safe environment and moving the process forward with everyone involved appropriately, participants feel it is safe to push the boundaries and be more courageous. If facilitated expertly, those participating in a collaboration exercise will not remember the facilitator, but they will own and remember the positive value of the exercise and will come together willingly again; if done badly, they remember a negative experience, poor facilitation and are wary of coming together again.

Snowden (2000) developed the Cynevin approach to complexity. This four quadrant model is applied in collaborative spaces globally as a pathway to decision making. It is acknowledged that effective leadership demands that a leader changes their leadership and decision-making styles to respond to changing contexts. Snowden and Boone (2007, p. 69) state that "Simple, complicated, complex and chaotic contexts each call for different managerial responses. By correctly identifying the governing context, staying aware of danger signals, and avoiding inappropriate reactions, managers can lead effectively in a variety of situations."

The quadrants are labelled: obvious, complicated, complex and chaotic. The use of an experienced facilitator is considered critical in the complex and chaos quadrants. Capable facilitators guide collaborations through the four quadrants, drawing them back from the experience of chaos to the space of complexity or complication. In this model, collaboration is identified as a complex space and needs cross-boundary facilitators to work within the boundaries. The intent is to move issues or problems from the chaotic to the complex, the complex to the complicated and on through the model, with the intent of clarifying and simplifying the issue to where responses can be developed.

Perspective or World View

The breadth of capabilities requisite in a successful cross-boundary facilitator have already been discussed. Rooke and Torbert (2005, p. 71) bring the concept of world view to this work. They identified seven transformational stages of leadership which are explored in executive leadership development programmes globally. The role of cross-boundary facilitator in the collaboration space requires individuals who are from the Strategist or even Alchemist levels who are "exploring the disciplines and commitments entailed in creating networks, strategic alliances, and whole organizations on the basis of collaborative inquiry. The path toward the Strategist and Alchemist action logics is qualitatively different from other leadership development processes." Individuals in the collaborative space may represent any of the seven stages, which offers further opportunity for misunderstanding of the thinking and practice of others.

Table 10.1 Questions to Ask

Level of leadership	Question	Focus
Opportunist	How can I survive?	Personal wins and see the world and others as opportunities to be exploited.
Diplomat	Do I belong?	Tactful, loyal, respectful, but may also find it difficult to deal with conflict, give or receive criticism or take unpopular decisions.
Expert	Who am I?	Lead through controlling the world around them through the quality of their knowledge, intellect and expert ability.
Achiever	Am I successful?	Manage people efficiently and effectively to achieve work goals.
Individualist	Who am I really?	Democratic, facilitative, team-oriented, empathetic and people-focused style of leadership.
Strategist	What can we contribute together to make a difference?	Clear about their gifts and are seeking to discover how to integrate them with the needs of their organisation and of society.
Alchemist	What does the planet need?	They and their organisation lead the way in creating a sustainable future for humanity and the planet.

As mentioned earlier, representatives of all of these levels of leadership thinking may be present in the collaborative space. By listening to the individuals and the language, and concepts they use and the questions they ask, the facilitator is able to support them to contribute more fully to the process. Rooke and Torbert describe some of these (Table 10.1).

Who Is Within the Boundaries?

A critical issue is that organisations and people create and are contained within the boundaries. They are sometimes within more than one boundary, e.g. they work for a health agency and have a disabled child for whom they receive support from community organisation(s) or one organisation is funded by another. The need to identify, disclose and discuss conflicts of interests is constant.

The emergence of place-based collaboration, which creates collaborations within defined geographical spaces, supports local culture and allows for peer support though shared experience, language and understanding of challenging social issues. Representatives of government,

Table 10.2 Examples of Boundary Objects; Use and Impact

Boundary Object	Examples of Use	Possible Impacts
Political policy position	'the government's position is'	Shuts down creative dialogue
Ministerial Portfolios	Portfolio competition for ownership of the space, resources 'the Minister wants'	Inhibits departments working together
Budget/financial power	There is not enough money to We can't do that because it is risk to	Shuts down innovative thinking or rewards
Positional power	I am the CEO I am a ministerial adviser	Participants listen rather than discuss or question
Language	Use of catch phrases, e.g. 'granularity in the narrative' or buzzwords Use of language specific to profession, e.g. IT	Shuts down conversation Use of language to confuse or diminish others People stop listening and engaging
Artefacts of identity (badges, uniforms, logos)	I represent X I am a X	Authority, threat, fear, power
Organisational identity	I am from X department, group	The most influential may be given more 'airtime'
Community group affiliation	I represent	Lack of empowerment depending on position in the hierarchy of organisations/ groups present
Individual identity	I am feeling racial or gender discrimination I identify as a colour, religion, race	Conflict, controversy Shutting down of debate Introducing the element of uncertainty in how to relate
Organisational culture	We don't believe that! We are the longest established! It goes against our values or principles!	Adversarial challenge (us v them), controversy Shuts down others who may feel less experienced
Community culture	I cannot speak This is not our way	Misunderstood language or behaviour Erosion of confidence in working together

Source: Authors' own

public sector and academia are often outliers in the core collaboration which is taking place within the place-based boundaries.

Williams (2013, p. 18) describes "both structural factors such as, social, economic and environmental context, institutional and organizational configurations, cultural and collaborative capital, resource, accountability and planning frameworks, and agential factors relating to leadership, management, professionalism and personal capabilities." Kets de Vries (2004) argues that *organisations as systems have their own life—a life that is not only conscious but also unconscious, not only rational but also irrational*.

To understand this and how it influences the collaborative space, it is worth examining the idea of relational systems: systems that explore how individuals and cultures relate to each other within and external to the organisation boundaries. Shaw (1997, p. 235), in her work on shadow systems in organisations, notes that "self organizing processes are to be found primarily in an organization's shadow system which is described as the complex web of interactions in which social, covert political and psycho dynamic systems co-exist in tension with the legitimate system."

Wheatley and Dalmau developed the Six Circle Model of organisation known colloquially as the 'Green Line Model.' It underpins the work of Wheatley and Rogers (1996) on the theory of self-organisation which describes the principle that collaboration seeks to bring order from potential chaos. The principle is based on the natural world where order will 'emerge' from chaos without seeking to control or impose the emergent order. Wheatley, in *Leadership and the New Science* (2006, p. 89) states "There is a path through change that leads to greater independence and resiliency. We dance along this path by maintaining a coherent identity and by honoring everybody's need for self-determination."

> The world of a simpler way has a natural and spontaneous tendency towards organization. It seeks order. Whatever chaos is present at the start, when elements combine, systems of organisation appear . . . order is gained through explorations into new relationships and new possibilities.
>
> (Wheatley and Rogers, 1996, p. 12)

In the Six Circle Model, all six circles are important to creating organisational success. Traditionally, the greatest amount of attention has been focused on the top three circles. Working within this framework allows the facilitator to see the critical and interdependent impacts of people as reflected by the bottom three circles. This is especially true as groups seek to understand how bias, conscious and unconscious, may be impacting teaching and learning at the individual, institutional and structural levels—the seventh circle.

The three circles above the 'Green Line' of an organisation's structures, systems and capabilities are rational. They are controllable through management direction, empirical through quantitative reporting, logical, visible and tangible through organisational artefacts such as organisational charts, annual reports, role descriptions on the intranet.

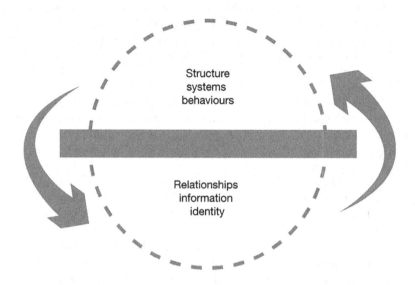

Figure 10.2 Six Circle Model or 'Green Line' Model (from Margaret Wheatley and Myron Rogers 1996)

Leaders, often newly appointed to role, move to change these elements of organisation rapidly, 'putting their mark' on the organisation system. They restructure the organisation and introduce new systems. They are then faced with the outcome of such disruption that, despite all this activity, nothing has really changed.

Collaborative and organisational conversations are informed by what is below as well as what is above the 'Green Line.' Within all conversations information is exchanged, shared meaning is developed and mediated, agendas modified and adapted aligned to the vision, values and policies as well as to the structure, plan and process.

The three circles below the 'Green Line' represent the non-rational space where the identity of the organisation and its individuals are evidenced by beliefs and values, which evolve from assumptions, feelings and emotions; individual roles, ambitions and aspirations, organisational visions and the psychological histories of individuals and organisations. In this part of the model the organisation's relationships, information flows and identity are non-rational, qualitative, hard to control, and not logical, visible or tangible—but they are felt. Management has little control over these elements of organisation. They are an essential part of the narrative of the organisation. Fuzzy visibility is there in employee morale surveys or organisational values statements where more is unsaid than is said.

The temptation for leaders to change these elements of organisation in an effort to change culture is almost irresistible. These are boundary objects of organisations. Yet the culture does not change. In fact, it burrows down, and slows or erodes organisational change.

The lead journey of changing structure, systems and skills profiles can happen quickly, but the lag journey of culture change takes much longer.

This is evident in collaboration space where groups seek to understand how bias, conscious and unconscious may impact the collaborative process. The challenge for the cross-boundary facilitator is to influence groups of people to value the work 'below the green line,' and self-organise to identify and implement the innovative strategies and the infrastructure to achieve powerful and creative results.

This is where cross-boundary facilitators and leaders need to focus to affect change. They do so through surfacing the difficult and often undiscussable issues of organisation and culture (and sometimes individuals) to work with the structural, systemic and capability elements. The change leader needs to discern the systems and behaviours underpinning organisational socialisation in the organisation they are about to change, to pay attention to the presenting internal and social dynamics, to the intricate playing field between leaders and follower (Kets de Vries, 2004). Chief executives have been appointed to lead an organisation to meet performance objectives. There is often a high capability organisation development professional who clearly and impartially sees the organisation and its culture and translates these for the CEO. Working with these systems and behaviours, making them visible and discussable, contributes to successful change (Shaw, 1997). It is also what experienced boundary spanners work with to dilute or create connections between members of a collaborative network.

The Participants

There is often a mix of critical roles representing a breadth of organisations and their boundaries; academics, citizens, community bodies—not for profit organisations, NGOs, clients/customers of services, public servants; policy experts, practitioners, communications experts, private sector, community leaders who often represent other cultures.

When establishing or being invited to enter into collaboration, leaders of organisations need to consider and include those who are 'best and brightest' in the space. These are often the high performing members of the organisation and the temptation to include someone less capable and less busy is often taken. This risks getting the best value out of the collaboration for that organisation and may damage the reputation of individuals. The leaders also need to consider who would benefit from the capability development opportunity provided through the exposure to the collaborative process.

Every individual in a collaborative process faces the challenge of expected contribution. For an individual, having the capability to do this is essential. These capabilities are in the interpersonal domain; personal mastery, courage, reflection and self-management, knowing when to listen, question and to value and respect others. These individuals and their behaviours are in and of themselves boundary objects and they bring the values, purpose and language of their organisations to the table.

Every individual brings filters, or concerns about others in the space:

> I know that they (academics) will baulk at providing questions as they will say 'it is more complex than that'—but I am not prepared to let them handle it this way to justify going off on some rambling tangent with their diagrams, products and schemas and then providing me with a report and a whole lot of vague 'options' or things to consider.
>
> (Public Sector Senior Executive, 2016)

> We don't want any more lectures, we want practical approaches.
>
> (Defence Force, Senior Officer, 2016)

In establishing a collaborative network, stakeholders are, in effect, establishing a short-term form of organisation which is greater than any one entity that is part of its whole. It develops an identity of its own. Flynn and Thompson (2012) describe (stakeholder) organisational receptivity as likely to be higher when the organisation has (1) an adaptation orientation rather than an efficiency orientation, (2) when boundary spanning as opposed to technical core units is dominant, (3) in simple and adhocracy configuration than in machine bureaucracy, professional bureaucracy or divisional configuration, and (4) when an organisation has a clan mode of governance than either market or bureaucratic modes of governance.

When people come together, they bring multiple roles and identities to the table: academics, citizens, community bodies, not for profits, NGOs, clients/customers of services, public servants, leaders, policy experts, practitioners, communications experts, private sector.

Much of the research literature focuses on the partnership and process elements of the collaboration. There is a gap in the research when we explore the boundary spanners—those individuals who, through specific capabilities and orientation, enable thinking, talking and working across boundaries to happen more easily. They facilitate it happening. They are the boundary-spanning facilitators.

Boundary Objects and Collaboration

Boundary objects have multiple faces and uses. They are used as facilitative objects and they are used as risk artefacts to shut down an avenue of discussion and exploration. In some cases they may be used as weapons to force through a position. The choice of how they are used rests with the individual or organisation. A facilitator needs to recognise the use of boundary objects in the collaboration, identify them, and clarify their value in the process. If being used as a 'big stick,' a facilitator must be capable of managing what may be experienced as 'bullying' tactics.

Experienced facilitators recognise boundary objects and know how to work with them to manage their impact on the whole collaborative stakeholder group. They acknowledge, respect and dilute boundaries and boundary objects. They know how to 'call behaviour' and name the boundary objects which may be 'the elephant in the room.' This often leads to a tangible release of tension. Once something is tabled openly and its role described and discussed by the group, it loses much of its power to disrupt.

What is common language to one group may be unknown or different to another. In this case a facilitator is the learning or dialogue guide to assist a group to think deeply about meaning, assumptions, beliefs and values and to assist in decoding the codes. An example of such codes is the ever present use of acronyms to create shortcuts to lengthy policy, programme or project titles or concepts. Acronyms are a powerful boundary object which quickly create a group 'in the know' and exclude everyone else. Stopping the process to ask for clarification of acronyms takes courage on the part of participants.

Table 10.2 is representative only and by no means covers the breadth of boundary objects. It does highlight the possibility that boundary objects may be found under the Wheatley and Rogers (1996) description of organisation: structures, systems, capabilities and relationships, information and identity. These are often the objects of authorising environments, but only so far as they are enacting the core purpose of the individual organisation; they have less power and influence in the collaborative space.

Boundary spanners/practitioners from all sides experience the boundaries between:

- Academic research and policy thinking
- Public sector practice, policy development and implementation
- Boundaries between public sector agencies and their internal structural divisions and teams

Table 10.3 Leadership Types

Theme 1	Mandate to undertake change, broad scope of discretion and support from client
Theme 2	Previous successful boundary-spanning facilitator experience
Theme 3	An understanding of the socialisation tactics of organisations, and the role of culture in assisting or creating obstacles to change
Theme 4	Highly developed understanding of group dynamics
Theme 5	Self-efficacy

- Boundaries between academia and public sector, third sector and community implementation
- Boundaries between communities
- Boundaries between individual actors
- Boundary between public sector and NFPs, NGOs.

One example is the wearing of uniforms to collaborative stakeholder workshops where they are a visible statement of identity, power and control. In a social policy collaboration exercise, those wearing uniforms may be seen as the adversary in the room to those who receive their services; the victims, the unemployed, the ex-prisoners or parolees, the homeless, the abused. If one group represents a uniformed culture (e.g. police, corrections, fire and emergency, ambulance, Defence forces), a facilitator may request in advance that everyone attending wears casual clothes to minimise the impact and create a visible level of equality.

There are individual expressions of identity, e.g. skin colour, accent, dress, self-management and behaviour, which may influence the interactions in a collaborative space.

Experienced cross-boundary facilitators are experienced in multiple processes and approaches, many of which are embedded in organisational development or systems thinking including relational systems: relationships between organisations, groups and individuals. They work with chief executives and at the most senior levels of organisation and across boundaries where the criticality of their capability in this space is emerging. They work with the individual not the position and are adept at handling the many expressions of ego that emerge in the space. They are accepted by the senior leaders as a trusted adviser or equal in the space, often bringing capability not present in the senior leadership cohort.

Williams (2002) ascribes knowledge of how to operate within the formal organisational system coupled with effective relational and interpersonal competencies as essential elements of cross-boundary work. Some of those described in the literature are linked to personality, including being extroverted, honest, respectful, trustworthy, open, sociable, diplomatic and persistent.

It is important to highlight here that introversion does not limit successful boundary spanning or cross-boundary facilitation.

A cross-boundary facilitator adds value through experience, wisdom and capability every step of the way through:

- Being authentic and congruent
- Genuine interest in the issues and the individuals
- Ability to 'rescue' when things are going off track badly
- Manages time, but not rigidly
- Accesses agile process responses
- Valuing diversity

- Rapid acquisition and understanding of context and purpose
- Exceptional management of group dynamics
- Remaining impartial and external to the content, while rapidly assimilating the critical aspects
- Use of energy and strength of presence.

(Flynn, 2016, p. 236)

At this level of organisational cross-boundary work, they also need to be across the current research literature in the field and the latest development in models and practice. They are able to add value to the thinking in the room by referencing current research and international trends. The use of illustrative stories as metaphors for what is happening may be used sparingly.

An emerging element in this research is the importance of cross-boundary facilitator's self-efficacy, which Jones (1986, p. 262) argues "may moderate the effects of socialization tactics on role orientation." Heifetz and Linsky (2002) describe the varied aspects of the self as leader which are encapsulated in this term: *self-knowledge, self-definition, self-protection and self-reflection.* The Australian Public Service Commission (2006), in describing the necessary capabilities of a senior executive leader, suggests that the individual should "display resilience, one element of which is to monitor own emotional reactions and respond to pressure in a controlled manner . . . displays a positive outlook in difficult situations" (Flynn and Thompson, 2013, p. 12).

Building this self-knowledge and self-mastery takes time. This deep understanding often emerges from experience and reflection. These practitioners have developed boundary-spanning capability as a craft. Other roles emerge from this space depending on type of collaborative process; panel chair, mediator, convenor. Not all processes are face-to-face—blogs, Skype and teleconference calls, chat rooms all need facilitation. They do not happen without someone energising the process.

As with any craft there are levels of development, mirroring the journey from apprentice through journeyman to master. What is the right, most effective process for the outcomes sought and the collaborative group working together?

The role of the cross-boundary facilitator should be one of designing and facilitating the transdisciplinary process. This should be a long-term relationship, not a 'seagull' event, usually described as swoop in, do the work (or make a mess) and swoop out. It is usually not just one event; it is a series of dialogues, workshops, seminars over time used to build networks with shared knowledge and understanding between groups with a shared interest in collaboration to achieve a positive outcome. The linking of events and milestones in the collaboration journey and the presence of a trusted cross-boundary facilitator committed to the journey is a contributing factor to success.

Shared Language and Meaning

What is the meaning when one of these terms is used and how do they differ?

- Co-design
- Co-production
- Collaboration
- Networks
- Borderlands
- Shared space
- Boundaries

There is a significant research body exploring each of these and further discussion of the comparative meaning and value of each. This is not the subject of this section. What is important is how the boundary spanner seeks to clarify the shared meanings within the collaborative space.

Flynn (2011) argues that the differences in language, in meaning-making and in relationships, influence the outcomes of academic, policy and practitioner engagement. Public policy is a complex field with many roles:

- Governments and politicians decide the policy
- Academics influence the policy
- Policy leaders in public administration develop the policy
- Public administration practitioners administer or implement the policy
- Stakeholders and community engagement demand inclusion and a voice in policy implementation, as well are being the receptors of the service and/or products of policy.

Terry Moran, as Secretary of Prime Minister and Cabinet, in the Government *Blueprint for Reform*, Commonwealth of Australia (2010), articulated a challenge to the relationship between academics and practitioners in describing the Australian Public Service experience of working across that boundary:

> Academics have limited influence on public policy because they don't give bureaucrats what they need . . . academic research is too slow and inaccessible for them to spend time reading it. It's always late, and it's always in a form that . . . has to be translated before it can be used.

He goes on to describe

> a disconnect between academics and public servants had driven policy maker to eschew academic input into public policy documents. There's a problem about translation, . . . relationships, . . . timeliness.

The Australian Government report *Empowering change—fostering innovation in the Australian Public Service,* (MAC, 2010) Management Advisory Committee Report (9), was more positive in its view that "Academia is rich in ideas, data and knowledge. It also provides insight, analysis and evaluation of ideas and innovations . . . there is evidence that the collaboration between academia and the public sector is underdone."

Other Challenges

Time is a critical issue. In the 'busyness' of day-to-day work and with a focus on efficiency, the challenge of committing enough time to the collaborative process to achieve the best outcomes is constantly present. Experience has taught facilitators to know how much time is needed, when to extend or shorten time in a process or discussion to be able to do their work in the time allocated. Often leaders want the work done quickly, sometimes too quickly, to achieve the best outcomes. They run the risk of being accused of 'skating over' critical issues or 'going through the motions' to be seen to have collaborated. This type of shortcutting damages the collaborative intent.

Some processes are designed to reinforce boundaries. Some facilitators are briefed to seek out and emphasise boundary tensions leading to erosion of trust in the process and possible failure of the collaboration. Some individuals are filtered negatively. There is also the possibility of collaborative process being used as a front to achieve already decided outcomes. This means the facilitator colludes with powerful agents to drive the collaborative dialogue towards the required end. Again the outcome is erosion of trust in the process and damage to the facilitator's reputation as unethical.

Credibility is based on the building of trust and congruent and consistent behaviour by the facilitator and is critical to the cross-boundary facilitator. Being seen to be colluding or to fail means credibility is lost.

> Don't treat us like fools. We know what you are doing. You have been told to get to this point by X. Why bother inviting us?
>
> (Senior Executive, National Association
> Strategy Workshop, 2014)

Each group is using different entry points to the dialogue and different value sets. There are variations in who they view as clients and stakeholders. They bring differing assumptions about what will occur within the collaborative space.

One critical issue is the degree of respect and value for what each group brings to the collaborative process. This is where boundaries can be the most impenetrable. One client of a collaborative process, where specialist academics the fields were central to the process, stated:

> I do not want any of the researchers writing a thesis on their own view of the world in relation to the constructs. I am particularly

worried about X and feel that the 'lecture' . . . and the 'geeing' up of the people in the room to go back and do something in relation to culture in their organisation was inappropriate . . . not what X was asked to do . . . X didn't let the room report back on what was done at the group discussions as X could not wait to have the stage again.
(Public Sector, Senior Executive, post collaboration network workshop email to facilitator, 2015)

This statement captures two pieces of perception by the Senior Executive:

1.   Concern that the 'academic specialists,' as they were termed in the contract, would not deliver what was required by the client;
2.   One of the 'academic specialists' had used the opportunity with the network to promote their own thinking and models, using a 'team trainer' frame despite being directly told not to promote their own models.

Case Studies

In the remainder of this section I outline two case studies. The overall purpose is to provide examples of collaboration in practice. The role of the cross-boundary facilitator is explored in both of these examples.

The first case focuses on a question of the value of the development of facilitation capability at the highest level of organisation supported by the facilitation of multiple commercial stakeholders and their public management counterparts to deliver a major piece of state-owned roads infrastructure; while the second case focuses on the question of when to introduce the facilitator to the collaboration exercise involving multiple state public management stakeholders and community groups to work on the challenges in the social policy space around families and children.

Case Study 1—State Infrastructure Organisation

From 1999–2000 a significant corporate and cultural change programme was undertaken in a technically oriented public service organisation (road stewardship and construction) which sought to work with both 'above' and 'below' the green line concepts to shift the agency in its thinking and practice about how it worked with government and community. Viewed by the government of the day as 'maverick' (working outside the rules) and identifying more as a civil construction organisation than a public service one, where staff identified as engineers or road workers, not as public servants, a major change was required to work in an improved way with government, community and the private civil construction sector in public-private partnerships. This was deep organisational development and impacted each of the 4000 employees.

The purpose was to move the organisation from being a civil construction organisation focused on the design, construction and maintenance of roads and bridges through its own staff, equipment and processes to being the steward of the road system and contracting out of the construction and maintenance functions to the private sector and local government. The organisation retained its own small road construction commercial arm which had to compete at the tender box with the private sector civil construction organisations, and found it difficult to win work as the perception of insider favouritism (though they were subjected to the same transparency controls) was strong.

The organisational change was documented in a long-term evaluation study by the Queensland University of Technology and the subject of numerous academic articles and conference papers from 1999–2006.

The critical Issues which were identified included:

- Strong assumption of monoculture identity—civil construction and engineering
- Shared values base embedded though tertiary engineering study
- Multi cultures between districts, regions, teams
- Strong, competitive individual personalities in senior executive leadership roles
- Resistance to change—'if nothing is broken why change it?'
- New Director General from a non-engineering background
- Change of Director General after two years
- Existing capability to lead and facilitate the change
- Lack of trust between key leadership roles leading to disrespectful and passive sabotage.

The Collaboration for Change

The change agenda encompassed improving communication and relationships both within and without the organisation. It also linked into achieving whole of government objectives with respect to engaging with the community, preserving the environment, recognising cultural heritage and adopting principles of social justice within a commercialisation context.

(Brown and Flynn, Osborne and Brown, 2005).

Strong sub-cultures existed within the organisation. The design engineers were perceived by the construction engineers to have little in the way of 'on the ground experience.' The road construction group contained over 1800 blue-collar workers who were road builders, maintenance gangs, line markers, safety teams—each with their own culture. The artefacts of civil construction: the large machinery, the tools of the trade, the bitumen and gravel they worked with, the IT systems supporting design, the uniforms representing each district and region, were all being lost through the process of change.

The practice elements involved large-scale ongoing facilitation, interventions and capability development, both internally and externally with stakeholders and community. The small departmental Organisational Development team was tasked to work directly with the Director General on the design, facilitation and delivery of these elements. A high level of trust and permission, coupled with highly effective cross-boundary facilitation, was essential to the success of this work.

Private sector consultants introduced different thinking and cultural frames to the organisation through multiple co-delivery iterations of three levels of leadership development programmes focused on behaviour change. These were aimed at building consistent behaviours at both leadership and staff levels across the organisation and with other public service organisations. These behaviours were then framed as evidence of values in the way the organisation worked with its collaboration partners: three levels of government, community and private sector. The work was undertaken across a large geographical spread and often in remote areas of Queensland. Consistent models, language and behaviours were cascaded through organisation to all levels of staff. Everyone, including the Director General, was held to account against consistent, required change concepts and the behaviours required to support them. A rolling programme of collaboration exercises with senior leaders and stakeholders was maintained for the next five years.

Competitive individual behaviours at the highest levels of organisation were surfaced and discussed robustly; ways of working differently across the silos were developed. Once the critical mass of leaders understood and committed to the behavioural changes required for them to lead, the organisational change moved forward rapidly.

At the same time the organisation was constructing a major national road link—the M1—with six individual contracts let to private civil construction firms for the construction of separate lengths of the highway. The Chief Engineer assumed the role of relationships manager and facilitated the cross-boundary interactions between public service agencies and private sector contractors. This case study demonstrates that no matter how clearly the terms of the traditional contract can be documented, relational abilities can improve the ability to balance stakeholder interests. (Brown et al., 2005)

This work was begun in 1998 and continued through to 2005 under two Directors General, who were both committed to the change. The smooth handover from one to the other was essential to this. The facilitator linked the work of the first leader to the work of the second leader, which was evidence of trust in their capability.

Case Study 2—Development of a Culture Evaluation Toolkit

This case study explores the journey of collaboration over two months and highlights the challenges that emerge and the role of the cross-boundary facilitator.

A State Government organisation with responsibility for the protection of families and children was tasked with the design and dissemination of a Culture Evaluation Toolkit to assist agencies to measure the underlying behavioural attitudes referred to in the Report as being critical to reform success in the child protection sector. These were seen to be changes in organisational culture, leadership, collaboration and cultural practices, e.g. from a culture of blame and conflict to one of learning from mistakes, working together and empowerment.

Two stages of collaborative process were conducted. The first was an Evaluation Leaders Forum which was to inform and guide the implementation and evaluation of the recommended reform with critical insight from experienced researchers involved in:

- Evaluation of child reforms in other sectors
- Child protection systems and practice
- Essential attributes of the reform process.

This first stage was a combination of 'talking heads' and round table discussion, with the intent of establishing the meaning of the following constructs in the context of child protection reform:

- Leadership
- Organisation culture
- Culturally appropriate practice (applied to working with Aboriginal and Torres Strait Islander Families)
- Collaboration.

Feedback from this session was mixed with one senior researcher commenting that the facilitation/convening of some panels was poor, and that some of the specialists were 'more trainers than researchers/ practitioners.'

The second stage was a Culture Change Expert Workshop. Over 60 people from 17 organisations representing public service, NGOs and not-for-profit organisations were invited to a 2-day residential workshop. All attendance costs were paid by the public agency, which represented a significant expenditure against annual budget.

Sixty-five participants were invited from a wide geographic distribution, days allocated and money expended on airfares and accommodation for a 2-day collaborative process which represented a significant expenditure to the lead agency.

Two weeks prior to the 2-day workshop, the design team had broken down in confusion about what they going to do and how they would do it (purpose and process), with poor behaviours (competition, disrespect, verbal attacks) evident among the team members. The senior executive, accountable for the success of the collaborative project, was advised by the lead academic to bring in an external facilitator with the intent of building the most effective approach to the collaboration and a way to work towards the outcomes.

The facilitator was engaged and observed the first half hour of a design team meeting before asking for permission to clarify the design elements. Several factors which were evident:

- There was a lack of clear leadership by the Senior Executive
- The intent was to run a collaboration exercise
- The purpose for the 2-day Culture Change Expert workshop was not clearly defined
- The critical issues were not identified
- The contract project manager was not prepared to relinquish control

- The contract project manager had a design in mind which relied on 'talking heads' rather than collaborative process
- The other members of the design team did not believe the design would deliver
- Competing agendas between public service agencies that each had a different understanding of who owned the agenda
- Interpersonal tensions emerging from control and ego needs
- Evidence of lack of capability in the design and presentation of some key individuals
- Evidence of a lack of due diligence into who would be the best people to put forward as 'specialists' in the collaborative space.

The facilitator used a rigorous systems design framework to co-design the workshop and respond to the challenge of "What needs to be clear from the outset?" After a month of indecision and conflict by the team, this decision-making process, drawn from systems leadership thinking (Macdonald et al., 2006), provided the framework in which the design for the workshop was completed in two hours.

- Context
- Purpose
- Critical Issues
- Role clarity
- Process Design
- Decision and clear decision maker
- Reflection and modification.

This facilitated process provided the leadership rigour needed to move forward and showed that the required outcomes could have been achieved in one day, with savings on budget and time expenditure

The 2-day workshop used a range of group processes and existing artefacts to engage and encourage contribution from all participants present. These included stakeholder mapping, world café and group reporting to identify shared language and concepts and obstacles to change. Sessions led by lead academics on collaboration, evidence-based data and evaluation established a shared language and understanding of these concepts with everyone in the room. Videos, discussion and debriefs were included on Day 2. Two further factors were evident:

- Despite agreeing to process, some individuals chose to go their own way when the facilitator handed over the group to them;

- What they had confirmed as their input to the session drifted into personal journey stores that bored the participants.

Post workshop feedback to the facilitator was positive:

> We had a debrief yesterday morning with everyone who was involved . . . and there was a lot of comment about how people felt that no-one else could have helped shape it the way 'the facilitator' did and also bring the level of energy to the room. The only negative, which I think is a compliment, is that we didn't have enough of 'the facilitator' day two.
>
> (Senior Executive, 2015)

While the workshop itself was a success, the breakdown in relationships between the 'academic specialists' (only one of whom was a university-based professor) emerged and threatened the process output of toolkit development and feedback to stakeholder participants. Labels and terms carry weight in collaborative spaces, and infer capability and understanding that was not evident in this particular situation.

The senior executive leader accountable for the success of the process stated that they were

> adamant that I don't want the researchers going off on a tangent and writing their own reports; and that I want them to provide a list of the most important questions to ask for a range of circumstances before they do anything else. I do not want any of the researchers writing a thesis on their own view of the world in relation to the constructs.

The facilitator was engaged to facilitate post workshop sessions as the output documents were drawn together in a consistent manner to meet the senior executive's expectations as

> I am worried that she (and possibly the others) will go off and do what they want and give me something that is totally useless. I would like to 'manage' what they do more closely than I originally thought would be necessary and ask for them to send us something every week. I also DO NOT want four reports, and I don't want any of their (or anyone else's) theory around the constructs other than where it is absolutely necessary to provide guidance in how to use the survey questions.
>
> (Senior executive, 2016)

Conclusion

Any individual working in organisations has, at some time, experienced a poorly facilitated exercise which led them to say or think that it had been a waste of time with the facilitator having 'no idea of what they are doing,' or been subjected to the 'enthusiastic amateur' airing ill-considered views on sensitive issues or taking valuable collaborative discussion time to share their own stories. An example of this is a leader who has experienced a failed exercise which makes them wary of all facilitators. The approach taken next time is to control the process to such an extent that the opportunity for successful boundary spanning, relationship building, learning and connection is lost.

As with any craft there are levels of development, mirroring the journey from apprentice through journeyman to master. What is the right, most effective process for the outcomes sought and the collaborative group working together?

The cross-boundary facilitators bring something intangible beyond facilitation process and capability to the process. They build trust and rapport with majority of participants in the process. They work intuitively and connect to the people and work in the space. They pick up on cues from participants and draw them out.

> I really appreciate that you saved us from a disaster, and will be for-ever grateful. Thank you.
>
> (Senior Executive, Queensland State
> Government 2015)

The Facilitation Relationship

Co-facilitation occurs often, either with another external facilitator or an internal one. Role clarity about who is the lead facilitator and who makes the final call on process and process changes is essential in these relationships. Norms need to be established to create agreed ways of working together, how and when to intervene when the other is leading a process, redirection and closure processes of synthesis. Above all, visible conflict between facilitators must be avoided, as the group observes this and it erodes trust and respect.

Translation of Research Into Practice

Building understanding of the research literature, maintaining its currency, coupled with developing robust and rigorous self-knowledge and self-mastery takes time and commitment on the part of the cross-boundary facilitator. This deep understanding emerges from study, investment in learning, experience and reflection. Building strong relationships with the academic researchers exploring this space leads to powerful dialogue about how to put the thinking into practice. It can lead to partnerships where the synergy of researcher and facilitator delivers a better outcome from a collaboration. We need to create the space within which practitioners, academics and professionals can share ideas, reflect on their respective boundary spanning practice and co-create new ways of engaging *with* and learning *from* each other.

Cross-boundary facilitators have developed boundary-spanning capability as their craft. Other roles emerge from this space depending on type of collaborative process; panel chair, mediator, convenor. Not all processes are physically face-to-face—blogs, Ted talks, webinars, and teleconference calls, chat rooms all need facilitation. These events do not happen without someone energising and guiding the process.

As with any craft there are levels of development, mirroring the journey from apprentice through journeyman to master. The practice of the cross-boundary facilitator is explored in the next section.

11 Towards the Craft and Practice of Facilitation Across Collaborative Boundaries

Christine Flynn

Introduction

Much of the collaboration research focuses on the partnership and process elements of the collaboration. There is a gap in the research when we explore the practice of boundary spanners who facilitate and enable, through specific capabilities and orientation, insight and thinking, talking and working across boundaries to happen more easily. They are the boundary-spanning facilitators. They combine deep practice experience with process expertise, and understanding of interpersonal dynamics framed in a research base.

One critical element of collaboration is that it is strengthened by a platform of physical presence: face-to-face connection and communication. This has been explored in the previous chapter which draws together some of the research literature and explores case studies on the role of the cross-boundary facilitator. This chapter is not about the theory of facilitation but about the practice of complex facilitation and the partnership between the cross-boundary facilitator and their collaboration partner.

The chapter explores the practice of the craft of cross-boundary facilitation. As with any craft there are levels of development, mirroring the journey from apprentice through journeyman to master. What is the right, most effective process for the outcomes sought and the collaborative group working together?

The practice of cross-boundary facilitators, as critical actors, helps to shape and design the collaboration and transdisciplinary processes when groups of stakeholders are brought together in one place for a common purpose. They facilitate and enable network development through stages of exploration, clarification and implementation design.

I do not delve into the many processes which are used to work in collaborative space.

The facilitator role is usually associated with the world of professional practice rather than the world of academic scholarship, and is often labelled 'practitioner.' The term 'practitioner' in itself challenges our thinking about language and labels. There are various 'worlds of practitioners' relevant to this section; there are at least three or more 'communities of practice'—such as public servants, service delivery providers and consultants/advisors. A neglected question is how well understood is the need to design and facilitate effective approaches, and in particular what the necessary capabilities are of a cross-boundary facilitator to support such interventions and processes. In effect, the cross-boundary facilitation role is a boundary-spanning role.

How successfully have we translated this knowledge back into the practices of academia, public management and service delivery providers as well as the community? As Williams (2002) observes, the literature has not been particularly forthcoming on the nature, characteristics and behaviours of these boundary spanners, nor has the literature explored the boundary-spanning facilitator.

Cross-Boundary Facilitation as a Craft

Dickinson (2014, p. 193), when discussing integration, points out that "we have forgotten those fundamental skills of public servants associated with 'craft.'" She describes "craft skills (as) those that take time to develop and which incorporate a great deal of implicit knowledge and careful judgement." When she goes on to describe the "craft and craft perspective of integration (as) . . . less concerned with isolating particular structures, processes and mechanisms that facilitate integration and . . . more concerned with the actual practice of integration," we could substitute the words 'collaboration' and 'facilitation' for 'integration' with ease. The development of skill as craft was reinforced by Gladwell's '10,000 hour rule' in his work on outliers. Pioneered by Ericsson, Gladwell (2008) posited that deep expertise—such as cross-boundary facilitation—develops with sustained learning and practice over many years. He also references the influence that culture, family, generation and idiosyncrasies have on an individual's expertise and success.

Rhodes (2014) spoke about recovering the 'craft' of public administration in network governance. He observed this craft as being devalued as the public sector embraced the principles of more scientific management like those associated with New Public Management. The implication is that more practical and locally situated knowledge and practice is not valued. I would further argue the understanding of interpersonal dynamics and culture, and how to work with these, are often dismissively described as 'soft skills,' and included in this loss of capability. In practice, they are complicated elements which require strength and experience when working with the multiple facets of collaboration. In any moment of a collaboration process, the experienced and successful cross-boundary facilitator seeks to grasp as full an understanding as possible of what is really happening in the collaboration space.

In his work on social innovation, Hogue (2017) explores the concept of the T-shaped person, first described by McKinsey in 2013. "A person is T-shaped when she possesses, and continually attends to, a breadth across many fields, accompanied by depth of knowledge in one—shallow and wide horizontal knowledge, deep and singular vertical expertise." Hogue's observation of effective social innovators (*facilitators*), led to a recognition of a third dimension which develops the concept into a three-dimensional approach. He describes the development of the social dimension as more than the development of interpersonal or 'soft skills.' Hogues believes it is essential to have the "will and a vision to alter structural impediments and commit to 'radical collaboration.'

In practice, all such discussions are anchored in a contextual and situational perspective, which is cultural and emotive one at the same time—in this instance, it is the perspective of experienced cross-boundary facilitation within a public sector and community context. The next section explores the capabilities that underpin engagement with critical actors in the collaboration space, e.g. academics, citizens, community bodies and others, and discusses professional facilitation as a craft.

An experienced cross-boundary facilitator, or a facilitation team familiar with each other's practice and thinking is critical for the success of any collaborative group process. Not all aspiring boundary spanners, researchers or facilitators are successful in their attempts to become cross-boundary facilitators, a role which merges two or more perspectives.

Problems in Building Shared Perspectives

Effective boundary spanners understand that these group processes and capabilities, centred on mutuality, are fundamental to building a successful collaboration. Behaving in ways contrary to these, such as seeking to control or close down differing thinking or voices, erodes the chance of success. In practice, not all facilitators working with other members from the collaborative network have the practice experience of working in complex spaces to succeed in the collaborative space, nor have developed the capability to do so. In many situations it is useful for the experienced facilitator with boundary-spanning capabilities to be knowledgeable about the network but not to be 'of' the network entities, in order to guide the processes and manage the interpersonal dynamics.

The preference to work solely on the structure(s) and systems of a collaboration, while seeking to develop rigour in evaluation and reporting, blinds both facilitator and collaboration group to the influence of other aspects of the intended and emerging collaborative community.

Public management agencies have become increasingly aware that achieving successful outcomes requires specialised processes for building shared understandings and commitments. As demand has grown by agencies, universities and community groups for successful collaborative processes, practitioners and consultants have developed a wide range of advice (Adams and Tovey, 2010) on the best available approaches, tools and processes to assist in building connections. In the struggle for attention, many approaches have been touted as the best. Most processes and mixes of tools have some credibility, provided that they are well facilitated.

As discussed earlier, the public sector is not prepared to invest in the time, money, people and capability needed to achieve true collaboration. The constant pressure to do, deliver and report more quickly with the implication that this will lead to the most effective and efficient way, reinforces the devaluing of the craft of how to enable people to work together on the complex issues of the current time, e.g. migration, drugs, homelessness, child safety and the multiple health challenges.

It is not only in the sphere of social, community and health policy challenges that collaboration is emerging as a powerful way of achieving successful outcomes that satisfy multiple stakeholders. Collaboration has emerged as a critical element in the asset and infrastructure sphere, where the cost of major projects may only be delivered through collaborations due to the funding costs they represent.

Dimensions of Collaboration in Practice

While various distillations have been attempted concerning the key elements of effective collaboration (Gray, 1989; Ring and Van De Ven, 1994; Huxham and Vangen, 2003), there is a consensus that the following dimensions are involved: an interpersonal orientation (trust, reciprocity, respect, reputation), interdependency (shared reliance on each other for results), mutuality (common vision, values and communication), and the undertaking of joint programmes that meet both individual and collective goals (the collaborators dilemma) (Keast, 2015). These are behavioural elements underpinned by thinking and are essential to cross-boundary facilitation practice.

An individual with the right mix of capabilities, emotional intelligence and experience is able to develop the complex capabilities to do the work. These are some of the key facets of expert facilitation. For some, life experience has taught individuals to pay attention to the emotions and behaviours of those around them; they track interpersonal dynamics, listen to voice tone, observe body language, defuse tension and harmonise the interactions of others. This may be based on childhood observation and experience in how to manage family dynamics.

Towards a Facilitated Design Model

The fundamental question in thinking about bringing large groups of differing stakeholders together in a collaborative space is how to design for success and how to facilitate the process and all its elements through each stage. Experience has shown that the projected collaborative journey rarely follows the path which was originally designed.

The cross-boundary facilitator is a critical voice in the design of any collaboration or collaborative intervention. In failing to include a facilitator from the design stage, the collaboration leadership runs the very real risk of not gaining full advantage from a complex collaboration. Often, they are brought in after the design phase has taken place and presented with a 'fait accompli'—a design into which they have had no input. Critical details may be missed and the design may of itself be flawed, resulting in less than optimal outcomes or even failure. They bring value to the design phase through their experience and rigour, particularly in the fields of process design and group dynamics. Often the design phase itself becomes a facilitated collaboration.

A key risk is the lack of shared understanding by leaders of the intent of the collaboration. Scattered understanding will erode the collaboration processes. If this is not clear, then the facilitator must work to build the shared understanding and align the leadership to one core purpose.

A university cooperative research centre with a focus on asset management was in the process of building a collaboration with its academic, public management and industry partners. One output expectation of the collaboration was the development of tools and processes for use by the industry partners who contributed financially to the centre. It became evident that the academic researchers developing some of these tools were viewing the work for publication purposes, not for industry practice. The language used was not the language of public management or industry; validated tests and questionnaires, regression analysis were not valued by these members of the collaboration as they viewed it has having no practical application or value in their daily work. This information was interesting and valuable to the academic partners but was not practice ready. Collaboration workshops were needed to translate it and work together on how best to apply it. Some individuals were unable to understand why their work was not valued by industry and displayed passive aggressive attitudes when changes were required. These workshops required cross-boundary facilitation to build shared understanding of purpose, manage the discussion and relationships, move the work forward and enable delivery of expected (and paid for) products.

A key part of this critical first stage is the understanding of what has gone before (e.g. previous critical elements such as events, successes, failures, personalities). These are captured and retold in the stories of collaboration partners, and may be used to block future collaboration efforts.

The Nine-Step Design Model

The key elements of design which are discussed repeatedly in action research and systems thinking literature are deceptively simple and familiar to both academics and practitioners. They may not be as familiar to the broader community who may want to 'cut to the chase' and get the solution. By working through each step, a shared understanding of what is really going on is built. The intent is to frame a structure which enables improvisation.

Each collaboration requires a first principles approach to how it will roll out over time. No two collaborations are the same as each brings its own mix of intent, stakeholders, cultures and dynamics.

One design map for collaboration recommends nine steps which are viewed as organic rather than linear:

1. Reaching a shared understanding of the context and purpose of the collaboration though a sense-making process of dialogue and negotiation with the client(s) (What? and Why?)
2. Critical stakeholder and network mapping (Who?)
3. Identifying other critical issues (What else?)
4. Co-designing the options for detailed process design for collaboration interventions, e.g. workshops, surveys, focus groups, roundtables (How?)
5. Deciding on which option to follow (Which?)
   Note: this may need rapid change in the actual process if it is not working.
6. Cross-boundary facilitation of collaboration events, processes and interventions (Act)
7. Evaluation (Measure)
8. Developing the report at the completion of each step (Report)
9. Reflect, modify and co-design the next design step (Repeat).

(C. J. Flynn; Source: Author's Own)

There is a tendency with some clients to push for solutions without investing the time to identity and discuss the critical stakeholders and broader issues. Investing time in the ambiguous uncertainties of critical issues leads to deep insights into the real nature of what is being discussed. This is the space where tensions begin to emerge based on differing understanding and perspectives. A facilitator must remain constant, centred and hold the role authority in the face of such dynamics. As stated previously, it is an action and reflection loop and is not sequential, as each step feeds into the others, forward or backward, in a dialogue spiral.

As a facilitator and client working through the collaboration design model (Figure 11.1), they build a shared picture of how the collaboration is building, what it is revealing, how it may differ from what may have been experienced previously and to where to move. Insights occur which enrich the design, and may forestall what in hindsight could be 'deal breakers' in the collaboration process.

The spiral nature of this design as a fluid and emergent process and the value of ongoing dialogue as negotiation and sense making with

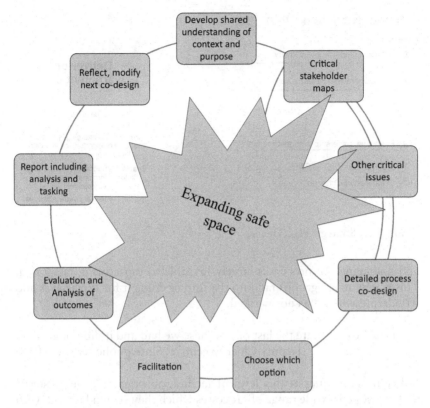

Figure 11.1 Collaborative Design Model

Source: Author's Own

stakeholders is captured in the example in Figure 11.2, which reflects the initiation phase of a collaborative process focused on developing a continuum of justice in an Australian context.

The intent is to create a collaboration design which is responsive to the direction of the collaboration and being open to the emergence of new spaces. This is where the sophisticated capability of the cross-boundary facilitator to identify and draw out possibilities and nuances from the collaboration members is highlighted. It is about what is possible in practice with collaboration members, and experience in what will work, how long a process will take, and other variables.

Process

The word 'facilitate' means to make an action or a process possible or easier. Experienced facilitators make it look easy; the complexity of what they are doing and how quickly they are thinking, observing, shaping

Strategic plan themes

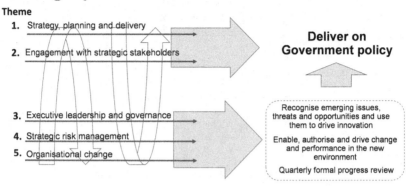

Figure 11.2 Strategic Plan Themes

and managing the process is largely invisible to those being facilitated. This is why many groups fall into the trap of doing it for themselves and wondering why it has not worked.

> I tried to facilitate the last one of these we had and it did not go well.
> (Deputy Chief Executive, State public service, 2018)

Individuals working at this level of facilitation practice have mastered and developed a wide range of processes which they switch between with ease to move a collaboration along. Participants may not even be aware that a process is being used. Years of developing the craft have honed the ability of the cross-boundary facilitators to judge how long a particular process will take and the energy level of the room. In the action and noise of a collaboration, they are paying attention at multiple levels: whole group, individual, progress and value, time and the overall energy level in the room. They know when it is time for a break.

The cross-boundary facilitator is facilitating and listening to the conversation which is not being spoken aloud, the ideas which are not being tabled courageously and the opportunities which are demanding to be recognised. They take these concepts, shape them and reflect them back to the collaboration membership. Having the ability to reflect on what is being heard at this shadow level of conversation, analyse it, draft what to say and present an elegantly articulated option results from deep experience and practice. This work requires rapid understanding, analysis and response. Timing is essential as leaving this response too long allows the energy around the issue to dissipate. A facilitator must be ready to manage the response as part of the next phase as there is no craft in 'throwing hand grenades' into the middle of the group just to get a reaction. What is the intent of putting the option out there? Is there an element of sabotage present?

Galford, Frisch and Green (2015) identify nine forms of sabotage in group or team situations.
"Sabotage by:

- Obedience: insist on doing everything through the correct channels
- Speech: speak as frequently as possible and at great length
- Committee: where possible refer matters to committee or working groups
- Irrelevant issues: introduce irrelevant issues as often as possible
- Haggling: haggle over semantics and syntax
- Reopening decisions: refer back to matters previously decided
- Excessive caution: urge others to be cautious, avoid risk and don't rush
- Is it really our call?: question the propriety of any decision
- CC everyone into all communications; send information frequently and to those only peripherally involved."

(p. 4)

An experienced facilitator will observe and identify these behaviours, naming it and moving the group along, which effectively limits the impact of sabotage.

Experienced facilitators are often termed process disturbers. With a question or a comment they disturb the equilibrium in the room, challenge the boundaries and know how to bring it back safely, usually after there is a significant shift in thinking and dialogue. They observe the individuals, the thinking and the behaviours. They are courageous in challenging the powerful voices in the room.

Some facilitators believe that in creating dissonance with groups or individuals, their job is done. This is far from the truth, as their reputation and credibility may suffer if this is a sustained process of choice. When dissonance emerges (or is created on purpose), a facilitator must seek a resolution which resolves the tension. If this does not happen, irretrievable damage can be done to individuals or client groups and organisations, and failure follows. Other actors are left to resolve and repair the damage of an ill-considered or unfinished intervention, which then becomes part of the mythologies of the organisations.

It is not necessarily always the case that facilitation is undertaken by an individual cross-boundary facilitator. A team of experienced facilitators may work together on collaborative events and processes. The need for trust, respect and connection between such facilitation teams is essential. A deep understanding of practice strengths and values frames is important for such a team.

Co-facilitation occurs often, either with another external facilitator or an internal one. Role clarity about who is the lead facilitator and who makes the final call on process and process changes is essential in these relationships. Norms need to be established to create agreed ways of working together, how and when to intervene when the other is leading a process, redirection and closure processes of synthesis. Above all visible conflict between facilitators must be avoided, as the group observes this and it erodes trust and respect. Any tension or disconnection is picked up quickly by group members and introduces a destructive element which can be leveraged to erode the success of the collaboration.

There are always 'informal' facilitators who are participants in the process and these people can play a critical and positive role in supporting and guiding the collaboration from within the group. If, however, participants are seeking to sabotage or derail the collaboration process, a facilitator needs to identify and manage them early. This management may take the form of a quiet conversation on the sides which seeks to understand what the individual is intending by their behaviour, and if it is intentional or not; or it may require robust naming of the behaviour in the whole group if it is overt.

The 'Right' Facilitator

When considering establishment of a collaborative stakeholder network journey, there are some critical design questions that the leaders of the collaboration need to ask:

- Do we need a facilitator?
- What is the role of a facilitator in the process of collaboration and co-production?
- When should a facilitator be brought in to the process?
- What capabilities does a facilitator in this space need?
- What is the shared understanding of the role of a facilitator?
- Will a facilitator be there for the long journey?
- Is a facilitator 'a fit' for the process?

Facilitators should have highly developed capabilities, backed by dexterity with a wide range of group processes, intuitive and empathic responses to individual and group needs. They need to rapidly process group dynamics to keep energy positive and moving forward. They build participation and participatory decision making through encouraging participation and a sense of shared responsibility. They support the development of shared solutions through building mutual trust, understanding and respect. They are committed to helping collaboration be effective.

Underpinning these skills is a deep familiarity with, understanding and application of the literature on organisational culture, leading change, group dynamics and personality types.

The term 'facilitator' may carry positive or negative filters. If done well, complex facilitation appears seamless. As one public service facilitator says 'we make it look easy.' Expert facilitators are victims of their refined practice, capability and expertise. Because it *looks* easy, many people think it is easy and attempt to do it themselves. Nothing could be farther from the truth. By creating the safe environment and moving the process forward with everyone involved appropriately, participants feel it is safe to push the boundaries and be more courageous.

The high capability facilitator must be a master of their own emotional, practice and energy states. Facilitators experience the full range of emotional states in doing this work; they are often targets for attack by group members who feel disenfranchised. This requires a facilitator to rapidly recognise these emotional states in others or in themselves, their own responses and their drivers and to have developed the ability to re-design, re-energise or reframe as required. This is where hours of research to familiarise themselves with the social and scientific research on group dynamics, coupled with reflective work to learn about themselves through group and individual exercises, builds the foundation for complex facilitation capability. Expert facilitators have been participants in group dynamics, and have been on the receiving end of robust dialogue and feedback. They have learned their craft from masters of the craft.

If facilitated expertly, those participating in a collaboration exercise will not remember a facilitator as a focus point, but they will own and remember the positive value of the exercise and will come together willingly again; if done badly, they remember a negative experience, poor facilitation and are wary of coming together again.

When the decision has been made to use a facilitator, the decision has to be made to use a facilitator who will best deliver on the outcomes. There is a need to consider:

- Complexity of purpose
- Complexity of collaboration
- Capability level of people in the room
- Capability level of a facilitator
- Reputation of a facilitator.

A national organisation recently ran an in-house workshop for experienced facilitators who delivered and facilitated complex leadership and board programmes on behalf of the organisation. The participants were all experienced professionals: lawyers, judges, academics, senior business people who undertook this work in addition to their daily roles. They experienced sales training '101' delivered by an in-house trainer and the overall feedback was it was a waste of their time. The wrong choice of facilitator had been made.

As the field of boundary spanning grows, it is helpful to identify the difference in complexity of policy issue or problem and the differing levels of facilitation required to work most effectively with the issues and the collaborative network. Understanding the complexity and impact of the policy issue, the level of stakeholder understanding and influence, particularly in the area of decision making, is essential in choosing what level of facilitator is required. Comments such as 'We had the wrong people in the room' are common and indicate a wasted opportunity. The facilitator needs to ask the 'Who else should be here?' " question during the design phase (see Figure 11.3)

Sometimes, a professional facilitator (or neutral outsider skilled in facilitation), who has no vested interested in the content of the discussion, is better able to help collaboration members reach consensus (Keast and Mandell, 2012).

In developing the four quadrant model described in Figure 11.3, it was important to recognise the understanding and application of adult learning principles (andragogy), as a long-accepted basis for supporting adults to learn and create something new.

The approach to adult learning is problem-based and collaborative rather than didactic, with a focus on more equality from the actors in the process.

Knowles (1950, p. 9) stated, in what can be viewed an early description of collaboration, that:

> The task of every leader of adult groups (is) real, specific, and clear: Every adult group, of whatever nature, must become a laboratory of democracy, a place where people may have the experience of learning to live co-operatively. Attitudes and opinions are formed primarily in the study groups, work groups, and play groups with which adults affiliate voluntarily. These groups are the foundation stones of our democracy. Their goals largely determine the goals of our society.

The first step to developing the craft of facilitation is often related to the training and development of adults. At this stage the level of capability is one of imparting knowledge and capability while delivering a clearly articulated curriculum, with learning objectives and competency levels to be achieved through some form of assessment. Group work in training scenarios is the trigger to developing facilitation capability.

There is a 'lock step' shift from training to facilitation which challenges a facilitator to move from the formal practice of training, such as modules, learning objectives, timelines and assessment, to the facilitation space. This is where the formal parameters of time, content and process shift to a more fluid and organic way of working with people.

The other three quadrants are representative of three levels of facilitation with each building on the other in cumulative and complexity of process, participation, purpose and dynamics. The increasing complexity of the policy issue and associated collaborative structures and stakeholders demands a high expertise facilitator who draws the four quadrants together. These facilitators draw on a broad knowledge and deep expertise base, not limited to facilitation but extending across teaching in the

INTERNAL	EXTERNAL
Participant-facilitator	**Cross boundary facilitator**
Context is complicated	Context is complex
Process is:	Process is:
• Internal • Outputs • Process • Pre-defined • Co-design • Consult • Control • Managing	• Networked • Creative • Strategic • Organic • Identifying connections • Emergent • Intuitive • Empathic • Multi-focused • Open space • Analytical
Outcome: internal purpose	**Outcome:** trust and mutuality on a shared journey
Outputs: defined and articulated	**Outputs:** uncertain
Trainer	**External process facilitator**
Context is transactional	Context is complicated
Process is	Process is
• Train/teach • Classroom style • Knowledge in • Formulaic • Control • Develop: capability and knowledge	• Process driven • Output driven • May manipulate group to desired place • Accepted practice e.g. strategic planning • Control with open group process
Outcome: Training modules delivered	**Outcome:** often predetermined
Outputs: measured capability/ skills improvement	**Outputs:** expected product

(Left vertical axis: INCREASING COMPLEXITY OF POLICY ISSUE — arrow pointing up)

INCREASING COMPLEXITY OF COLLABORATIVE STRUCTURES AND STAKEHOLDERS

(Bottom horizontal axis: arrow pointing right)

Figure 11.3 Types of Facilitation

Source: Author's Own

academic sense, organisation design and intervention. They move fluidly through the four quadrants as the collaborative situation requires.

Keast and Mandell (2011) point out that while a collaboration leader can guide the process for consensus—setting the ground rules for dialogue and interaction, reminding members of their common goals and their importance, and helping them reach decisions that are mutually acceptable—they are often constrained by their own membership of the collaboration and personal agenda.

When dealing with a complex policy issue or challenge where the majority of collaborative partners agree on what is needed, the participant-facilitator role can be successful. When faced with complex issues where collaboration group members are not aligned, the participant-facilitator is faced with the dilemma of taking themselves with their knowledge, expertise, wisdom and capability out of the process. Most find this difficult to do and become enmeshed in the discussion, allowing personal bias to filter through. This may polarise the participants or create an adversarial situation with the group coalescing against a facilitator. The outcomes may erode trust and engender failed collaboration relationships which will take time to rebuild.

In developing the four quadrant model described in Figure 11.3, I drew on the reflections and experience of many colleagues. The model draws out the differences at each level and guides organisations about which type of facilitation they need for their purpose. It also serves as a capability development map for those intending to become facilitators known for working in complexity.

Models of Facilitative Approaches and Capabilities

Thompson and Flynn (2014) describe seven themes of leadership for change leaders at the senior levels of organisations. These themes can be adapted to reflect five themes for cross-boundary facilitation in the collaboration space:

- Theme 1: Mandate to undertake change, broad scope of discretion and support from client
- Theme 2: Previous successful boundary spanning facilitator experience
- Theme 3: An understanding of the socialisation tactics of organisations, and the role of culture in assisting or creating obstacles to change
- Theme 4: Highly developed understanding of group dynamics
- Theme 5: Self-efficacy

(Source: Adapted from Thompson and Flynn, 2014)

As mentioned earlier, representatives of all of these modes of leadership thinking may be present in the collaborative space. By listening to the individuals, the language and concepts they use, and the questions

Table 11.1 Key Collaborative Practice Elements

- Mutual trust
- Open, respectful communication
- Empathy
- Openness to others' views, values and perspectives
- Shared decision making
- Clarity about roles and responsibilities
- Appreciation of each other's knowledge and experience
- Willingness to negotiate and compromise
- Commitment to resolving tensions and conflicts
- Shared aims or goals

Source: Keast, R. 2015

they ask, a facilitator is able to support them to contribute more fully to the process. Rooke and Torbert (2005) in their Seven Transformations of Leadership describe these roles and motivations which I explore in the section on the theory underpinning this level of cross-boundary facilitation. It is evident that the level of work of the cross-boundary facilitator aligns with the leadership level of assigned to the strategist.

Presence and Impact

The cross-boundary facilitator brings presence and impact to their role. Presence in the collaboration space is the act of centring the energy of the group, conveying authority in guiding the process and creating the safe space in which the collaboration is able to explore its work. Impact is the ability to bring order out of what appears to be chaos to bring about positive outcomes by introducing new concepts and ways of thinking and behaving.

Inexperienced facilitators may make the mistake of thinking they are the centre or focus of attention. In fact the opposite is closer to the truth. Knowing when to withdraw and when to be silent and allow the tension to build until the collaboration members speak is one key process tool. A facilitator should be as invisible as possible in the process while shaping and guiding the process. However, visibility becomes necessary when the interactions become challenging and conflicted. In the end, it is not about a facilitator but about the collaboration and its members' ownership of the work they do. Facilitators who seek to make themselves the centre of the interactions often draw criticism.

> Academic X did the same tangential stuff at the evaluation forum, but I don't think she can help herself.
> (Public Sector Senior Executive, 2015)

A facilitator is there to co-design, develop and facilitate, not to:

- be the centre of attention
- hold the floor

- share their views and biases
- to be right
- inflexibly hold to agendas.

When all is done, the collaborative group creates and owns the outcomes.

The underpinning idea is that order emerges from chaos and the creation and repetition of replicating fractals resonates with the expanding nature of collaborations, where the intent is that the thinking and behaviours will replicate across collaboration systems. Traditionally the greatest amount of attention has been focused on the top three elements, the hard systems which are visible, tangible, manageable and empirical. Working within this broader framework allows a facilitator to see the critical and interdependent impacts of people as reflected by the bottom three elements where culture, emotion, values and identity are situated which are invisible, intangible, unmanageable and difficult to capture and measure. They sit in direct contrast to the above the green line elements. If not identified and surfaced to be worked with, they pose a very real risk of eroding success. This is especially true as groups seek to understand how bias, conscious and unconscious, may be impacting teaching and learning at the individual, institutional and structural levels.

The complexity for a facilitator lies in identifying and surfacing the undiscussable issues from below the 'green line' and surfacing them to make them visible and tangible in the collaboration.

Dalmau developed several questions which may guide a facilitator in the use of the model:

- Who are the people affected by the current inequity being discussed?
- What historical patterns (around race, class, language etc.) may be informing the dynamics in this context?
- Who has power here? What is power based on here? Who is at the table?
- How are oppression, internalised oppression and transferred oppression playing out right here, right now?
- How safe is it here for different people to share their truth?
- What are the potential unintended consequences of our proposed solutions/actions?
- Do the proposed solutions ignore or worsen existing disparities for the group in which we are focused?

(Source: Seven Circle Model; © National Equity Project,
Oakland California, adapted from the Dalmau
Network Group, www.dalmau.com)

When people come together they bring multiple roles and identities to the table: academics, citizens, community bodies, not for profits, NGOs, clients/customers of services, public servants, leaders, policy experts, practitioners, communications experts, private sector.

Table 11.2 Action Logics in Collaboration (Torbert and Rooke, 2005)

Action logic	Characteristics	Strengths	Focus	% of population
Opportunist	*Wins any way possible.* Self-oriented; manipulative; 'might makes right.'	Good in emergencies and in sales opportunities.	internal	1%
Diplomat	*Avoids overt conflict.* Wants to belong; obeys group norms; rarely rocks the boat.	Good as supportive glue within an office; helps bring people together.	external	4%
Expert	*Rules by logic and expertise.* Seeks rational efficiency.	Good as an individual contributor	internal	10%
Achiever	*Meets strategic goals.* Effectively achieves goals through teams; juggles managerial duties and market demands.	Well suited to managerial roles; action and goal oriented	external	30%
Individualist	*Interweaves competing personal and company action logics.* Creates unique structures to resolve gaps between strategy and performance.	Effective in venture and consulting roles.	internal	38%
Strategist	*Generates organisational and personal transformations.* Exercises the power of mutual inquiry, vigilance and vulnerability for both the short and long term.	Effective as a transformational leader	external	12%
Alchemist	*Generates social transformations.* Integrates material, spiritual and societal transformation.	Good at leading society-wide transformations	internal	5%

Boundary spanning and collaboration combines practice, research and relational systems. Keast (2016) describes the key elements of collaborative practice. Tested in practice with large public service systems (e.g. health, education, family and child support), and the public-private partnership contexts of asset management and infrastructure, these elements resonate strongly for senior leadership groups seeking to collaborate.

Boundary spanners/practitioners from all sides experience the boundaries between:

- Academic research and policy thinking
- Public sector practice, policy development and implementation
- Boundaries between public sector agencies and their internal structural divisions and teams
- Boundaries between academia and public sector, third sector and community implementation
- Boundaries between communities
- Boundaries between individual actors
- Boundary between public sector and NFPs, NGOs.

Trust and the Safe Space

A facilitator understands and accepts responsibility for creating a safe environment in which the collaborative work is enabled. They recognise the need to keep every individual safe. They have no hesitation in calling poor behaviour, closing it down and if required, excluding people from the space. This is always done with respect.

This is done by:

- establishing norms for behaviour in the room
- rapidly building rapport with the collaboration participants present
- enabling the collaboration participants to build connection among themselves
- observing the process, the people and the interactions simultaneously
- managing all interactions within the collaborative space
- being aware of issues of sensitivity
- knowing when to intervene
- managing time
- creating a safe physical space with room for individuals to spread out, sit and move freely.

Individuals working in this space have developed capabilities, both formal and informal, accredited or intuitively, that enable them to work with people, their emotions and behaviours. They know how to create 'safe space' where people feel they are able to be honest, emotional or controversial. Many of the tools and practices have foundations in organisational psychology as well as some management group processes that grew out of thinking, like applied system thinking and behaviours. They are often accredited in a range of psychometric testing instruments. The key to successful interactions is to debrief processes and to de-escalate tension when the time is right as conflict may be a positive if managed well.

The establishment of confidentiality agreements (or Chatham House rules) is an essential first step. What happens or is said in the space belongs to the participants. It may be discussed outside the space with no attribution of individual.

There needs to be commitment to building the relationship between the cross-boundary facilitator and the members or participants in the collaborative process. This engenders trust, shared understanding and enables more robust and rapid movement through processes as the relationship strengthens.

For the duration of a facilitated collaborative process, everyone in the space should feel they are able to suspend or air conflicts, surrender control of the process and be heard, valued and acknowledged without fear of conflict or judgement. Safety in the collaborative process is essential. As with any coming together of groups with different identities, values and boundaries, the collaboration space can become tense at times. A facilitator who avoids or ignores tension or conflict within the collaboration or who seeks to shut it down is not practising complex facilitation through exploration or resolution.

This sense of being in a safe space is created by the cross-boundary facilitator who establishes some boundaries for individual safety. How quickly the cross-boundary facilitator can build rapport and associated trust with the group influences how quickly the sphere of safety is created. Knowing how hard and fast to go, when to pull back and where to apply pressure is part of the craft. A facilitator accepts responsibility for this. Within that safe space, robust discussion including direct conflict may often emerge, and a facilitator must have the capability to manage the dynamics and the courage to intervene when necessary. Above all the leader(s) present, (Chief Executives(s), Directors-general, CEOs), should have a robust level of trust in the boundary scanner/facilitator that allows them to surrender their need for control and direction in the collaborative space to a facilitator, who is then able to practise their craft of building the collaborative relationships, culture and processes—using these to move the strategy forward. Bachmann (2001) defines trust as a mechanism for coping with uncertainty and complexity and positions it as personal and system level. The higher the level of trust between the organisational leadership and the cross-boundary facilitator, the more control the leadership is prepared to accede to a facilitator to co-ordinate the social interactions and the greater the chance of success

An example of the need for this level of trust is evident in a recent exchange with a Chief Executive when he asked the facilitator to describe the design for a process in a collaboration start-up workshop:

CHIEF EXECUTIVE: *'What's World Café?'*
The facilitator described the large-group process known as World Café which builds rapid connections between members and deep insights into critical questions through a tightly managed process including

> *collaborative dialogue and knowledge-sharing, particularly for large and diverse groups.*
> CHIEF EXECUTIVE: *'Good luck with that!'*

The Chief Executive's assumption was that this would not work with his own group of senior executives; nevertheless, he did not veto the approach. Ultimately he was surprised by the level of energy, relationship connection and above all, the rapid deep insights developed when the process enabled rich and robust conversations to develop.

Conclusion

Any individual with significant work experience in large organisations has, at some time, experienced a poorly facilitated exercise. This experience may be recalled as 'a waste of time' or with a facilitator having 'no idea of what they are doing.' In some cases they may also feel they have been subjected to an 'enthusiastic amateur' airing ill-considered views on sensitive issues or taking valuable discussion time to share their own stories rather than facilitating the group interaction. A leader who has experienced a failed exercise becomes wary of all facilitators. The approach taken next time may be to control the process so closely that the opportunity for successful boundary spanning, relationship building, learning and connection is diminished.

A cross-boundary facilitator adds value through experience, wisdom and capability every step of the way as shown in the following section.

Collaboration In Multi-Cultural Contexts

Most countries are experiencing a growth and shift in the multi-cultural profile of their populations. These social shifts demand new policy and service responses. How different cultures relate in a collaboration space to contribute to these dialogues is dependent on multiple factors. These are not being explored in this section.

Cultural differences need to be respected. The style of facilitation that is acceptable in one culture may not be acceptable in another. For example, many of the processes based on game-playing, role-playing and team celebration which is valued in some cultures is not well received in others. Some local communities have very different behavioural norms than others. In the context of the incoming government in the Northern Territory of Australia in 2016, the political leadership stated that the new government would consult widely with a view to empowering local Indigenous communities and partnering with non-government agencies to ensure the cultural component of delivery. This statement reflects the fact that working with these communities on their traditional lands demands a specific skill set which reflects time spent in developing cultural understanding and capabilities.

Thinking about how to facilitate in these emerging spaces is important— the need for early involvement in design, the value of rigorous explora- tion of how to work best with other cultures and the due diligence in what matters for all cultures in the space is the pre-collaboration chal- lenge for cross-boundary facilitators.

Conclusion

In exploring the research literature, working with existing models, devel- oping some new ones and reflecting on the challenges of the craft of cross-boundary facilitation the following themes emerge.

Expert cross boundary facilitation is the result of the combination of many hours spent developing the craft, researching the literature and moments of success and failure in the collaboration journey. It stems from working across the many expressions of collaboration.

Collaboration is a way of people being together working towards a shared purpose. Each person brings difference in thinking, culture, val- ues, language and emotion and this difference needs to be valued. It all contributes to the rich picture that emerges during the collaboration.

An experienced cross-boundary facilitator will contribute best value when included from the design stage of a potential collaboration. They will follow a design process which allows for feedback loops, re-design, critical reflection and decision points. They understand it is an organic and emerging design, not a linear one.

They understand boundaries, boundary spanning, boundary objects and how to work effectively and respectfully with these in a positive way.

They model refined group process behaviours, including:

- authentic and congruent dialogue
- rapidly building relationships and rapport
- creating safe environments for all
- developing common vision and shared understanding of purpose
- creating synergies and alignments
- identifying points of connection
- energising and encouraging
- accessing a range of large and small group processes and individual processes. No group will sit and wait while the facilitator discovers something isn't working and cannot move agilely to a more suitable process.
- Deep understanding of group dynamics and individual states
- Accreditation in psychometric tests.

This is the beginning of an exploration of the practice value of cross- boundary facilitation. More importantly, it reinforces that practice and research do not stand alone. More work is needed to develop improved outcomes from the connections between the two.

12 Conclusion

Gemma Carey, Luke Craven, and Helen Dickinson

The examination of boundaries is of central interest, and importance, to the field of public administration. Current literature on boundary spanners has consistently shown that they are important players in public policy and administration. While this previous work shows that boundary spanners are important, examination of how boundary spanners work across and within different contexts or domains is in its infancy.

This Part has aimed to provide a comprehensive practical and theoretical overview of 'how' boundary spanners go about their practice, and to draw clear links between the theory and practice of *being* a boundary spanner. It presented a detailed typology of boundary spanners that theorises why and how they operate and, crucially, the likelihood that they produce institutional gains. This acknowledgement that boundary-spanning activities can have both negative and positive implications is a key development for the literature, and thread that runs through each of the contributions of this book.

The final two chapters of this Part explored in detail the practices and capabilities that underpin engagement with critical actors in the collaboration space, e.g. academics, citizens, community bodies and others. It highlighted the role of case cross-boundary facilitators, showing that good practice requires they integrate a range of research and strategic insights, on a broad range of public management challenges and themes into their craft. In doing so, it presented a range of new models for the craft of complex facilitation and approaches to the actions of collaboration by exploring the current research discussions about boundary spanning in collaboration, and explores two recent Australian case studies where these practices worked, with uneven results.

References

Adams, R., and Tovey, W., 2010. *Consultancy in public services: Empowerment and transformation.* Bristol: Policy Press.

Aldrich, H., and Herker, D., 1977. Boundary spanning roles and organization structure. *The Academy of Management Review*, 2, 217–240. doi:10.2307/257905.

Australian Public Service Commission, 2006. *The integrated leadership system.* Canberra: APSC.

Bachmann, R., 2001. Trust, power and control in trans-organizational relations. *Organization Studies,* 22 (2), 337–365.

Bandura, A., 1997. *Self-efficacy: The exercise of control.* New York: W. H. Freeman.

Barraket, J., Keast, R., and Furneaux C. (eds), 2015. *Social procurement and new public governance.* London: Routledge.

Blackman, D. A., Buick, F., and O'Flynn, J, 2016. From engaging to enabling: Could an asset-based approach transform Indigenous affairs? *Environment and Planning C: Government and Policy,* 34 (8), 1632–1651.

Bourdieu, P., 1977. *A theory of practice.* Cambridge, MA: Harvard University Press.

Bourdieu, P., 1984. *Distinction: A social critique of the judgement of taste.* London: Routledge.

Bourdieu, P., 1991. Genesis and structure of the religious field. *Comparative Social Research,* 13, 1–44.

Bourdieu, P., 1996. *The rules of art.* California: Stanford University Press.

Bourdieu, P., 1998. *Practical reason.* Cambridge: Polity Press.

Bourdieu, P., Wacquant, L.J.D., and Farage, S., 1994. Rethinking the state: Genesis and structure of the bureaucratic field. *Sociological Theory,* 12, 1. doi:10.2307/202032

Bourgon, J., 2011. *A new synthesis of public administration: Serving in the 21st century.* Montreal: McGill-Queen's University Press.

Brown, K.A., and Flynn, C.J., 2005. Managing change in public service organisations: A case study, in Osborne, S., and Brown, K., (Eds.), *Managing change and innovation in public service organisations.* London: Routledge.

Brown, K.A., Keast, R.L., Waterhouse, J.M., Murphy, G.D., & Mandell, M., 2012. Co-management to solve homelessness: Wicked solutions to wicked problems, in Pestoff, V., Brandsen, T., and Verschuere, B. (Eds.) *New public governance, the third sector, and co-production.* New York: Routledge, Taylor & Francis Group, pp. 211–226.

Buick, F., 2014a. Boundary spanning to address indigenous disadvantage in Australia, in *Boundary-spanning in organizations: Network, influence, and conflict.* New York: Routledge.

Buick, F., 2014b. The culture solution? Culture and common purpose in Australia, in O'Flynn, J., Blackman, D., and Halligan, J. (Eds.), *Crossing boundaries in public management and policy: The international experience.* Oxon: Routledge, pp. 78–91.

Carey, G., Buick, F., Pescud, M., and Malbon, E., In press. Preventing dysfunction and improving policy advice: The role of intra-departmental boundary spanners. *Australian Journal of Public Administration.*

Commonwealth of Australia. 2010. https://www.campusreview.com.au/2011/03/academic-research-lost-without-translation/

Dickinson, H., 2014. Making a reality of integration: Less science, more craft and graft. *Journal of Integrated Care,* 22(5–6), 189–196.

Dickinson, H., 2018. *The concept challenge, crossing boundaries in public management and policy: Tackling the critical challenges,* Ed. Craven, Dickinson, Carey. New York: Routledge.

Flynn, C.J., 2011. *Lost in translation*. Presentation to IRSPM Conference, Dublin, April.

Flynn, C.J., 2016. *Invisible and invaluable—facilitation as a critical trans-disciplinary process in collaboration, consensus building and co-production*. Presentation to IRSPM Conference, Hong Kong.

Flynn, C.J., and Thompson, R. M., 2013. *Thrown in the deep end: Newcomers and public sector reform*. Presentation to IRSPM Conference, Bern.

Flynn, C.J., and Thompson R.M., 2012. *Between a rock and a hard place*. Presentation to IRSPM Conference, Rome, April.

Galford, R.M., Frisch, B., and Greene C., 2015. *Simple Sabotage: A Modern Field Manual for Detecting and Rooting Out Everyday Behaviours That Undermine Your Workplace*. New York: Harper Collins.

Giddens, A. 1979. *Central problems in social theory*. Berkeley: University of California.

Giddens, A., 1984. *The constitution of society*. Cambridge: Polity Press.

Gladwell, M., 2008. *Outliers: The story of success*. London: Hachette, p. 40.

Gray, B., 1989. *Collaborating: Finding common ground for multiparty problems*. San Francisco, CA: Jossey Bass.

Head, B., 2008. Assessing network-based collaborations: Effectiveness for whom? *Public Management Review*, 10 (6), 733–749.

Head, B., 2014. The collaboration solution? Factors for collaborative success, in O'Flynn, J., Blackman, D., and Halligan, J. (Eds.), *Crossing boundaries in public management and policy: The international experience*. Oxon: Routledge, pp. 142–157.

Heifetz, R.A., and Linsky, M., 2002. *Leadership on the line*. Boston: Harvard Business School Press.

Hilgers, M., and Mangez, E., 2014. Introduction to Pierre Bourdieu's social fields, in Hilgers, A., and Mangez, E. (Eds.), *Bourdieu's theory of social fields: Concepts and applications*. New York: Routledge, pp. 1–35.

Hogue, A., 2017. *Social innovation in 3 D*, Stanford, Social Innovation Review, https://ssir.org/articles/entry/social_innovation_in_3_d?utm_soure=Enews&utm_me

Huxham, C., and Vangen, S. 2003. Researching organizational practice through action research: Case studies and design choices. *Organizational Research Methods*, 6 (3), 383–403.

Innes, J.E., and Booher, D., 2000. *Collaborative dialogue as a policy making strategy*. Working Paper, Institute of Urban and Regional Development, University of California, Berkeley.

Jones, G.R. 1986. Socialization tactics, self-efficacy, and newcomers' adjustments to organizations. *Academy of Management Journal*, 29 (2), 262–279.

Kaner, S., Lind, J., Toldi, C., Fisk, S., and Berger, D., 2014. *Facilitator's guide to participatory decision-making*. San Francisco, CA: Jossey Bass.

Keast, R.L., 2015. *Shining a light on the 'Black Box' of collaboration: Mapping the prerequisites for cross-sector working*. Presentation to workshop on cross sector working for complex problems, Canberra.

Keast, R., 2016. Integration terms: Same or different?, in Carey, G. (Ed.), *Grass roots to government: Joined-up working in Australia*. Melbourne: Melbourne University Press, pp. 25–46.

Keast, R.L., and Mandell, M.P., 2011. *Consensus building and facilitation*. Fact-Sheet. Australian Research Alliance for Children and Youth.

Kets de Vries, M.F.R., 2004. Organizations on the couch: A clinical perspective on organizational dynamics. *European Management Journal*, 22 (2), 183–200.

Knowles, M., 1950. *Informal adult education*. Chicago: Association Press.

Klijn, E-H., 1997. An overview, in Kickert, W., Klijn, E-H., Koppenjan, J. (Eds.), *Managing complex networks: Strategies for the public sector*. London: Sage Publications Ltd, pp. 166–191.

Macdonald, I., Burke, C., and Stewart, K., 2006. *Systems leadership*. Farnham, Surrey: Gower.

Mahoney, J., Thelan, K., 2010. *Explaining institutional change: Ambiguity, agency and power*. Cambridge: Cambridge University Press.

Management Advisory Committee, 2010. *Empowering change—fostering innovation in the Australian Public Service*. Canberra: Australian Government.

Mandell, M., and Keast, R., 2009. A new look at leadership in collaborative networks: Process catalysts, in Raffel, J., Lesienk, P., and Middlelbrooks, A. (Eds.), *Public sector leadership: International challenges and perspectives*. Cheltenham: Edward Elgar.

McKinsey & Company, 2013. http:/working with mckinsy.blogspot.com/2013/01/t-shaped-problem-solving-at-mckinsey.html

O'Flynn, J., 2009. The cult of collaboration in public policy. *Australian Journal of Public Administration*, 68, 112–116. doi:10.1111/j.1467-8500.2009.00616.x

O'Flynn, J., 2014. Crossing boundaries: The fundamental questions in public management, in O'Flynn, J., Blackman, D., and Halligan, D., (Eds.), *Crossing boundaries in public management and policy: The international experience*. London: Routledge, pp. 11–44.

Osborne, S.P., (Ed.), 2010. *The new public governance*. New York: Routledge.

Parston, G., and Timmins, N., 1998. *Joined-up management*. London: Public Management Foundation.

Quick, K., and Feldman, M., 2014. Boundaries as junctures: Collaborative boundary work for building efficient resilience. *Journal of Public Administration Research and Theory*, 24 (3), 673–695.

Rhodes, R.A.W., 2014. *Recovering the 'craft' of public administration in network governance*. Plenary Address to the international Political Science Association World Congress, Montreal, 19–24 July. www.ipsa.org/my-ipsa/events/montreal2014/plenary/plenary-recovering

Ring, P.S., and Van de Ven, A.H., 1994. Developmental processes of cooperative interorganizational relationships. *Academy of Management Review*, 19 (1), 90–118.

Rogers, R., 1969. *Max Weber's ideal type theory*. New York: Philosophical Library Inc.

Rooke, D., and Torbert, W.R., 2005. Seven transformations of leadership. *Harvard Business Review*, 83 (4), 66–76.

Roth, L., 2011. *Social impact bonds*. NSW: NSW Parliament.

Shaw, P., 1997. Intervening in the shadow systems of organizations: Consulting from a complexity perspective. *Journal of Organizational Change Management*, 10 (3): 235–250.

Snowden, D.J., 2000. The social ecology of knowledge management: Cynefin, in Despres, C., and Chauvel, D. (Eds.), *Knowledge horizons*. London: Butterworth-Heinemann, pp. 237–266.

Snowden, D.J., and Boone, M.E., 2007. A leader's framework for decision making. *Harvard Business Review*, 85 (11), 68–76.

Star, S.L., and Griesemer, J., 1989. Institutional ecology, translations, and boundary objects: Amateurs and professionals in Berkeley's museum of vertebrate zoology, 1907–39. *Social Studies of Science*, 19 (3), 387–420.

Stones, R., 2005. *Structuration theory*. New York: Palgrave Macmillan.

Szakolczai, A., 2009. Liminality and experience: Structuring transitory situations and transformative events. *International Political Anthropology*, 2 (1), 141–172.

Thompson, R. McLeay, and Flynn, C. 2014. Inter-sector senior leader transitions: experience and outcomes. *International Journal of Public Sector Management*, 27 (1), 85–93. http://www.emeraldinsight.com/doi/abs/10.1108/IJPSM-03-2012-0034

Torbert, W. R., and Rooke, D. 2005. Seven transformations of leadership. *Harvard Business Review*, 83 (4), 66–76.

Thompson, J., 1984. Symbolic violence: Language and power in the sociology of Pierre Bourdieu, in *Studies in the theory of ideology*. Cambridge: Polity Press, pp. 42–72.

Weber, M., 1922. *Economy and society: An outline of interpretive sociology*. New York: Bedminster Press.

Wheatley, M.J., 2006. *Leadership and the new science*, 3rd edition. San Francisco, CA: Berrett-Koehler Publishers.

Wheatley, M.J., and Rogers, M., 1996. *A simpler way*. San Francisco, CA: Berrett-Koehler Publishers.

Whittington, R., 1992. Putting Giddens into action: Social systems and managerial agency. *Journal of Management Studies*, 29, 693–712.

Williams, P.M., 2002. The competent boundary spanner. *Public Administration*, 80 (1), 103–124.

Williams, P.M., 2010. Special agents: The nature and role of boundary spanners, in ESRC Research Seminar Series, *Collaborative futures: New insights from intra and inter-sectoral collaboration*. Birmingham, UK: University of Birmingham.

Williams, P.M., 2012. *Collaboration in public policy and practice: The role of boundary spanners*. Bristol: Policy Press.

Williams, P.M., 2013. We are all boundary spanners now? *International Journal of Public Sector Management*, 26 (1), 17–32.

Part 4
The Methodology Challenge

Introduction

This Part explores the methodological challenges of research on boundary-spanning issues. Specifically it asks, what *can* we know about the boundary-spanning challenge through current research approaches? And, what needs to be done to further this knowledge through more innovative approaches?

Currently, much of the research on boundary issues reflects more general limitations in studies on the complexity of policy problems. The field is predominantly comprised of single case studies, from which we hope to generalise (Macaulay, 2016). In addition, research is often caught between being too specific, creating challenges for generalisation, or not specific enough in that it does not provide an in-depth and nuanced investigation into the social practices that sit at the core of boundary work.

In this Part, we focus on two methodological challenges key to understanding effective boundary crossing, which are reflected in two chapters. The first chapter explores how different methodologies have been used to investigate and understand the nature of boundary crossing—what works or what might work in collaborative settings. That is, given a particular understanding of complexity in the social world, how can we generate knowledge about the craft of working across boundaries in public policy contexts? We conducted a systematic review of the boundary-spanning literature, which identified a number of common approaches to understanding boundary crossing. We identified three common approaches: practice-based methods, single case studies and socio-metric analyses. We assess how these different methods are applied, as well as discussing their benefits and drawbacks. Building on this analysis, we argue that we must further develop new and existing methodological approaches simultaneously to address the generalisation challenge, while maintaining a level of fidelity to the context of particular boundary-spanning initiatives, such as meta-synthesis and meta-analyses.

In the second chapter, we explore how the use of methods can help us conceptualise issues, problems and social conditions that themselves cross boundaries and domains. Much of the work in public policy and administration is premised on the idea that the challenges we face are inter-sectoral (Klijn and Koppenjan, 2000; Osborne, 2006; Rhodes, 2014). But, to more effectively utilise boundary-crossing strategies, we need methods to understand how wickedness and complexity exist in real world settings (Head and Alford, 2008, 2015). The discussion focuses on new approaches to modelling systems dynamics, group model building and other approaches to generating systems understandings from qualitative data, many of which will be new to scholars of public policy and management. However, as previous contributions to this collection have made clear, the governance challenges that we face require us to cross a range of academic boundaries and seek out disciplines which can offer new methodological tools and insights. This means that we must also continue to critically examine boundaries between disciplines, their normative standards and approaches to knowledge, and how these might be overcome in order for us to capture, examine and progress the boundary problems faced by practitioners and policy makers.

The key point in both chapters is that methods shape how and what we see with respect to boundary crossing. Our choice of method actively delimits the conclusions we are able to draw from our research and practice, and therefore what comes to be seen as important or necessary for supporting effective boundary crossing. As we make clear, for example, the use of case studies and comparative case studies tends to emphasise roles of organisations or structures, just as an interest in understanding these structures drives researchers to certain case-based or comparative methodologies. Put simply, our methodologies affect what we understand about boundaries, just as our understanding of boundaries influences our methodological choice. This Part aims to begin to address the *complexity* of this relationship to support boundary crossing in research, policy and practice.

13 Review, Methodological Approaches to Understanding Collaborative Practice

Luke Craven, Gemma Carey,
Helen Dickinson, and Iona Rennie

This chapter discusses a range of methods and methodologies that have been used to understand different forms of collaborative practice. Our discussion is based on a systematic review of the boundary-spanning literature, which identified a number of common approaches to understanding boundary crossing. We explore three common approaches: practice-based methods, single case studies, and socio-metric analyses. We assess how these different methods are applied, as well as discussing their benefits and drawbacks. Finally, we suggest a range of methodological approaches that could be more widely used in boundary-spanning research, which address many of the limitations of the individual methods we explore.

The Epistemological Question

Before examining methodological approaches to exploring boundary issues, it is important to examine epistemological debates in the field. Epistemology refers to our understanding of the social world, the ways by which we can construct knowledge about it and notions of what constitutes 'truth' (Blaikie, 1993). Before any research can be conducted, researchers need to make choices about: the research problem to be investigated, the research questions, the strategy and posture to be adopted by the researcher and the research paradigm. All of these contain assumptions about the nature of social reality and how it can be studied (Blaikie, 1993). Questions of epistemology underpin any research; however, in relation to boundary spanning they are also shaped by the perspectives and demands of governments. That is, the research that we conduct is influenced by how governments perceive truth and the construction of knowledge about policy and governance issues.

In recent years, changes in the way governments think about truth and research have influenced the construction of knowledge in the fields of public policy and governance. This, in turn, has affected the ways in which we conceptualise and then investigate boundary issues. Sullivan (2011) argues that the combination of decentred governance and wicked policy problems led to a search for 'truth' in order to comfort citizens that governments are 'still in control,' so to speak. This has manifested in a growth in evaluations and a focus on evidence-based policy which were not rooted in the positivist epistemologies traditionally associated with the natural sciences (i.e. where a single observable truth can be discovered) (Cairney, 2018, 2016; Sullivan, 2011). This first emerged in an explicit way (i.e. the linking of uncertainty and an aim to valorise evidence over ideology) with third way politics in the UK under New Labour (Giddens, 2000), and has subsequently spread across other Westminster systems and western democracies (Buckmasters and Thomas, 2009). Evaluations and evidence-based policy would provide governments with concrete evidence about what works, with a renewed emphasis on the role of social sciences (Sullivan, 2011). More specifically, it reshaped how evaluation was done.

In place of outputs-focused evaluations—concerned with questions of additionality, displacement and substitution of different programmes—approaches emerged that encouraged a more interactive and formative style evaluation (Sullivan, 2011). This was part of a broader effort to reconfigure the ways in which citizens engaged in policy. Consistent with the engaged citizen that sits at the heart of third way politics, participatory research methods were favoured, such as action research and action learning (Giddens, 2000; Sullivan and Stewart, 2006). In addition to a shift away from positivist paradigms, this also represented a departure from the approaches to evaluation and policy research employed in earlier decades. During the 1970s, for example, there had been an emphasis in research and evaluation that would inform meta theories (e.g. Marxism) (Sullivan, 2011). Instead, there was a growing interest in micro and meso level theories that help to unpack the experiences of individuals and groups and their responses to policy. Hence, the challenge for research is to capture and explain complexity, rather than bracket it out or attempt to simplify it.

This trend can be seen in our review of research methods in the field of boundary spanning, where later research has both a participatory and interpretive flavour. Interpretive research aims to understand the social world from the perspective of the actors creating and experiencing it, consistent with participatory approaches (Blaikie, 1993). While interpretive research does not necessarily involve participatory methods, it requires prolonged and deep engagement with the subjectivities and experiences of those being researched—immersing the researcher in the same 'tacit' (or taken for granted) knowledge that individuals draw on to construct their social world and make decisions about how to proceed (Blaikie, 1993). Hence, in addition to participatory research we have seen a growth in ethnographic and qualitative research both within evaluations of policy and research, as Dickinson and Smith explored in the Conceptual Part, which covers questions of both governance and boundary crossing from decentred perspectives (Sullivan, 2016).

In addition to engaging citizens and policy actors in a different way, the interpretivist turn in public policy has helped to establish why actors do not necessarily act in predictable ways (Sullivan, 2016). Moreover, it enables us to understand why this is the case. This is particularly important in an era of networked governance, whereby actions in one policy domain or sector may have unanticipated flow on effects for another area or set of actors (Carey et al., 2015). However, the transition to new approaches to evaluation and policy learning was not complete. Sullivan (2011) argues that old preoccupations with particular forms of 'truth' combined with new networked governance agendas to create cultures of strict performance management and audit, as seen in new public management. Here, the newly elevated role of evaluators led to a preoccupation with generating 'better' truth through the use of increasingly sophisticated methods and models which ultimately privileged particular types of data (e.g. performance statistics) (Sullivan 2011). This suggests that a disconnect between evidence, argument and policy grew (Cairney, 2018; Sullivan, 2011).

In the last five to ten years there has also been a growth in realist approaches to research and evaluation in public policy. This is, in many ways, an attempt to bridge the divide between old positivist approaches and the interpretive turn in public policy. Realist approaches seek to understand what works for whom under what circumstances, seeking a single but highly contextualised truth (Dickinson and O'Flynn, 2016; Bonell et al., 2012; Greenhalgh and Russell, 2009). This is different from realist philosophy (i.e. that there is a single understanding about the nature of the world), but rather seeks a more nuanced view of the reasons why collaboration might exist (Dickinson and O'Flynn, 2016). As Dickinson and O'Flynn (2016, p. 46) note, "the crux of this perspective is how organisations change in response to the wider environment and how they might achieve either (or both) gains through collaboration" or boundary crossing.

Systematic Review of Boundary-Spanning Research Methods

In reviewing methods to understand collaborative practice, first, we must consider how we have come to understand what works or might work in collaborative cross-boundary settings. That is, given a particular understanding of complexity in the social world, how can we generate knowledge about the craft of working across boundaries in public policy and administration? To answer this, we conducted a review that adopted a systematised approach to get a good survey of the existing literature on boundary crossing and the approaches that have been taken. Our review found that current research falls into three broad categories of methodology:

- Single-N case studies, which are often mixed methods
- Social network analysis and other socio-metrics

- Practice as method, either reflections of the author, or engaging with the insights, reflection and experiences of boundary-crossing practitioners

Following this review, we turn to a range of strategies that can be used to simultaneously address the generalisation challenge, while maintaining a level of fidelity to the context of particular boundary-spanning initiatives, such as meta-synthesis and meta-analyses, comparative analysis and systems approaches that go beyond the current use of socio-metrics.

Reviewing the Boundary-Spanning Literature

The review approach adopted for this section sought to identify methodological approaches used to analyse boundary spanning at either the organisational, team or individual level. Searches were conducted from 1960 to 2017 in policy, public service and public administration contexts. While the review collected both conceptual and empirical work, the focus of this chapter is on empirical studies and the methodologies and methods that they employed. Ultimately, what we sought to address through this process is the question 'what methods have been used in empirical research into boundary spanning?'

Searches were conducted in the following databases: Business Source Premier (EBSCO, ProQuest Web of Science, EMERALD SCOPUS, WILEY, Taylor & Francis). Search terms included are given in Table 13.1.

Studies not published in English and outside of academic peer-review journals were excluded. It is worth noting here that the decision to exclude grey literature from the review is a deliberate one.

Key Terminology Explained

Before we continue with the findings of the review, it is prudent to explain some key terms relating to method and methodology that will be used throughout. Many of our readers will be familiar with these, and should

Table 13.1 Search Terms Used as Part of the Review

Boundary spanning	Policy	Competencies and skills
Boundary spanner	Public service	Leadership
Reticulist	Civil service	Collaboration
Network manager	Public administration	
	Public sector	
	Public management	

feel welcome to skip directly to the next section. For others, we have defined a number of relevant terms in Table 13.2. Dickinson and O'Flynn (2016) also provide a helpful and accessible introduction to these key research terms and the distinctions between them, and which provides a useful supplement to Table 13.2.

Table 13.2 Key Terms Defined

Term	Definition
Method	A method is simply the tool used to answer your research questions—how, in short, you will go about collecting your data. If you are choosing between methods, you might say, 'what method should I use?' and settle on one or more methods to answer your research question.
Methodology	A methodology is the rationale for the research approach, and the lens through which the analysis occurs. Said another way, a methodology describes the "general research strategy that outlines the way in which research is to be undertaken" (Howell, 2012, p. 4). The methodology should impact which method(s) for a research endeavour are selected in order to generate the compelling data.
Qualitative	Qualitative Research is a form of research used to gain an understanding of underlying reasons, opinions and motivations. It provides insights into the problem or helps to develop ideas or hypotheses for potential quantitative research. Qualitative Research is also used to uncover trends in thought and opinions, and dive deeper into the problem. Qualitative data collection methods vary using unstructured or semi-structured techniques. Some common methods include focus groups (group discussions), individual interviews and participation/observations.
Quantitative	Quantitative Research is used to quantify the problem by way of generating numerical data or data that can be transformed into usable statistics. It is used to quantify attitudes, opinions, behaviours and other defined variables—and generalise results from a larger sample population. Quantitative Research uses measurable data to formulate facts and uncover patterns in research. Quantitative data collection methods are much more structured than Qualitative data collection methods. Quantitative data collection methods include various forms of surveys—online surveys, paper surveys, mobile surveys and kiosk surveys, face-to-face interviews, telephone interviews, longitudinal studies, website interceptors, online polls and systematic observations.

(Continued)

Table 13.2 (Continued)

Term	Definition
Mixed-method	Mixed-methods research is a methodology for conducting research that involves collecting, analysing and integrating **quantitative** (e.g., experiments, surveys) and **qualitative** (e.g., focus groups, interviews) research. This approach to research is used when this integration provides a better understanding of the research problem than either of each alone. By mixing both quantitative and qualitative research and data, the researcher gains in breadth and depth of understanding and corroboration, while offsetting the weaknesses inherent to using each approach by itself. One of the most advantageous characteristics of conducting mixed-methods research is the possibility of triangulation, i.e. the use of several means (methods, data sources and researchers) to examine the same phenomenon. Triangulation allows one to identify aspects of a phenomenon more accurately by approaching it from different vantage points using different methods and techniques. Successful triangulation requires careful analysis of the type of information provided by each method, including its strengths and weaknesses.

Three Methods Used to Investigate Collaboration

Table 13.3 provides an overview of the finding from our systematic review of methods used in boundary spanning. We found that current research tends to use single-N case studies, social network analysis and other socio-metrics and 'practice as method,' whereby an author provides reflections on boundary-spanning practices. In this section we provide a review of these approaches before suggesting ways that they can be combined and re-analysed in ways that boost their generalisability and usefulness to the field.

Single Case Study Research—Current State and Future Possibilities

Single case studies are a prominent part of the public policy literature broadly, but they especially dominate the examination of wicked policy issues where cross-boundary work is most needed (Macaulay, 2016). Our review of this literature found that these studies often take a qualitative mixed-methods approach. For example, Gasson (2006) used an ethnographic approach that conducted interrupted field observations of the team activities of business process re-design and IT system definition over

Table 13.3 Characteristic Methodologies Employed Across Boundary-Crossing Research

	Approach	Example studies
Single-N case studies, which are often mixed methods	An intensive study about a group of people or a unit, which is aimed to generalise over several units. In a single-N case study the focus is based on a special unit.	(Austin et al., 2012; Carey et al., 2017 Drach-Zahavy, 2011; Dudau et al., 2016; Evans and Scarbrough, 2014; Fleming and Waguespack, 2007; Friedman and Podolny, 1992; Gasson, 2006; Harting et al., 2011; Hunt et al., 2010; Johnson, 2011; Leung, 2013; Guarneros-Meza and Martin, 2016; Sørensen and Waldorff, 2014)
Social network analysis and other socio-metrics	Social network and socio-metrics approaches aim to study the structures of social interactions. With regard to boundary spanning and collaborative activities, social network analysis has sought to understand and make visible flows of information and connections between actors.	(Akoumianakis, 2014; Behrend and Erwee, 2009; Brion et al., 2012; Hinds and Kiesler, 1995; Hoeijmakers et al., 2013; Manev and Stevenson, 2001)
Practice as method	Studies that tend to focus on reflections of the author, or that engage with the insights, reflection and experiences of boundary-crossing practitioners.	(Aungst et al., 2012; Broussine, 2003; Curnin and Owen, 2014; Druskat et al., 2003; Hsiao et al., 2012; Lewis, 2012; Miller, 2008; Wilson-Prangley and Oliver, 2016)

a period of 18 months. The unit of analysis was the local actor-network perpetuated by the process of design. The study observed the trajectory of actions and interactions engaged in by a team of seven organisational managers involved in the co-design of business and IT systems. Here, information systems were seen as a genealogical process that reflects the emergent negotiation of normative definitions and requirements across the boundaries between organisational interest groups.

Other authors also attempt to take a real-time semi-longitudinal approach. Arguably this is an effort to overcome single case study limitations by providing both greater contextual knowledge and by analysing change over time in order to draw out broader learning. Leung (2013), for example, used a qualitative mixed-method approach consisting of semi-structured interviews, conducted twice with each of the five agency directors combined with a semi-ethnographic approach and field notes taken at 16 project steering committee meetings. The first round of interviews was conducted in the first year of the project, in which the interviewees were asked for their reasons and goals in joining the venture. The second was conducted near the end of the period and they were asked to evaluate the success of their alliance and its contributing factors. The steering committee was composed of the five agency directors and it possessed the highest decision-making power in the project. Leung was centrally concerned with individual-level factors, recording interactions among the members, such as their communications and processes of problem-solving and conflict resolution.

Both of these studies reflect an effort to combine methodological approaches that take account of context (i.e. thick description of individuals' practices through ethnographic or semi-ethnographic inquiry). This deeply qualitative approach can also be found in Austin et al. (2012) and Johnson (2011). For example, Austin et al. (2012) used ethnographic life-history interviews to document the career trajectories of senior managers who crossed the public-non-profit boundaries. Using an adaptation competence framework to analyse the cases, this study identified three archetypes of boundary crossers that include client advocates, organisational change agents, and team leaders. Across these archetypes, the boundary crossers all had preconceptions about the other sector, and each came away from the experience with a changed view as well as a new appreciation of their former sector. Arguably this represents an effort to engage in the practices of boundary spanners, while aiming to also make some normative claims about the nature of working across boundaries that can be generalised beyond the single case study. This work provides important and rich contextual information, from which other authors can compare and contrast future work in order to build towards consensus or more refined knowledge of boundary spanning. This is consistent with proponents of case study approaches. Flyvbjerg (2006), for example, has argued for the natural generalisability of case studies. Here, the responsibility of the researcher is to provide as accurate and detailed account of a single case as possible. Drawing lessons and applying them to other cases becomes the responsibility of future researchers (Flyvbjerg, 2006). Hence, individual cases can generate testable hypotheses and elicit some causal claims.

The distinctiveness of case studies as a method of analysis also has the potential to go beyond the qualitative/quantitative divide. Several studies

(Guareneros-Meza and Martin, 2016; Drach-Zahavy, 2011; Hunt et al., 2010) used not just mixed qualitative approaches as the examples described earlier, but also combined qualitative and quantitative methods. For example, Guareneros-Meza and Martin (2016) analysed the role of senior civil servants who work directly with local public service partnerships in the UK using a mixed-methods approach that had both qualitative and quantitative elements. First, the study examined the reasons for the formation of Local Service Boards (LSB) and the decision to allocate Welsh Government Representatives (WGR) to work with them. An in-depth analysis was undertaken of government policy statements and reports and the minutes of regular meetings of WGRs, in which they talked with each other about their roles and the issues emerging from the partnerships with which they were working. Interviews were then conducted with the senior civil service team that was responsible for the LSB policy and for recruiting and supporting WGRs in their work with local partnerships. Next, seven (of the 32) past and present WGRs were interviewed.

The qualitative data guided the development of a structured survey, which asked a series of questions about the activities WGRs should undertake; the activities they had actually engaged in; and the achievements of the LSBs with which they worked. The survey was sent to all 32 past and present WGRs and to 283 members or local public service leaders of the 22 LSBs. Respondents were asked to answer a series of statements on a 7-point Likert scale (from 1 = strongly disagree to 7 = strongly agree with 4 = neither agree nor disagree). They were also invited to add any open comments they wished to make by asking at the end of survey to write any points that clarified the responses from the closed questions. The survey data were analysed through descriptive statistics, and significance tests between the two types of respondents were run. Tests to confirm differences between vertical and horizontal boundary spanning were carried out. Correlations between the actual activities of WGRs and LSB achievements were also calculated. Finally, the qualitative data collected in the initial phase were triangulated with the survey data to help contextualise the impact of the role of WGRs and LSBs' achievements of the most salient partnerships. The study is clearly an example of a rigorous mixed-method study that included both qualitative and quantitative elements. This approach to research is used when this integration provides a better understanding of the research problem than either of each alone. By mixing both quantitative and qualitative research and data, the researcher gains in breadth and depth of understanding and corroboration, while offsetting the weaknesses inherent to using each approach by itself.

Whether qualitative or a combination of qualitative and quantitative approaches were used, these single case studies help establish realist analyses of boundary-spanning attempts or challenges. As we noted in the section earlier on how epistemology shapes and is shaped by our methodological choices, the realist approach is broadly viewed as a middle ground between approaches that focus too much on structure or too much on agency in their accounts of the social world (Pawson, 2006). Simply put, they help us focus on examining what works for whom and under what conditions, recognising that both structure and agency are important by focusing our attention on understanding the concepts of context, mechanism and outcome, and the relationships between them (Macaulay et al., 2011; Pawson, 2006). While each of these have long histories within the social sciences, within a realist approach analysis is geared towards understanding their usefulness and explanatory power within a particular case. Hence, context refers to aspects of background, people and research settings that can moderate action and outcomes. Mechanism refers to the mediating variables in the change process, while outcomes refers to the expected or unexpected intermediary outcomes as well as potentially the final outcomes (Macaulay et al., 2011; Pawson, 2006). In doing so these studies seek to get inside the 'black box' of practice in the context of boundary spanning, helping to elucidate elements of it that are often taken as a given.

There are, as previously noted, drawbacks to the single case approach. Single case studies can be too contextually embedded, providing an account that is rich but ultimately idiosyncratic and hard to draw broader learnings from. Moreover, they tend not to examine case-specific prerequisites for collaboration such as organisational or team design, the type of function of leaders, or the influence of historical success with collaboration. However, as Woolcock (2013, p. 229) notes,

> Upholding the canonical methodological principle that questions should guide methods, not vice versa, is required if a truly rigorous basis for generalizing claims about likely impact across time, groups, contexts and scales of operation is to be discerned for different kinds of development intervention.

Hence, removing a deep appreciation of context will not overcome single case study challenges. Woolcock argues that we need to deploy case studies to better identify the conditions under which diverse outcomes are observed, focusing in particular on the salience of contextual idiosyncrasies, implementation capabilities and trajectories of change.

Overcoming Limitations of Single Case Studies—A Case for Research Synthesis

There are also a range of methodological approaches that can help us aggregate learning from single case study approaches. Many of these have developed out of the field of health and medicine, but are gaining traction in policy studies and public administration more broadly (Carey and Crammond, 2015; van der Heijden and Kuhlmann, 2017)—demonstrating the need to address disciplinary boundaries in boundary research. Bacchi (2009) has argued for the importance of research synthesis for policy and public administration studies as a means to overcoming the limitations of single case analysis. Approaches such as meta-analysis

> provide a forum by which disparate empirical studies can be reduced to a common metric, and so if policy formulation is desired on some topic, issue or problem, what better way to proceed then to show that some 'effect' or direction can be shown to be better than others?
> (Miller and Fredericks, 2008, p. 6)

In short,

> meta-synthesis/analysis is an intentional and coherent approach to analyzing data across qualitative studies. It is a process that enables researchers to identify a specific research question and then search for, select, appraise, summarize, and combine qualitative evidence to address the research question.
> (Erwin et al., 2011, p. 186)

Such approaches help us to establish patterns. While not a basis for establishing causality, these patterns tell us much about what is likely to work in different contexts (Pawson, 2006). It is worth noting that meta-analysis can also be conducted qualitatively; however, this has tended to focus on problems which are analysed solely in quantitative terms which is not found (and arguably is not appropriate) for analysing boundary-spanning practices.

Currently there are no agreed upon methods of qualitative research synthesis, and debate in this area has continued for some time (Dixon-Woods et al., 2005; McDermott et al., 2004). Thematic approaches to meta-analysis seek to uncover concepts and their meanings from the data (rather than pre-determining them), using interpretive approaches to ground the analysis if that data (i.e. existing studies) (Carey and Crammond, 2015). Thematic approaches are useful for hypothesis generation and explanation of particular phenomena; however, they are unable to provide a picture of the context and quality of the individual studies (Dixon-Woods et al., 2005).

Many of the epistemological and methodological debates around qualitative meta-analysis centre on the very thing that makes single case studies useful—the contextual nature of qualitative research. McDermott et al. (2004) argue that "What this means is that we cannot assume that concepts, experiences and practices have homogenous meanings, which stay constant across time and place; different contexts support a variety of meanings" (McDermott et al., 2004, p. 11). This approach, however, is to deny the generalisability of qualitative research (Stake, 2005). While a qualitative case study is a comprehensive examination of a single phenomenon, it can provide 'trustworthy' information about the broader class to which it belongs. To claim that generalisation is not possible is to deny the transferability of any shared meanings or generative mechanisms (McDermott et al., 2004). Moreover, meta-analyses can take a realist approach, consistent with the goals of individual cases found in the boundary-spanning literature. While systematic reviews of experimental studies provide evidence of 'what works,' a realist review method opens a window to analyse how, for whom and in what circumstances does it work (Pawson, 2006). Arguably, this helps to strike a balance between the too specific and the not specific enough challenges of boundary-spanning research. The risks of such approaches are that they can abstract too far from context to provide truly actionable insights; however, a realist approach can help to overcome this.

Social Network Analysis and Other Socio-Metrics

Social network and socio-metric approaches aim to study the structures of social interactions (Berkman, 1977; Cross, 2002). With regard to boundary spanning and collaborative activities, social network analysis has sought to understand and make visible flows of information and connections that might otherwise be left invisible (Cross, 2002). Analysing these, often informal, connections helps to establish how work happens in particular organisational or cross-organisational contexts. Scholars in public administration have argued that social network analysis is an "invaluable tool for systematically assessing and then intervening at critical points within an informal network" (Cross, 2002, p. 26).

While social network analysis has a long history in public policy studies (Lewis, 2005), more specific examples focused on inter-agency collaboration were found in the boundary-spanning literature. For example, Behren and Erwee (2009) use social network analysis to examine how networks support knowledge creation and exchange between teams. The authors identify social network analysis as a method to map information and knowledge flow with individuals in diverse cultures in private and public sector companies in international contexts. Here, social network analysis is able to quantify diverse members' influence, prestige and specific team member-related brokerage roles, while revealing boundary-crossing knowledge sharing activities. Manev and Stevenson (2001) also explore the relationship between boundary-spanning communication and individual influence in a fairly large network with 108 organisational members. A survey was administered that issued background characteristics, followed by a socio-metric instrument that instructed the respondent to list individuals with whom they communicated to get the job done both within and outside the organisation. In doing so, they are able to quantify some of the effects of boundary spanning, finding that boundary spanning correlated with influence regardless of formal organisational hierarchical position.

Other studies used different types of socio-metric methodologies. Akoumianakis (2014), for example, analyses digital trace data compiled through a virtual ethnographic assessment of a cross-organisational tourism alliance. Data comprise electronic traces of online collaboration whose interpretive capacity is augmented using knowledge visualisation techniques capable of revealing dynamic and emergent features of boundary spanning. Using this approach, they were able to establish that boundary spanning in virtual settings requires micro-negotiation across a number of different boundaries, which are often enforced or inscribed into technology and practice. Akoumaianakis argues that these types of data visualisation techniques enable an excavation of different boundaries and assessment of their implications, uncovering critical hidden knowledge that drives boundary-spanning approaches within collaborations. Similarly, Hoeijmakers et al. (2013) used network analysis to understand the interconnectedness of actors from policy, research and practice as part of a broader study on the Academic Collaborative Centre Limburg (a Dutch boundary organisation in the health sector that brings together a range of practitioners). They showed the method is particularly useful in situating the achievements of the ACCL in terms of knowledge transfer and exchange.

There is the potential to expand systems analysis that goes beyond socio-metrics. Across other disciplines there are a range of innovative approaches and metrics already being used to explore networks, which could arguably be widely applied to the boundary-crossing context. Brion et al. (2012), for example, conducted a study on a sample of 73 project leaders in manufacturing firms and assessed the variables of new product development (NPD) outcomes, boundary-spanning activities, network characteristics and controls. The study used a sample of project leaders involved in NPD projects in a variety of industries. An online questionnaire was sent to 782 project leaders listed in two French databases: AFITEP (French Association of Project Management) and Rhône-Alpes Chamber of Commerce. The study used name generators, with respondents being asked to name contacts who played a role in their day-to-day professional activities. Project leaders were required to complete the questionnaire with reference to a completed NPD project. As the authors suggest, using this methodology enabled a new way to an understand how team leaders contribute to project performance, noting that (1) 'obtaining political support' and 'scanning for ideas' are the boundary activities with the greatest impact on performance, (2) project leaders with strong ties in their network are more effective at these activities, (3) project leaders with structural holes in their networks are more effective in another boundary activity. This is just one example, but the possibilities are virtually endless, particularly given the explosion of research on the analysis of networks. There are, of course, ongoing debates within this literature about how to use network methodologies to best understand the practice of boundary crossing, but engaging with these methods remains a key frontier for scholars and practitioners in public policy and management.

The benefits of social network analysis and other socio-metric tools are that they enable us to explore entire networks, rather than single actors within a small sample (as is often the case of qualitative research, where resource constraints limit sample size). They also provide quantitatively assessable insights. However, these approaches tend to not draw on or be embedded in richer qualitative insights. As a result, many analyses are unable to speak to the processes involved in connection between actors— noting instead that the connection merely exists. It is often difficult to assess the quality of these relationships or the flow of information unless a substantive qualitative component is built into the study design. There is significant potential, however, in using these approaches as part of a mixed-method study.

Practice as Method

A third category of studies we have classified as 'practice as method.' Here authors either reflected on their own practice, or of others, in order to provide insight into, and lessons for, boundary-spanning activities and initiatives. These used qualitative or ethnographic methods, or were purely conceptual in their approach. Another distinction of this approach is that authors applying it were most often interested in investigating leadership or capability across cases, rather than trying to understand specific cases of collaboration. These studies tend to be predominantly reflective in nature, rather than engaging in a structured comparison.

Wilson-Prangley and Oliver (2016), for example, explored the views of business leaders who had reached out across sector boundaries to work with government and others to raise and resolve key societal issues. Each of the interviewees emphasised the belief that they were able to be effective boundary spanners because of their individual capacity to be integrative leaders. By encouraging practitioners to reflect on their experiences, the authors attempted to situate these individual successes in the particular contexts and histories of each interviewer. Similarly, driven by a desire to gain a greater depth of understanding about the specific characteristics and influences of boundary-spanning leadership in education partnerships, Miller (2008) undertook a study that used observation and interviews to engage with the perspectives and reflections of boundary-spanning practitioners. They identified that boundary spanners were considered, and considered themselves, institutional infiltrators for community advancement, and that effective boundary spanners often work to establish sustainable boundary-spanning infrastructure within a community that exists beyond them.

Druskat et al. (2003) undertook in-depth critical incident interviews with the external leaders of self-managing work teams and their team members, and interviews and surveys provided by managers, to understand how effective leader behaviours and strategies unfold over time. Content analyses of the data produced a process model showing that effective external leaders move back and forth across boundaries to build relationships, scout necessary information, persuade their teams and outside constituents to support one another and empower their teams to achieve success. Similarly, Aungst et al. (2012) drew on 39 semi-structured interviews with senior emergency management practitioners spanning organisational boundaries, to propose a typology of boundary-spanning activities for emergency management. And, as a final example here, Broussine (2003) presented a range of ideas about boundary spanning that did not stem from a piece of systematic research, as the author himself notes. Instead, the ideas arise from numerous interactions with chief executives and directors in various settings—in one-to-one supervision sessions, informal talks, critical reflection in learning settings. It is a particularly good example of the approach we are referring to as 'practice as method' where the data is collected through regular but *informal* researcher engagements with local authority chief executives over a number of years

While each of these studies applies practice-based methodologies in slightly different ways, at their core is a shared belief that research must be conducted with an ethnographic sensibility to reliably adjudicate truth claims about the world (Shapiro, 2005). These ethnographies tend to proceed from two assumptions: that "the world consists of causal mechanisms that exist independently of our study—or even awareness—of them," and that ethnographic techniques "hold out the best possibility of grasping their true character" (Shapiro, 2005, pp. 8–9). This is consistent with emerging debates in the field, which have emphasised that we need to explore processes and practices of boundary spanning as a type of social and cultural performance, as outlined in Part 1 The Conceptual Challenge (Carey, Dickinson, et al., 2017; Dickinson and Sullivan, 2014). This work argues that boundary spanning and collaboration is a highly contextual set of practices that necessarily vary across contexts, rather than more instrumentalist arguments that often dominate the literature. From this perspective we can better appreciate the values, norms and practices of different actors or groups engaged in boundary spanning and the ways in which we can derive policy value from these differences (Carey, Dickinson, et al., 2017).

While critical for informing practice, these approaches do not solve the questions of generalisability. Without taking the form of a structured comparison, the benefits which we have described in the previous section, have only a limited capacity to show what success looks like, or why, or how the data can be used to inform more effective boundary-spanning practice. Put another way, practice-as-method should be seen as an exploratory methodology that generates research questions or hypotheses that can be used as the foundation for future research.

Further Methodological Advancements

When analysing the methodological approaches used in boundary-spanning research as a whole, comparative analysis is strangely absent and underdeveloped—despite the huge potential for addressing many of the limitations of individual methods and studies and creating more generalisable and actionable knowledge.

There are some notable exceptions to this (Hunt et al., 2010; Lewis, 2012; Levina and Vaast, 2005: Lindsay and Dutton, 2012; Ratcheva, 2009). Lewis (2012), for example, draws on a cross-country comparative study based on field data collected in Bangladesh, the Philippines and England. The qualitative study undertook 20 semi-structured interviews to construct individual means of navigating power, policy and politics within their respective countries. The life history method was endorsed so as to allow individuals to speak from personal experience, allowing work, politics and policy to be investigated. Using this methodology in cross-country settings provided a typology of boundary-spanning archetypes based on motivations and the negotiation of micro-politics of policies. Similarly, Hunt et al. (2010) undertook a comprehensive study across five general practices (GPs) and a Community Mental Health Team (CMHT) in the Northwest of England as part of a process evaluation. Framework analysis was used to manage and interpret this comparative data, which led to conclusions that would not have been possible from within individual cases. Using this methodology, the study was able to verify that cross-group meetings are effective mechanisms for collaboration and coordination, which the authors themselves concede would not have been possible from a single case study design.

Comparative approaches can also be quantitative. Peters et al. (2017), for example, studied the role of network management and trust in the realisation of integrated public health policy and network performance, as well as the relation between integrated public health policy and network performance. In 34 Dutch local policy networks, we measured the perceptions of 278 actors through a Web-based survey and used regression analyses to assess the relations between policy variables. Using this comparative method, the authors established that management and trust were positively related to perceived integration and network performance.

The particular value of comparison in helping us to understand 'what works' in boundary crossing is that it is crucial to understanding causality. As Emma Uprichard and David Bryne (2012, p. 112) suggest:

> we can go beyond the ideographic description of causality in relation to the individual case and do this through processes of systematic comparison of cases of much the same kind. In the language of complexity theory, we can explore the trajectories of ensembles of systems that in crucial respects are near neighbours. To do this, we have to have some systematic process for establishing similarity and difference.

Expanding the horizons of comparative work opens up the possibilities systematic comparison. This could be qualitative. For example, one such method that has received much attention as being particularly suitable for analysing the complexity of reality is Charles Ragin's qualitative comparative analysis (QCA) (Ragin, 2000). The main feature of this case-based method is that it is able to account for the contingency of a social phenomenon. In addition (and not instead of doing so), it allows for an exploration of causal patterns. As such, it is a viable means by which to understand the systemic nature of case studies *and* to identify recurring patterns across such cases. However, there are challenges. Such work is often time consuming and requires access and resources, which are often hard to secure.

When considering comparative work, it is important to think through an effective approach for generating insights. This enables a study to maximise the utility of information from small samples and single cases. Cases are selected on the basis of expectations about their information content. This could involve examining 'extreme' cases, variant cases or critical cases (Flyvbjerg, 2006), for which Flyvbjerg provides concise definitions

- Extreme/deviant cases: to obtain information on unusual cases, which can be especially problematic or especially good in a more closely defined sense
- Maximum variation cases: to obtain information about the significance of various circumstances for case process and outcome; e.g., three to four cases which are very different on one dimension: size, form of organisation, location, budget, etc.
- Critical cases: to achieve information that permits logical deductions of the type, "if this is (not) valid for this case, then it applies to all (no) cases"
- Paradigmatic cases: to develop a metaphor or establish a school for the domain that the case concerns.

While these approaches are well established and seen as non-controversial ways to generate generalisable insights from the process of comparison, we are not suggesting that comparison is a panacea to the complexity of the real world: that is, as Yin (2002, p. 112) notes, any attempt at generalisation as an attempt "to build a general explanation that fits each of the individual cases, even though the cases will vary in their details." This process is always going to involve a certain level of imprecision, and different research designs will always demand different types of comparison. However, as the preceding discussion makes clear, comparison—as a broad and pluralistic form of inquiry—is a valuable tool for researchers and practitioners seeking to understand 'what works' in boundary crossing.

Summary

The aim of this section has been to first explore the epistemological debates and trends within the field, then explore how boundary crossing is being researched at present. The review provides a robust survey of the literature and identified a number of common approaches to understanding boundary crossing, namely practice-based methods, single case studies and socio-metric analyses. We have presented a number of examples of how these different methods are applied, as well as discussing their benefits and drawbacks. Building on this analysis, we have argued that we must further develop new and existing methodological approaches simultaneously to address the generalisation challenge, while maintaining a level of fidelity to the context of particular boundary-spanning initiatives, such as meta-analysis and structured case comparison. The next section extends upon this analysis to show that we also face methodological challenges to the study of policy problems that cross boundaries, which are often referred to as 'complex' or 'wicked.' We suggest that attention must be paid to both of these methodological challenges *in tandem* to develop and apply methodological approaches that will support effective boundary crossing in practice.

14 A Spotlight on Systems Methodologies

Methods to Understand Complex Issues

Luke Craven, Gemma Carey, Helen Dickinson, and Iona Rennie

This chapter discusses methods to help us conceptualise issues, problems and social conditions that themselves cross boundaries and domains. Much of the work in public policy and administration is premised on the idea that the challenges we face are inter-sectoral, but to more effectively utilise boundary-crossing strategies we need methods to understand the *structure* and *form* of wicked and complex problems and how they cross boundaries. Our discussion will focus on new approaches to modelling systems dynamics, group model building and other approaches to building systems understandings from qualitative data. Before this, though, it is important to understand what complexity is, and how it can and should be mobilised to understand the issues that scholars of public policy and management are interested in addressing.

What Is Complexity?

There is considerable variation in the way that complexity theory is described, used and understood and we cannot claim to speak here to all complexity theories. Instead we take our lead from the so-called 'British School' of complexity that seeks to apply the complexity sciences to social scientific research and stems largely from the work of David Byrne (1998) and Paul Cilliers (1998). Taking Bryne and Cilliers as our starting point, we consider key ideas from complexity theory to be interdependence, nonlinearity, emergent features, adaptive agents and open systems.

In this section we first describe each of these features and establish relevance for a understanding policy issues. Although they may seem somewhat self-evident, placing them at the core of the methodological justifications is a fundamental part of any strategy to think of a policy problem as a complex system of causal determinants. It is crucial to note, however, that while these characteristics help with talking about complexity in an abstract way, we also need to develop methods to measure and understand how complexity manifests in everyday life. Second, therefore, this section offers philosophical guidelines to help researchers more effectively engage with complexity in the real world. That is, as Paul Cilliers (1998, p. 13) has suggested, "science without philosophy is blind, and philosophy without science is paralysed"—we need both if complexity is to become successful in social scientific practice.

Five Characteristics of Complex Systems

First, a complex system cannot be explained merely by breaking it down into its component parts because those parts are interdependent: elements interact with each other, share information and combine to produce systemic behaviour. This forces us to be more holistic about the causes and effects of a particular problem. The analytic focus should not be on particular causes but on the 'rules' that govern their interaction at the individual and community level. It is in those interdependencies that we will come to understand problems as systemic and complex. Methodologically, this necessitates researchers attempt to capture information about the logical and causal relationships between different relevant factors helping to identify core points of circularity and feedback.

Second, the behaviour of complex systems exhibits nonlinear dynamics produced by feedback loops in which some forms of energy or action are dampened (negative feedback) while others are amplified (positive feedback). Feedback is a core part of interdependence and makes the outcome of systemic dynamics difficult to predict. As Bob Jervis (1997, p. 125) notes, "feedbacks are central to the way [complex] systems behave. A change in an element or relationship often alters others, which in turn affect the original one." In complex systems, as Byrne (1998) suggests, feedback is about the consequences of nonlinear, random change over time. While in simpler systems, feedback may be linear, predictable and consistent, nonlinearity guarantees that seemingly minor actions can have large effects and large actions can have small effects. It is a precondition for complexity. Charles Perrow's (1984) work illustrates dramatically the implications of interdependence and nonlinearity by distinguishing between accidents that occur in tightly coupled systems and in loosely coupled systems. In tightly coupled systems—like poverty or disadvantage—relatively trivial changes in one element or dimension can spread rapidly and unpredictably through the system and have dramatic and unpredictable effects. The core point here is that the relations that lead to the emergence of particular problems are likely to be nonlinear.

Third, complex systems exhibit emergence, or behaviour that evolves from the interaction between elements in which, as the colloquialism goes, the whole is greater than the sum of its parts, as seen in Figure 14.1. Put another way, in a nonlinear system adding two base elements to one another can induce dramatic new effects reflecting the onset of cooperativity between the constituent elements. This can give rise to unexpected structures and events whose properties can be quite different from those

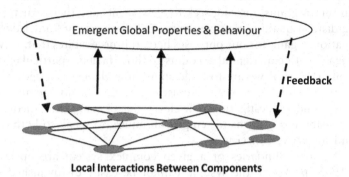

Figure 14.1 Emergence in Complex Systems

base elements (Nicholis, 1995, pp. 1–2). This makes the system difficult to control and, again, focuses our attention on the rules of interaction and the extent to which they are followed. The problematic tendency in the social sciences is to engage with the social world in terms of correlations between variables, which are then evaluated using standard methodological techniques oriented toward the evaluation of the 'net effects' of causal variables. That is, as Charles Ragin (2000, p. 15) has put it, "each causal condition [is] conceived as an analytically distinct variable [that] has an independent impact on the outcome." But if we take interconnectedness and nonlinearity as a given, these practices lose their practical purchase. Net effects are impossible to isolate. The focus, instead, must be to view the components of particular issues as attribute configurations, which can be expressed in set theoretic terms. That is, we must seek to look at particular instances of a problem, the contextual factors at play and the interactions between them as wholes, so that policy issues are seen as a systemic phenomenon, which is seen as an emergent property.

Fourth, in complex systems the behaviour of adaptive agents has a role in shaping the structure of the system. Adaptation here describes a process within which an agent changes to respond to its environment, seeking to gain equilibrium. Complex systems are in dialectic with the agents that operate within them. As Reed and Harvey (1992, p. 370) argue "far-from-equilibrium conditions can originate in the values and actions of humans themselves." Systemic dynamics, then, emerge from the agency of their actors, their collective goals, their conflicts and their negotiations, but the existing structure of the system plays a significant role in conditioning the actors. It is this coevolution that produces change in a system (Mitchell, 2011; Cilliers, 1998). Crucially, though, we must resist the temptation to dissolve agents into their structures or to see structures as the result of agential emergence. Doing so creates, as Donati and Archer (2015) have noted, a theoretical problem of 'central conflation' in which agents and structures are fused so that they become analytically inseparable. We must instead, seek to view agents and their structures as having distinct qualities that can be treated as objects of knowledge and explanation. Again, for our purposes here, this necessitates that we value and engage with experiential accounts of those facing a particular social problem. That is, if we are to understand how elements of agency contribute to systemic outcomes, we must talk to those who operate within the system under investigation. The clear value of complexity theory here is the possibilities it opens for empirical inquiry to speak to both objective and subjective concerns.

Finally, the boundaries of a given complex system are open (Cilliers, 1998, p. 4), as 'the system' cannot be easily distinguished from the broader dynamics in which it is situated, as seen in Figure 14.2. For example, while we could analyse Australia as a complex bounded system, doing so would exclude elements of the international environment that undoubtedly influence Australian outcomes. Similarly, while the experience of food in/security is innately local, the food systems within which individuals operate extend beyond spatial boundaries. The core point here is that where and how we draw or define the boundary of a system is a methodological choice rather than something intrinsic or essential to the system itself (Cilliers, 2000, pp. 27–28). This has implications for understanding any problem as a discrete social phenomenon. If academic engagements with a particular problem always involve boundary judgements, we need to more deeply interrogate the benefits and limitations of particular framing practices.

The concepts outlined here illustrate a range of ideas and perspectives, many of which are closely related to each other. How these concepts and categories are defined is contentious. As Mitchell (2011, p. 95) notes, "there is not yet a single science of complexity but rather several different sciences of complexity with different notions of what complexity means. Some of these notions are formal, and some are still very informal." We should view therefore the idea of complexity as a 'sensitising concept'

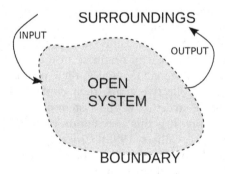

Figure 14.2 Boundaries in Complex Systems

(Blumer, 1954) that can provide some initial direction in understanding how to evaluate complex social phenomena. Others have begun to apply these foundations to the areas of public policy and management. French and Lowe (2018), for example, have recently argued that there are four aspects of complexity which such policy problems present:

- Compositional complexity, which results from the interdependence and interdeterminance of causal factors leading to the creation of outcomes
- Dynamic complexity, which results from the coevolution of interacting factors and the instability inherent to complex systems
- Experiential complexity, which results from the variation in how outcomes are experienced by individuals, and the multiplicity of pathways to shared outcomes across the population
- Governance complexity, which results from the autonomy of public service organisations and other agents, increased by the fragmentation of modern public service landscapes

Similarly, Alford and Head (2017) have recently argued that many accounts of wicked problems tend to totalise the level or degree or complexity present in particular situations, often levelling the argument that policy or policy makers are unable to make sense of or respond to the resulting 'mess.' They argued for a more nuanced analysis, where complex problems vary in the extent of their wickedness, via such dimensions as their cognitive complexity or the diversity and irreconcilability of the actors or institutions involved, which results in the following typology (Figure 14.3).

The two-dimensional matrix they present is oriented around two particular elements of wicked situations: the problem and the actors involved. Alford and Head (2017, p. 405) refer to this first dimension as 'structural complexity' and note that this is

> basically about complexities in the technical aspects of the situation— i.e. the relative tractability of the objective conditions, rather than complexities to do with the stakeholders (who are considered within the horizontal (stakeholder) dimension of [the matrix]). The focus here concerns the *inherent structure* of the problem, that is, the extent to which problem clarity allows for effective interventions, without simply generating other problems.

This definition of structural complexity is clearly an amalgamation of French and Lowe's first three aspects of complexity, those being compositional, dynamic and experiential. The key point here is that problems *themselves* are complex. However, as the earlier section makes clear, much of the work on boundary spanning in public policy and

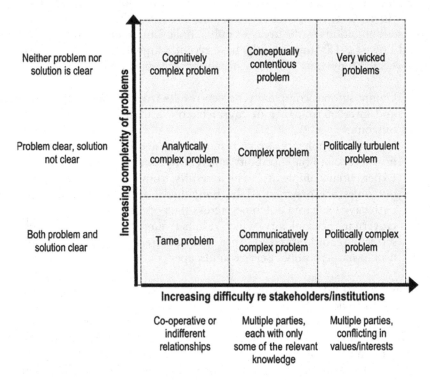

Figure 14.3 A Typology of Wicked Problems (from Alford and Head, 2017)

administration is focused on the governance (on French and Lowe's definition) or stakeholder (on Alford and Head) dimensions. As this discussion makes clear, though, it is crucial to bring these dimensions together.
In order to effectively utilise boundary-crossing strategies, we first need
methods to understand the *how* of wickedness and complexity, how it is
composed, how it is experienced and how it shifts over time.

Our argument, then, is that the concepts offered by complexity theory
aid understanding of social problems by situating their dynamics as a
complex system of causal determinants. That is, if the emergence particular problems is a complex process, this must be reflected in the ways that
process is operationalised and measured and of interest to researchers
and practitioners in the areas of public policy and management.

Toward a Theory of Modelling Complexity

The question at hand, then, is how we can effectively deploy these concepts in social scientific practice. It is prudent to consider some of the
general challenges for using complexity theory to model the social world

and problems within it. Two are particularly relevant for the discussion here: (1) any description of complexity is a reduction of that complexity, and (2) comparing systems is key if our objective is to understand the structure of their internal dynamics. We consider each of these in turn.

The first of these, which we term the 'problem of perspective,' relates to the fact that any attempt to understand a complex system is a reduction of that system from a particular perspective (Cilliers, 2000, 2002). In order to function as a model, all system descriptions necessarily reduce the system and its dynamics, and a limited number of characteristics of the system can be taken into account by any specific description. These descriptions also, by necessity, draw arbitrary boundaries around a set of open systemic dynamics that exclude important environmental factors from consideration (Byrne, 2005; Cilliers, 2005). The result of these challenges is that more than one description of a complex system is possible, as different descriptions decompose the same system in different ways. Paul Cilliers (2005, p. 258) puts it well when he notes:

> Since different descriptions of a complex system decompose the system in different ways, the knowledge gained by any description is always relative to the perspective from which the description was made. This does not imply that any description is as good as any other. It is merely the result of the fact that only a limited number of characteristics of the system can be taken into account by any specific description.

What does this mean for how one might come to understand the complex system of causal determinants from which a problem emerges? As Cilliers and others have noted, the problem of perspective does not mean that no objective knowledge of a complex system is possible, but that all knowledge about complex phenomena is local, a product of the conditions in which complexity arose and in which it was understood (Byrne, 2005, p. 98). The result is that we have to think critically about methods that might speak to and across these different knowledges. As Donna Haraway (1988, p. 584) suggests, "the alternative to relativism is partial, locatable, critical knowledges," which should embolden the political and epistemic project of building "webs of connections" between and across them. Actionable understandings are not possible without connectivity.

The implication here is that we need to develop concrete methodological strategies to connect the plurality of partial and incomplete experiences of, and reflections on, systems. Different system descriptions, though, are not the only barrier to a more connected understanding. The boundary between a particular system model and the broader environment is also a product of how it is deconstructed (Cilliers, 2001). The result is a messy one in which systemic understandings will be varied and inconsistent. If our intention is to speak to individual system-experiences of a problem whilst developing tools to assist the design of interventions at the community level, individuals' system models must be put in conversation. That is, as Haraway (1988, p. 593) suggests, accounts of the " 'real' world do not depend on a logic of 'discovery' but on a power-charged social relation of 'conversation." We must therefore engender conversations between different individuals, their models, perspectives and knowledges, recognising that these conversations are about the identification of similarity and difference.

Relatedly, then, the second key implication of thinking of instances of a problem as a complex system of causal determinants is that those systems are best understood through comparison. Indeed, as Paul Cilliers (2010, p. 8) put it, we cannot understand complex systems "without the making of profuse distinctions." This is not an entirely new insight. In the social sciences sans complexity comparison has long been a methodological strategy to explore causal relationships. As prominent sociologist Robert Morison McIvor noted in his 1942 book Social Causation, the search for causes is always directed to the differences between things, as "underneath all of our questioning lies the implicit acceptance of the axiom that no difference exists without a cause" (McIvor, 1942, pp. 27–28).

The characteristics of complexity explored previously further confirm that comparison is necessary to establish causation in systemic analyses of a given problem. Within a complex system, the factors that contribute to a given outcome are conjunctural and multiple—they exist as attribute configurations that are greater than the sum of their parts (Byrne, 2013; Byrne and Uprichard, 2012). Across individual determinant systems, attribute configurations that contribute to the same outcome—a policy problem—differ based on the particular nonlinear and emergent dynamics present. This function of complex systems is known as equifinality where "factors in different systems combine in different and sometimes contradictory ways to produce the same outcome, revealing different causal pathways" (Ragin, 2000, p. 102; George and Bennett, 2005, pp. 25–27).

If we concede that causation is the result of attribute configurations, it becomes very difficult to deconstruct their nonlinear and emergent interactions within a single case. Comparison, in contrast, helps identify the internal relations between and across systems that produce particular outcomes. This is not to suggest that comparison is a panacea. Our systemic comparisons must engage methodically across different models to identify the impact of particular attribute configurations on the dynamics that emerge from their interactions. As David Bryne and Emma Uprichard (2012, p. 112) put it:

> we can go beyond the ideographic description of causality in relation to the individual case and do this through processes of systematic comparison of cases of much the same kind. In the language of

complexity theory, we can explore the trajectories of ensembles of systems that in crucial respects are near neighbors. To do this, we have to have some systematic process for establishing similarity and difference.

There are, of course, various methodological strategies that could assist in the identification of similarity and difference across complex systems both within and across cases, a selection of which we explore later. Whatever form they take, the implication here is that they must focus on how different attribute configurations produce a particular outcome for particular individuals or communities.

Additionally, mixing methods within particular studies of a given problem is crucial if a researcher is to attend to and be receptive toward different perspectives and knowledges. That is, whatever methods of engagement a researcher uses to engage individual systemic perspectives in practice, they should be multiple. This could include, for example, combining interviews, focus groups, participatory mapping exercises, graph theoretical analysis and quasi-deliberative workshops. In empirical political science, mixing methods is traditionally advocated as a way to triangulate or confirm particular conclusions using various data points (King et al., 1994; Yin, 2002). In contrast, the role of mixing methods to understand complex phenomena is a response to the partiality of knowledge, which entails recognition that many of these differences between 'data points' will be difficult to resolve.

The comparative value of mixing methods, though, goes beyond collecting different types of data and triangulation, to include collecting the same type of data in different ways; or, taking a different route to the resolution of the same question. If knowledge is partial, then the way individuals are able to express certain perspectives is limited by the method of elicitation. There may be many insights or perspectives, for example, which simply cannot be accessed through traditional modes of qualitative research, such as the interview or focus group. Systemic inquiry must therefore be comparative, mixing methods that have the potential to draw out different perspectives from within particular participant-collaborators. Doing so enables a process that can more readily engage with the wholeness of individual experiences in context. The various methods we present help achieve this in light of complexity.

The above notwithstanding, there is no doubt that complexity remains a contentious theoretical concept in the modern academy. Its uses (and abuses) are most often metaphorical, rather than shaping the actual tools of academic research (Geyer and Cairney, 2015; Byrne and Callaghan, 2014). Many still claim that an interconnected, nonlinear and emergent world is 'too complex' to understand with methodological strategies we have at our disposal (Geyer and Cairney, 2015; Byrne and Callaghan, 2014). Similarly, various commentators have argued that the reductionism necessary to methodologically engage with complexity is a hopeless and internally conflicted exercise (see, in particular, Luhmann, 1995). As Law and Mol (2002, p. 6) put it, however, "the endless mobilisation of the single [critical] trope in which simplification figures as a reduction of complexity, leaves a great deal to discover." Their core point is that we need to find new ways of relating to the complexity of the social world. That is, there is little point in describing problems as complex systems if these attempts are simply denounced as over-simplifications. The tendency in the academy is to reject simplification or to embrace complexity's scholarly impossibilities as though the poles of this dichotomy exhaust the possibilities. Instead, the focus should be theories and methods that attempt to more effectively speak to the experiences of complexity in everyday life, but that embrace epistemic humility in doing so. Put simply, responding to the complex as complex becomes possible by acknowledging the limits of our explanatory and normative academic practices.

In sum, as Byrne (1998, p. 7) puts it, "the point about complexity is that it is useful—it helps us to understand the things we are trying to understand." In particular, complexity theory helps us understand the dynamic relations between the social and material determinants of a given policy problem and the ways they are embedded in and interact with individual contexts.

We suggest that following methods sufficiently achieve this bar, and should be more widely adopted by the public policy and management community, as they engage both with eliciting different perspective on systems *and* exploring them through different means of comparison:

1. Using mental models to understand mental models
2. Generating systems maps from qualitative data
3. Group model building exercises

We discuss each in turn.

Using Mental Models to Understand System Dynamics

Mental models are a representation of how individuals structure and organise concepts cognitively, revealing understandings of dynamic and interconnected elements of the world around them (Jones et al., 2011; Checkland, 2000, 2006). They are based on a person's knowledge, experience, values, beliefs and aspirations, explaining how they reason, make decisions, behave and selectively filter and interpret information (Easterby-Smith, 1980). Mental models are functional but incomplete representations of 'reality' that are context-dependent and change over time through learning (Jones et al., 2011; Pearson and Moon, 2014).

Unlike existing methodological approaches that emphasise linear associations, mental model frameworks are well suited to capturing the *complexity* of particular phenomena to understand the interrelation of factors that produce certain outcomes, and the ways in which they are characterised by nonlinearity, emergence and dynamic feedbacks (see also Luke and Stamatakis, 2012). In addition, most members of the public have a perceptive bias toward linear causality, which presents a problem for theorising the social world in and for systems (Sterman, 1994). New research has shown, however, that having people engage in mental model exercises that focus on systemic phenomena heightens their ability to engage in 'systems thinking' (Thibodeau et al., 2016). Mental modelling, therefore, is able to engage people in understanding issues as systemic and complex, and presents a useful tool for researchers and practitioners in public policy and management that are interested in acting on wicked or complex problems.

These mental models can be elicited in a variety of ways, but most are grounded on the epistemological assumption that individuals see and understand the world in terms of systems given the opportunity. Many practitioners use a variation of soft systems methodology (Checkland, 2000, 2006) to elicit these models, in which a device known as a 'rich picture' is used to capture different perspectives on a given system. A rich picture a freehand representation (map) of whatever an individual regards as the most salient features of the system at hand. Rich pictures are generally regarded as "a better medium than linear prose for expressing relationships" and can be taken in as a whole and help to encourage holistic—and complex—rather than reductionist thinking about a situation (Checkland, 2000, p. S22).

The challenge, however, is using these individual mental models or rich pictures to generate actionable insights about the structure and form of particular problems. There are a number of ways that these models can be analysed, at both the individual and group level. At the individual level, Lavin et al. (2018) show that while modelling approaches can support policy coherence by helping to understand a problem from multiple perspectives, we need methods to identify agreement among individuals. This may be achieved through intensive qualitative methods such as interviews, or by automatically comparing models. Current comparisons are limited as they either assess whether individuals think of the same factors, or see the same causal connections between factors. Systems science suggests that, to test whether individuals really share a paradigm, we should mobilise their entire models. Lavin et al. (2018) suggest that an effective way to do this is to use metrics of network centrality—which identifies the factors that *interact most* with other factors in the system—to understand similarities between mental models. They performed experiments on mental models from 264 participants in the context of fishery management. Their results suggest that if stakeholder groups agree on the central factors, they also tend to agree on simulation outcomes and thus share a paradigm. McGlashan et al. (2016) have similarly used the application of network analytic methods as a new way to gain quantitative insight into the structure of mental models to inform intervention design. While their study focused on analysing one specific model, they note explicitly that these analytic methods provide means to contrast and compare multiple mental models of a given complex problem. As the discussion in the previous section suggestions, building these methods of *comparison* are crucial if we are to build actionable understandings of these wicked policy problems.

At the group or aggregate level, network analysis tools can be used on adjacency matrices of individual, team or shared models to identify similarities between individuals in the content and structure of their mental models (e.g. Craven, 2017; Jones et al., 2011). Network analysis methods are useful for examining team and shared models, presenting an opportunity for researchers to identify dominant structural components of the system across participants to explore the complexity and heterogeneity of individual models. Measures include path length (average distance between variables), measures of centrality, maximum distance between variables and the total number of connections (see Pearson and Moon, 2014; Craven, 2017). One example of this approach is the System Effects methodology, developed by Craven (2017) which we explore in further detail in Box 14.1.

Box 14.1 'System Effects' Mapping as a Tool for Intervention Design

System Effects is a methodology developed by Craven (2017) to explore the 'user' or citizen experience of complex forms of disadvantage, such as poor health, malnutrition and other health inequities. The methodology emphasises the heterogeneous nature of disadvantage and its determinants, while at the same time giving policy makers tools to understand the complex nature of how disadvantage manifests at the community or population level. System Effects can be used to support the design, implementation and evaluation of interventions aimed at promoting health and well-being in disadvantaged communities.

1. Theory

    System Effects draws on soft systems methodology, fuzzy cognitive mapping and graph theoretical analysis. Its objective is to *aggregate* and *quantify* participant-generated system models of a given problem (e.g. poor health or malnutrition) and its determinants to inform intervention design.

2. Method

    The participant-led approach begins by asking research participants to visually map or depict the range of variables they perceive to be causes of the problem at hand, drawing arrows between the variables to indicate causality. Participants identify whatever they perceive to be relevant, and the researcher codes variables for consistency across the sample in the analysis stage.

3. Analysis

Once completed, the researcher creates an adjacency matrix for each participant response, using a coding scheme to ensure variable consistency across the sample. The foundation of this method is that individual participant maps represent network diagrams, with the barriers between them acting as 'nodes' and the connections between them as 'edges' or links. As an example, a truncated participant map from Craven's work understanding the primary determinants of food insecurity:

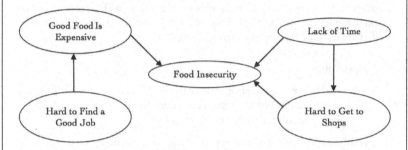

Will result in the matrix below:

	Food Insecurity	Lack of Time	Hard to Get to Shops	Good Food is Expensive	Hard to Find Job
Food Insecurity	0	0	0	0	0
Lack of Time	1	0	1	0	0
Hard to Get to Shops	1	0	0	0	0
Good Food is Expensive	1	0	0	0	0
Hard to Find Job	0	0	0	1	0

Next, these individual adjacency matrices are aggregated into one matrix that brings together individual perceptions. The aggregate weight of connections between variables depends on the frequency with which that connection is identified across the sample. Aggregating individual mental models in this way accounts for every variable identified across the sample, and the diverse range of causal pathways present, as well as making clear the intensity and frequency of particular connections at the community or population level.

Next, this aggregate adjacency matrix can be used to create a directed network graph, where the nodes represent barriers to food access and each connection represents the number of participants identifying particular links between them. This is done using a force-directed layout algorithm in the network mapping software *Gephi*.

Finally, these aggregate models can then be explored using graphic theoretical analysis to identify key structural components of the system. Unlike many analytical approaches that emphasise linear associations, System Effects emphasises the complexity and heterogeneity of participant responses. These statistics provide a way to 'navigate' the complexity of a given problem and its determinants in aggregate at the community or population level, providing evidence to assist in the design, implementation and evaluation of interventions to address it.

4. Application

    The methods present opportunities to identify key structural features of systemic problems across communities, providing insights into their structure as complex systems.

The results can be used to inform policy and programme:

*   **Design:** How can policies most effectively address *systemic* and *complex* determinants of disadvantage, given its heterogeneous nature?
*   **Implementation:** How can the implementation of policies be effectively tailored to the systemic dynamics of particular contexts?
*   **Evaluation:** How can we assess the systemic impact of particular interventions and their interactions with the contexts in which they are deployed?

The System Effects approach can be adapted to help answer each of these questions providing a range of tools to assist policy makers in promoting systems change in disadvantaged communities.

As mentioned in Box 14.1, one of the methodological foundations of Craven's (2017) System Effects methodology is known as fuzzy cognitive mapping (Özesmi and Özesmi, 2003, 2004; Fairweather, 2010; Christen et al., 2015). A fuzzy cognitive map is much like a mental model, but has a mathematical structure that helps explore the strength of particular connections in a mental model. The approach stems from seminal work by Axelrod (1976) that showed that fuzzy logic could be used as a formal way of representing social scientific knowledge and modelling decision making in social and political systems. Fuzzy cognitive maps, much like other mental models, are visual devices in which the relations between the elements (e.g. concepts, events, project resources) of a 'mental landscape' can be used to compute the 'strength of impact' of these elements. The particular power of fuzzy cognitive maps is that their mathematical structure enables them to be used for modelling and simulation, to ask questions about the likely impact of changing the structure or form of different parts of the system. The use of this part of fuzzy cognitive mapping is widespread in disciplines such as ecological economics and systems engineering (Özesmi and Özesmi, 2003, 2004; Fairweather, 2010; Christen et al., 2015), but its use by public policy and management scholars and practitioners has been limited. We suggest that it is time that we begin to dabble, as using mental models to explore systems dynamics is a powerful way to understand the structure and form of particular problems.

That said, there are of course limitations to these approaches. Worth emphasising, in particular, is that as Wood et al. (2012) note, an important distinction exists between the structure of individual mental models 'on the page' and the how people use those models in practice to make decisions and navigate the world around them. The structure on its own, however, does not tell us explicitly how people will behave or necessarily how their model matches with 'reality,' but it can provide important context for motivations and behaviours. As we suggested in the previous section, no method alone will be sufficient to understand a complex problem, but using different methods or mixing methodologies within the same study will reveal different elements of how it manifests in practice. If we are wary of and accept these limitations, there is scope to use them more widely, in combination with more traditional approaches, to understand those issues that cross boundaries.

Generating Systems Maps from Qualitative Data

While system maps have most commonly been elicited from individuals in a visual form, as fuzzy cognitive maps or soft systems maps, researchers have begun to explore how to generate system maps from other forms of qualitative data. Doing so presents an opportunity to engage with existing data, whether interviews, focus groups or documentary analysis, to understand the relationships and interactions present.

Understanding the systemic dynamics present in qualitative data is important for a range of reasons. As Craven (2017) has shown, most qualitative research tends to be premised on a tabular understanding of the world, which establishes boundaries between different factors, causes or variables. That is, while many studies mention or attempt to engage with complexity, it tends to be applied as a loose metaphor—a complexity gloss—that adopts the language but not the fundamental logic of principles of the complexity sciences, such as interconnectedness or emergence.

For example, in research on food security and food access, it is common to suggest that outcomes are determined by a system that is a "complex mix of factors" (Friel and Ford, 2015, p. 437) that is then followed by a presentation of those factors that is tantamount to listing (see, in particular, Lang et al., 2009; Friel and Ford, 2015; Pettygrove and Ghose, 2016). While authors that fall into this *listing trap* often acknowledge that their view is based on a systemic or complex perspective, the structure of their presentation works against this imperative, as it underemphasises the interconnected and interactive nature of the factors presented. The challenge here is that most traditional approaches to analysing qualitative data are not well suited to understanding systems, and themselves work to establish boundaries between different parts of the systems with which we are trying to grapple.

A range of researchers have begun, however, to develop new approaches to generating systems models from qualitative data. Kim and Andersen (2012) and Spicer (2015), for example, have presented innovative ways to building causal diagrams from purposive text data. Purposive text data arise from a discussion involving key stakeholders in the system under study and are particularly focused on the systemic dynamics of the problem at hand. As a result, focus group or interview data frequently depict causally and dynamically rich discussions. Both approaches use a causal coding approach, which utilises Grounded Theory (Corbin and Strauss, 2008) to identify problems, key variables and their structural relationships in the transcripts of focus group discussions.

The process operates as follows. First, transcripts from interviews or focus groups are open coded to reveal different parts of the data (key variables and the relationships between them). An example of a coding chart from Craven's (2017) work on food access in migrant communities is presented in Table 14.1, where the data is broken down into small segments that contain the different components of causal arguments made by participants in focus group conversations. During the open coding process, a chart similar to Table 14.1 is created for every argument in the dataset that reveals mental models of the system.

Each of the tables is likely to contain multiple columns summarising the different relationships identified for a given context. As a result, the coding process generates a significant number of coding charts, which then require analysis. In the second stage of this process, therefore, the researcher must axially code these open codes to reveal patterns in the data that identify common causal relationships. The purpose of this variation on axial coding is to merge the open-coded variables and causal

Table 14.1 A Truncated Example of One Coding Chart (process adapted from Spicer, 2015)

Chart# Focus group		27	CIN CONTEXT	F02-065 to F02-231 Answering questions about diet quality			
Source			F02-064; F02-200	F02-075	F02-064; F02-166	F02-170	F02-229
Causal Structure	Cause var		Bad food environment	Children like junk	Bad food environment	Unhealthy food=cheap	Unhealthy food=cheap
	Effect var		Diet quality	Junk is an easy option	Children like junk	Diet quality	Unhealthy food=easy
	Relationship		Causal negative	Causal positive	Causal positive	Causal negative	Causal positive
Var behaviour	Cause var		lots of junk food here	N/A	advertising; surplus	it's all we can afford	saving money
	Effect var		so we eat it	pester power	gets in their heads	N/A	just makes sense

Notes:

Explanatory notes, adapted from Spicer (2015)

1. Each paragraph in the focus groups has a CIN (conversation identification number) in the form of FX-YYY where X is the number assigned to the focus group and YYY is the paragraph of the focus group transcript. Paragraphs are grouped thematically in the process of coding.

2. The coding chart contains the following information:

   a. Chart#: each chart contains codes with a common context.

   b. CIN: all CINs from which the chart is generated (can be a range).

   c. Context: normally the question being responded to at a particular moment in the focus group discussion.

   d. Source: the exact CIN(s) identifying the source of the text for the code.

   e. Cause variable: if a relationship is identified between two variables, the name of the cause variable occupies this space (otherwise insert 'N/A').

   f. Effect variable: the name of the effect variable or the data variable (in cases where there is no cause variable) occupies this space.

(Continued)

Table 14.1 (Continued)

g. Relationship: if there is a causal relationship between the two variables, then this space is either Causal Positive or Causal Negative. Other relationships include: 'Type of' (identifying a category for a variable), 'Equivalent' (identifying relationship) and 'N/A' for standalone variables.

h. Var behaviour for cause variable: if any behaviour of the cause variable has been identified, then it is entered here.

i. Var behaviour for effect variable: if any behaviour of the effect or data variable has been identified, then it is entered here.

3. In addition, special characteristics of the codes are represented by background colour:

a. Grey: for straightforward causal codes and reference modes or data identified.

b. Green: for identifying or categorical relationships between variables ('Type of,' 'Equivalent').

c. Blue: for codes identified as *implicit* in the data, where, for example (1) a participant does not explicitly state the relationship between two variables, but it can be assumed to be present based on the explanation provided by interviewee, or (2) in some cases, the relationship is omitted from the participant's explanation because of how obvious the relationship is.

d. Red: for codes that arise from major assumptions by the coder, where, for example, (1) the participant's explanation was unclear and incomplete, or (2) a major leap in logic had to be taken by the coder to fill a gap.

relationships where possible, for the purposes of more easily building causal loop diagrams. A resulting table of this part of the process is presented in Table 14.2. Methods for eliciting word-and-arrow diagrams directly from qualitative data have been developed by early cognitive mapping works such as Axelrod (1976). Axelrod's cognitive mapping derives structural relationships among a set of causal assertions made by an individual or a group. Each concept is represented by a word or a phrase, and the relationships between concepts are specified with an arrow with either positive or negative polarity to show the nature of the causal relationship.

Finally, these causal relationship tables are transferred into the causal mapping software *Vensim* (see the example in Figure 14.4). The numbers in Table 14.1 and Figure 14.4 show how each causal link in Table 14.1 is represented in the combined map. For every coding chart generated in the previous stage of the coding process, a diagram similar to Figure 14.4 can be produced.

The key point is that some parts of system are simply better suited to visual depiction than verbal elicitation and vice versa. Coding qualitative data in this way to generate system maps offers researchers a different *perspective* on the structure of a given problem as complex. Crucially, it offers additional tools to pinpoint relationships and points of intervention that would otherwise remain unseen. And there are a range of ways to use and analyse the resulting system maps. It would be possible, for example, to ask service providers and policy makers questions how and where on the systems map to which they respond is the problem different. What dynamics do they know have the most influence? Which do they fund programmes to target? For which do they measure outcomes? Understanding the answers to these questions would offer a new form of data on how we work to influence systems change. The resulting diagrams can also be used to run simulations much like as we suggested in the previous section about fuzzy cognitive maps or analysed using a range of network measures to gain quantitative insight into the structure of the system to inform intervention design.

Group Model Building

The final approach worth briefly mentioning here is group model building. While it shares a number of key similarities with the previous two methodological approaches, namely that it seeks to understand system dynamics through visualisation, it also exhibits some key differences. As Vennix (1999) notes, group model building is a system dynamics model building process in a particular group that is deeply involved in an issue which comes together *as a group* to produce the model. The problem that is modelled can be reasonably well defined, but it can also take the form of an ill-defined or wicked problem, i.e. situations in which group,

Table 14.2 Axially Coded Causal Arguments From Chart 2 (process adapted from Kim and Andersen, 2012)

Cause	Effect	+/-	Word-and-arrow diagrams	#
Children's desire for unhealthy food	Belief that unhealthy food is easy	+	Children want unhealthy food → (+) Unhealthy food = cheap	1
Belief that unhealthy food is easy	Children's desire for unhealthy food is easy	+	Unhealthy food = cheap → (+) Children want unhealthy food	2
Belief that unhealthy food is cost effective	Belief that unhealthy food is easy	+	Unhealthy food = cheap → (+) Unhealthy food = easy	3
Belief that unhealthy food is easy	Diet quality	−	Unhealthy food = easy → (−) Unhealthy food = easy	4
Belief that unhealthy food is cost effective	Diet quality	−	Unhealthy food = cheap → Diet quality	5
Availability of the unhealthy food in immediate environment	Children's desire for unhealthy food	+	Unhealthy food available → Children want unhealthy food	6
Availability of unhealthy food in the immediate environment	Diet quality	−	Unhealthy food available → Diet quality	7

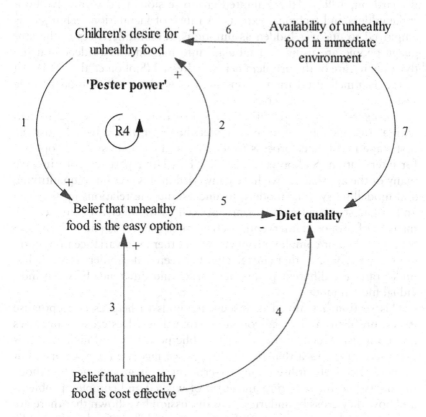

Figure 14.4 Connecting the Axially Coded Components Into a Resulting System Map

community or team opinions differ considerably (see also Rouwette et al., 2002). As we explored in the previous section, this wickedness and experiential complexity takes a number of different forms, many of which would be amenable to exploration using a group model building exercise. As Vennix (1999, p. 391) suggests, group model building is

> a process in which team members exchange their perceptions of a problem and explore questions such as: what exactly is the problem we face? How did the problematic situation originate? What might be its underlying causes? How can the problem be tackled?

In general, facilitated process is used much like those explored by Flynn et al. in the Craft Part, involving several scripted group exercises to develop a visual depiction of a problem of interest that can be used to guide policy and practice (Hovmand et al., 2012; Andersen and

Richardson, 1997). The facilitated group sessions tend to involve both stakeholders and technical experts. A range of facilitation techniques is employed to uncover hidden assumptions, reveal differences in the language people are using and tabulate information and evidence on the dynamic nature of the problem being addressed (Siokou et al., 2014). All of this is aimed at creating a consensus view about which model of the system of interest can be constructed.

The exercise can end with the construction of a causal loop map such as the ones shown in this chapter; however, this is usually just the first stage in a longer process to identify and evaluate systemic options for intervention (Siokou et al., 2014). This latter part tends to involve many of the approaches we have canvassed in this section to quantifying and modelling systems models, to understand the relationship between and amongst the system elements, as well as the likely systemic consequences of proposed interventions. The methodology is particularly useful for wicked or complex problems where there is a variance in opinion amongst a group, so that engagement between stakeholders is needed to understand the different points of overlap and difference between individual mental models

This section has aimed to discuss methods to help us conceptualise issues, problems and social conditions that themselves cross boundaries and domains. Much of the work in public policy and administration is premised on the idea that the challenges we face are inter-sectoral, but to more effectively utilise boundary-crossing strategies we need methods to understand the *structure* and *form* of wicked and complex problems and how they cross boundaries. This discussion has shown that there are a number of generative approaches, currently underutilised in the public policy and management community that deserve wider application.

Conclusion

Our overall aim here has been to argue that methodology is not a solely a technical decision. The methodological choices that researchers and practitioners in public policy in management make have a marked influence on what they are able to comprehend about the social world, the boundaries that are most evident to them, and which come to be seen as important. Most notably, as we have showed throughout this Part, different methodologies construct the same boundaries in different ways. That is, the way we come to understand a given boundary—using different practices of data collection, analysis and dissemination—cause that boundary to become real. This point might seem counterintuitive, but a raft of scholarship has shown that data never merely represents an objective reality, but rather intervenes in nature to create such a reality (Coopmans et al., 2013; Lynch and Woolgar, 1990), privileging particular ways of seeing and interacting with the world (Haraway, 1997). As such, the notion that a particular boundary exists absent our engagement with it is a false one. Instead, boundaries are actively created and enacted by researchers and practitioners in specific, situated ways, which are intertwined with the methodologies they use.

The key point here is that while the public policy and management community undoubtedly give a disproportionate amount of attention to particular types of boundaries, this does not have to be a given. Our effort here has been to show how new approaches to understanding boundaries and boundary crossing are possible by taking stock of the disparate and multi-disciplinary literature on these and related issues. Our systematic review of the literature that sought to understand boundary crossing showed that a range of strategies are available that can help researchers and scholars produce generalisable insights, while also being responsive to the richness and context contained in individual cases. Similarly, the overview we provided of complexity theory, how it relates to theories of governance and 'wicked problems,' and how it can be operationalised in practice emphasises that there is a value remaining in seeking out new methodologies and approaches to generating knowledge in order to more effectively examine and progress boundary problems. Being committed to the development of new methodologies, and staying critical of the boundaries between them, will help scholars and practitioners remain engaged with these many complexities.

References

Akoumianakis, D. (2014). Boundary spanning tactics and 'traceable' connections in cross-organizational virtual alliances: A case study. *Journal of Enterprise Information Management*, 27(2), 197–227.

Alford, J., & Head, B. W. (2017). Wicked and less wicked problems: A typology and a contingency framework. *Policy and Society*, 36(3), 397–413.

Andersen, D. F., & Richardson, G. P. (1997). Scripts for group model building. *System Dynamics Review*, 13(2), 107–129.

Aungst, H. et al. (2012). Boundary spanning and health: Invitation to a learning community. *London Journal of Primary Care*, 4(2), 109–115. DOI:10.1080/1 7571472.2012.11493346

Austin, M. J., Dal Santo, T., & Lewis, D. (2012). Boundary-crossing careers of senior human service administrators: A cross-case analysis. *Administration in Social Work*, 36, 109–132.

Axelrod, R. (1976). *Structure of the Decision: The Cognitive Maps of Political Elites*. Princeton, NJ: Princeton University Press.

Bacchi, C. (2009). *Analysing Policy*. Sydney, Australia: Pearson Higher Education AU.

Behren, F. D., & Erwee, R. (2009). Mapping knowledge flows in virtual teams with SNA. *Journal of Knowledge Management*, 13(4), 99–114.

Berkman, L. (1977). *Social Networks and Health*. Berkley: University of Berkeley.

Blaikie, N. (1993). *Approaches to Social Enquiry*. Cambridge: Polity Press.

Blumer, H. (1954). What is wrong with social theory? *American Sociological Review*, 19(1), 3–10.

Bonell, C., Fletcher, A., Morton, M., Lorenc, T., & Moore, L. (2012). Realist randomised controlled trials: A new approach to evaluating complex public health interventions. *Social Science & Medicine*, 75, 2299–2306. https://doi.org/10.1016/j.socscimed.2012.08.032

Brion, S., Chauvet, V., Chollet, B., & Mothe, C. (2012). Project leaders as boundary spanners: Relational antecedents and performance outcomes. *International Journal of Project Management*, 30(6).

Broussine, M. (2003). Leading and managing at the boundary: Perspectives created by joined up working. *Local Government Studies*, 29(3).

Buckmasters, L., & Thomas, M. (2009). *Social inclusion and social citizenship—towards a truly inclusive society*. Research Paper no. 08 2009–10. Parliamentary Library, Parliament of Australia, Canberra.

Byrne, D. (1998). *Complexity Theory and the Social Sciences: An Introduction*. London: Routledge.

Byrne, D. (2005). Complexity, configuration and cases. *Theory, Culture and Society*, 22(5), 95–111.

Byrne, D. (2013). Evaluating complex social interventions in a complex world. *Evaluation*, 19(3), 217–228.

Byrne, D., & Callaghan, G. (2014). *Complexity Theory and the Social Sciences: The State of the Art*. London: Routledge.

Byrne, D., & Uprichard, E. (2012). Useful complex causality. In H. Kinkard (Ed.), *Oxford Handbook of Philosophy of Social Science* (pp. 109–129). Oxford: Oxford University Press.

Cairney, P. (2016). *The Politics of Evidence Based Policy*. London: Palgrave Pivot.

Cairney, P. (2018). The UK government's imaginative use of evidence to make policy. *British Politics*, 1–22. https://doi.org/10.1057/s41293-017-0068-2

Carey, G., Buick, F., Pescud, M., & Malbon, E. (2017). Preventing dysfunction and improving policy advice: The role of intra-departmental boundary spanners. *Australian Journal of Public Administration*, 76(2).

Carey, G., & Crammond, B. (2015a). Systems change for the social determinants of health. *BMC Public Health*, 15(1), 662.

Carey, G., & Crammond, B. (2015b). What works in joined-up government? An evidence synthesis. *International Journal of Public Administration*, 18, 1020–1029.

Carey, G., Crammond, B., & Riley, T. (2015). Top-down approaches to joined-up government: Examining the unintended consequences of weak implementation. *International Journal of Public Administration*, 1–12. https://doi.org/10.1080/01900692.2014.903276

Carey, G., Dickinson, H., & Olney, S. (2017). What can feminist theory offer policy implementation challenges? *Evidence and Policy*. https://doi.org/10.1332/174426417X14881935664929

Checkland, P. (2000). Soft systems methodology: A thirty year retrospective. *Systems Research and Behavioral Science*, 17(S1), S11–S58.

Checkland, P. (2006). *Learning for Action: A Short Definitive Account of Soft Systems Methodology and Its Use for Practitioners, Teachers and Students*. Hoboken, NJ: John Wiley & Sons.

Christen, B., Kjeldsen, C., Dalgaard, T., & Martin-Ortega, J. (2015). Can fuzzy cognitive mapping help in agricultural policy design and communication? *Land Use Policy,* 45, 64–75.

Cilliers, P. (1998). *Complexity and Postmodernism.* London: Routledge.

Cilliers, P. (2000). What can we learn from a theory of complexity? *Emergence,* 2(1), 23–33.

Cilliers, P. (2002). Why we cannot know complex things completely. *Emergence,* 4(1–2), 77–84.

Cilliers, P. (2005). Complexity, deconstruction and relativism. *Theory, Culture and Society,* 22(5), 255–267.

Cilliers, P. (2010). Difference, identity and complexity. In P. Cilliers & R. Preiser (Eds.), *Complexity, Difference and Identity* (pp. 3–18). London: Springer.

Coopmans, C., Vertesi, J., Lynch, M. E., & Woolgar, S. (Eds.). (2013). *Representation in Scientific Practice Revisited.* Cambridge, MA: MIT Press.

Corbin, J., & Strauss, A. L. (2008). *Basics of Qualitative Research: Techniques and Procedures for Developing Grounded Theory* (3rd ed.). Thousand Oaks, CA: Sage Publications Ltd.

Craven, L. K. (2017). System effects: A hybrid methodology for exploring the determinants of food in/security. *Annals of the Association of American Geographers,* 107(5), 1011–1027.

Cross, R. (2002). Making invisible work visible: Using social network analysis to support strategic collaboration. *Strategy Organ,* 44, 25–46.

Curnin, S., & Owen, C. (2014). Spanning organizational boundaries in emergency management. *International Journal of Public Administration,* 37(5), 259–270.

Dickinson, H., & O'Flynn, J. (2016). *Evaluating Outcomes in Health and Social Care* (2nd ed.). Bristol: Policy Press.

Dickinson, H., & Sullivan, H. (2014). Towards a general theory of collaborative performance. *Public Administration,* 92, 161–177. https://doi.org/10.1111/padm.12048

Dixon-Woods, M., Agarwal, S., Jones, D., Young, B., & Sutton, A. (2005). Synthesising qualitative and quantitative evidence: A review of possible methods. *Journal of Health Services Research and Policy,* 10, 45–53.

Donati, P., & Archer, M. S. (2015). *The Relational Subject.* Cambridge: Cambridge University Press.

Drach-Zahavy, A. (2011). Interorganizational teams as boundary spanners: The role of team diversity, boundedness, and extrateam links. *European Journal of Work and Organizational Psychology,* 20(1).

Druskat, V. U., & Wheeler, J. V. (2003). Managing from the boundary: The effective leadership of self-managing work teams. *The Academy of Management Journal,* 46(4), 435–457.

Dudau, A., Fischbacher-Smith, D., & McAllister, L. (2016). The unsung heroes of welfare collaboration: Complexities around individuals' contribution to effective inter-agency working in LSCBs. *Public Management Review,* 18(4).

Easterby-Smith, M. (1980). The design, analysis and interpretation of repertory grids. *International Journal of Man-Machine Studies,* 13, 3–24.

Erwin, E. J., Brotherson, M. J., & Summers, J. A. (2011). Understanding qualitative metasynthesis: Issues and opportunities in early childhood intervention research. *Journal of Early Intervention,* 33, 186–200. https://doi.org/10.1177/1053815111425493

Evans, S., & Scarbrough, H. (2014). Supporting knowledge translation through collaborative translational research initiatives: 'Bridging' versus 'blurring' boundary-spanning approaches in the UK CLAHRC initiative. *Social Science and Medicine*, 106.

Fairweather, J. (2010). Farmer models of socio-ecologic systems: Application of causal mapping across multiple locations. *Ecological Modelling*, 221(3), 555–562.

Fleming, L., & Waguespack, D. M. (2007). Brokerage, boundary spanning, and leadership in open innovation communities. *Organization Science*, 18(2), 165–180.

Flyvbjerg, B. (2006). Five misunderstandings about case-study research. *Qualitative Inqiry*, 12, 219–245. https://doi.org/10.1177/1077800405284363

French, M., & Lowe, T. (2018). *The Wickedness of Public Service Outcomes: Why We Need a New Public Management Paradigm*. Presentation to New thinking for wicked problems in public policy, International Research Society for Public Management 22nd Annual Conference.

Friedman, R. M., & Podolny, J. (1992). Differentiation of boundary spanning roles: Labor negotiations and implications for role conflict. *Administrative Science Quarterly*, 37, 28–47.

Friel, S., & Ford, L. (2015). Systems, food security, and human health. *Food Security*, 7(2), 437–451.

Gasson, S. (2006). A genealogical study of boundary-spanning IS design. *European Journal of Information Systems*, 15(1), 26–41.

George, A. L., & Bennett, A. (2005). *Case Studies and Theory Development in the Social Sciences*. Cambridge, MA: MIT Press.

Geyer, R., & Cairney, P. (Eds.). (2015). *Handbook on Complexity and Public Policy*. Cheltenham: Edward Elgar.

Giddens, A. (2000). *The Third Way and Its Critics*. Cambridge: Polity Press.

Greenhalgh, T., & Russell, J. (2009). Evidence-based policymaking: A critique. *Perspectives in Biology and Medicine*, 52, 304–318.

Guarneros-Meza, V., & Martin, S. (2016). Boundary spanning in local public service partnerships coaches, advocates or enforcers? *Public Management Review*, 18(2), 238–257.

Haraway, D. (1988). Situated knowledges: The science question in feminism and the privilege of partial perspective. *Feminist Studies*, 14(3), 575–599.

Haraway, D. (1997). *Modest_Witness@Second_Millennium.FemaleMan©_Meets_Oncomouse: Feminism and Technoscience*. New York: Routledge.

Harting, J., Kunst, A. E., Kwan, A., & Stronks, K. (2011). A 'health broker' role as a catalyst of change to promote health: An experiment in deprived Dutch neighbourhoods. *Health Promotion International*, 26(1).

Head, B. W., & Alford, J. (2008). *Wicked Problems: The Implications for Public Management*. Presentation to Panel on Public Management in Practice, International Research Society for Public Management 12th Annual Conference. pp. 26–28.

Head, B. W., & Alford, J. (2015). Wicked problems implications for public policy and management. *Administration and Society*, 47, 711–739.

Hinds, P., & Kiesler, S. (1995). Communication across boundaries: work, structure, and use of communication technologies in a large organization. *Organization Science*, 6(4), 373–393.

Hoeijmakers, M., Harting, J., & Jansen, M. (2013). Academic collaborative centre Limburg: A platform for knowledge transfer and exchange in public health policy, research and practice? *Health Policy*, 111(2).

Hovmand, P. S., Andersen, D. F., Rouwette, E., Richardson, G. P., Rux, K., & Calhoun, A. (2012). Group model-building 'scripts' as a collaborative planning tool. *Systems Research and Behavioral Science*, 29(2), 179–193.

Howell, K. E. (2012). *An Introduction to the Philosophy of Methodology*. London: Sage Publications Ltd.

Hsiao, R-L., Tsai, D-H., & Lee, C-F. (2012). Collaborative knowing: The adaptive nature of cross-boundary spanning. *Journal of Management Studies*, 49(3).

Hunt, C. M., Spence, M., & McBride, A. (2010). The role of boundary spanners in delivering collaborative care: A process evaluation. *BMC Family Practice*, 17(1).

Jervis, R. (1997). *System Effects: Complexity in Political and Social Life*. Princeton, NJ: Princeton University Press.

Johnson, T. R. (2011). Fishermen, scientists, and boundary spanners: Cooperative research in the U.S. Illex squid fishery. *Society & Natural Resources*, 24(3), 242–255.

Jones, N. A., Ross, H., Lynam, T., Perez, P., & Leitch, A. (2011). Mental models: An interdisciplinary synthesis of theory and methods. *Ecology and Society*, 16, 46.

King, G., Keohane, R. O., & Verba, S. (1994). *Designing Social Inquiry: Scientific Inference in Qualitative Research*. Princeton, NJ: Princeton University Press.

Kim, H., & Andersen, D. F. (2012). Building confidence in causal maps generated from purposive text data: Mapping transcripts of the federal reserve. *System Dynamics Review*, 28(4), 311–328.

Klijn, E-H., & Koppenjan, J. (2000). Public management and policy networks. *Public Management*, 2, 437–454.

Lang, T., Barling, D., & Caraher, M. (2009). *Food Policy: Integrating Health, Environment and Society*. Oxford: Oxford University Press.

Lavin, E. A., Giabbanelli, P. J., Stefanik, A. T., Gray, S. A., & Arlinghaus, R. (2018, April). Should we simulate mental models to assess whether they agree? *Proceedings of the Annual Simulation Symposium* (p. 6). Society for Computer Simulation International.

Law, J., & Mol, A. (Eds.). (2002). *Complexities: Social Studies of Knowledge*. Durham, NC: Duke University Press.

Leung, Z. C. S. (2013). Boundary spanning in interorganizational collaboration. *Administration in Social Work*, 37, 447–457.

Levina, N., & Vaast, E. (2005). The emergence of boundary spanning competence in practice: Implications for implementation and use of information systems. *MIS Quarterly*, 29(2).

Lewis, D. (2012). Across the little divide? Life histories of public and third sector 'boundary crossers'. *Journal of Organizational Ethnography*, 1(2), 158–177.

Lewis, J. (2005). *Health Policy and Politics: Networks, Ideas and Power*. Melbourne: IP Communications.

Lindsay, C., & Dutton, M. (2012). Promoting healthy routes back to work? Boundary spanning health professionals and employability programmes in Great Britain. *Social Policy & Administration*, 46(5).

Luhmann, N. (1995). *Social Systems*. Stanford, CA: Stanford University Press.

Luke, D. A., & Stamatakis, K. A. (2012). Systems science methods in public health: Dynamics, networks, and agents. *Annual Review of Public Health*, 33, 357–376.

Lynch, M., & Woolgar, S. (Eds.). (1990). *Representation in Scientific Practice*. Cambridge, MA: MIT Press.

Macaulay, A. C. (2016). *The Epistemological Evil of Wicked Problems*. Conference paper. http://programme.exordo.com/irspm2016/delegates/presentation/142/

Macaulay, A. C., Jagosh, J., Seller, R., Henderson, J., Cargo, M., Greenhalgh, T., Wong, G., Salsberg, J., Green, L.W., Herbert, C.P., & Pluye, P. (2011). Assessing the benefits of participatory research: A rationale for a realist review. *Global Health Promotion*, 18, 45–48. https://doi.org/10.1177/1757975910383936

Manev, I. M., & Stevenson, W. B. (2001). Balancing ties: Boundary spanning and influence in the organization's extended network of communication. *The Journal of Business Communication*, 38(2).

McDermott, E., Graham, H., Hamilton, V., & Glasgow, L. (2004). *Experiences of Being a Teenage Mother in the UK: A Report of a Systematic Review of Qualitative Studies*. Lancaster: Lancaster University.

McGlashan, J., Johnstone, M., Creighton, D., de la Haye, K., & Allender, S. (2016). Quantifying a systems map: Network analysis of a childhood obesity causal loop diagram. *PLoS ONE*, 11(10), e0165459.

McIvor, R. M. (1942). *Social Causation*. New York: Ginn and Company.

Miller, P. M. (2008). Examining the work of boundary spanning leaders in community contexts. *International Journal of Leadership in Education*, 11(4), 353–377.

Miller, S. I., & Fredericks, M. (2008). Social science research and policymaking: Meta-analysis and paradox. *Protosociology*, 25, 186–205.

Mitchell, M. (2011). *Complexity: A Guided Tour*. New York: Oxford University Press.

Nicholis, G. (1995). *Introduction to Nonlinear Science*. Cambridge: Cambridge University Press.

Osborne, S. P. (2006). The new public governance? *Public Management Review*, 8, 377–387.

Özesmi, U., & Özesmi, S. L. 2003. A participatory approach to ecosystem conservation: Fuzzy cognitive maps and stakeholder group analysis in Ulubat Lake, Turkey. *Environmental Management*, 31(4), 518–531.

Özesmi, U., & Özesmi, S. L. (2004). Ecological models based on people's knowledge: A multi-step fuzzy cognitive mapping approach. *Ecological Modeling*, 176, 43–64.

Pawson, R. (2006). *Evidence-Based Policy: A Realist Perspective*. London: Sage Publications Ltd.

Pearson, L. J., & Moon, K. (2014). A novel method for assessing integration activities in landscape management. *Land and Urban Planning*, 130, 201–205.

Perrow, C. (1984). *Normal Accidents: Living with High-Risk Technologies*. New York: Basic Books.

Peters, D. T. J. M., Klijn, E. H., Stronks, K., & Harting, J. (2017). Policy coordination and integration, trust, management and performance in public health-related policy networks: A survey. *International Review of Administrative Sciences*, 83(1).

Pettygrove, M., & Ghose, R. (2016). Mapping urban geographies of food and dietary health: A synthesized framework. *Geography Compass*, 10(6), 268–281.

Ragin, C. C. (2000). *Fuzzy Set Social Science*. Chicago: University of Chicago Press.

Ratcheva, V. (2009). Integrating diverse knowledge through boundary spanning processes—the case of multidisciplinary project teams. *International Journal of Project Management*, 27(3), 206–215.

Reed, M., & Harvey, D. L. (1992). The new science and the old: Complexity and realism in the social sciences. *Journal for the Theory of Social Behaviour*, 22(4), 353–380.

Rhodes, R. (2014, July 19–24). *Recovering the 'craft' of Public Administration in Network Governance*. Plenary Address Int. Polit. Sci. Assoc. World Congr. Montr.

Rouwette, E. A., Vennix, J. A., and Mullekom, T. V. (2002). Group model building effectiveness: A review of assessment studies. *System Dynamics Review: The Journal of the System Dynamics Society*, 18(1), 5–45.

Shapiro, I. (2005). *The flight from reality in the human sciences*. Princeton NJ: Princeton University Press.

Siokou, C., Morgan, R., & Shiell, A. (2014). Group model building: A participatory approach to understanding and acting on systems. *Public Health Research and Practice*, 25(1), e2511404.

Spicer, J. (2015). *Representation and Dynamic Implications of Mental Models of Food Systems: A Case Study of Dynamic Decision Making of Small-Scale Farmers in Zambia*. Paper presented at the 33rd International Conference of the System Dynamics Society, Cambridge, MA.

Sørensen, E., & Waldorff, S. B. (2014). Collaborative policy innovation: Problems and potential. *The Innovation Journal: The Public Sector Innovation Journal*, 19(3).

Stake, R. (2005). Qualitative case studies. In N. Denzin & Y. Lincoln (Eds.), *The Sage Handbook of Qualitative Research* (3rd ed., pp. 443–482). California: Sage Publications Ltd.

Sterman, J. D. (1994). Learning in and about complex systems. *System Dynamics Review*, 10(2–3), 291–330.

Sullivan, H. (2016). Interpretivism and public policy research. In N. Turnball (Ed.), *Studies in Governance and Public Policy*. New York: Routledge.

Sullivan, H. (2011). 'Truth' junkies: Using evaluation in UK public policy. *Policy and Politics*, 39, 499–512. https://doi.org/10.1332/030557311X574216

Sullivan, H., & Stewart, M. (2006). Who owns the theory of change? *Evaluation*, 12, 179–199. https://doi.org/10.1177/1356389006066971

Thibodeau, P. H., Winneg, A., Frantz, C., & Flusberg, S. (2016). The mind is an ecosystem: Systemic metaphors promote systems thinking. *Metaphor and the Social World*, 6(2), 225–242.

van der Heijden, J., & Kuhlmann, J. (2017). Studying incremental institutional change: A systematic and critical metaanalysis of the literature from 2005 to 2015. *Policy Studies Journal*, 45(3), 535–554.

Vennix, J. A. M. (1999). Group model-building: Tackling messy problems. *System Dynamics Review*, 14(5), 379–401.

Wilson-Prangley, A., & Olivier, J. (2016). Integrative public leadership in the private sector in South Africa. *Development Southern Africa*, 33(2).

Wood, M. D., Bostrom, A., Convertino, M., Kovacs, D., & Linkov, I. (2012). A moment of mental model clarity: Response to Jones et al. 2011. *Ecology and Society*, 17.

Woolcock, M. (2013). Using case studies to explore the external validity of 'complex' development interventions. *Evaluation*, 19(3), 229–248.

Yin, R. K. (2002). *Case Study Research: Design and Methods* (3rd ed.). Thousand Oaks, CA: Sage Publications Ltd.

Conclusion

The Future of Boundary Spanning Research and Practice

Gemma Carey, Luke Craven, and Helen Dickinson

In "Crossing Boundaries in Public Management and Policy" (edited by Janine O'Flynn, Deborah Blackman and John Halligan), O'Flynn argues that modern societies are enmeshed in complex, interdependent, diverse, multilevel and shifting sets of boundaries—organisational, professional, sectoral, governance and personal—and these exert a huge influence on the core tasks of modern public management and policy. This first book brought together a highly fragmented and disorganised literature. Our book extends this work, aiming to deepen our knowledge of four key challenges that remain unresolved in the boundary-spanning literature, which span from the conceptual and methodological, to the practice, and to the translational. In doing so, the book tackles the question of boundary spanning from these four different angles—providing an in-depth investigation of the current state of the field in each of these realms, in addition to highlighting new directions for solving the identified challenges. Although boundaries are an important feature of the public administration and public policy literatures and have been for some time, in fleshing out each of these challenges, it becomes clear there are a number of unanswered questions still remaining for scholars and practitioners seeking to understand and operationalise boundary spanning.

Crucially, the challenges we deal with in this text are deeply interdependent. Our objective from the outset has been to identify and traverse the boundaries between them, the result being a form of 'boundary *bricolage*'—each comprising elements of the other. As such, we hope these contributions emerge as being more than simply the sum of their parts. In order to aid this process, this chapter concludes the text by summarising the key questions raised across the four 'Challenges,' bringing together important themes and setting out a roadmap for those seeking to work with, or study, boundaries or boundary work. We have identified a number of important questions that have arisen from the contributions within this book, namely:

- What is driving our interest in boundaries in public management?
- What types of boundaries are there?

- Why do we care about some boundaries more than others?
- What are the impacts of different boundaries?
- What do we want to do with boundaries?
- What do we need to know about those who cross boundaries? What is the process and practice of crossing boundaries?

These questions form the structure of this concluding chapter. Though we do not always have answers, raising these questions together in this collection provides a critical look at the issues in ways that are often overlooked by the broader literature, thereby opening new pathways for both policy and practice.

Key Themes Arising Out of the Text

1. *What Is Driving Our Interest in Boundaries in Public Management?*

Within both contemporary public service practice and the study of these organisations, it is often taken as a given that boundaries are an important unit of analysis. However, as this text has illustrated, there are a number of different reasons for this. This has important implications for the questions that follow, relating to the form that they take and the impact that they have on the design and delivery of policy and public services. As we have sought to demonstrate, knowing why boundaries matter is an important first step in engaging in working in and around these entities. In this section we provide a summary of the four major factors driving interest in boundaries in public management.

First, a shift towards specialisation has led to an increasing number of boundaries in the public sector. As Nicolini et al. (2012) observe, one of the "most notable characteristics of post-industrial society is that work is increasingly accomplished through collaboration among independent groups of disciplinary specialists" (p. 612). The rise of specialisation has created professionals who focus on particular areas (e.g. finance, information technology, administration, human resources) and agencies with narrow remits around a set of functions (e.g. regulatory and oversight, service delivery, policy development). The implication of this are the associated boundaries that come with specialisation in terms of particular knowledge and functions. As specialisation has grown, boundaries have become more acute and the need to find ways to traverse and bridge them more pressing.

Second, as more functions of government become externalised, so the number of boundaries proliferate. This is seen as a key part of New Public Management and New Public Governance. Both of these (overlapping) paradigms have precipitated the use of different mechanisms for externalisation of government services, from contracting to individual budgets and new forms of procurement. These mechanisms have drawn not just more non-government actors into the policy design and implementation space, but in new and often poorly understood ways. Concurrent with this, new roles for government have emerged that require cross-boundary action, such as market stewardship (where government facilitates the development and sustainability of quasi-markets that may contain a wide array of actors). For policies to be effective in reaching their aims, government officials—from senior levels through to street level bureaucrats—need to grapple with boundary issues.

Third, other trends in public administration have brought boundary issues to the fore—the 'cult of collaboration' (O'Flynn, 2009) highlights a whole host of boundary issues, which are addressed in Part 3 of this book: The Craft Challenge. As Flynn notes, the public sector has rapidly moved towards models for collaborative design and complex facilitation practice. The aim of these processes is to foster co-creation spaces as a guide to leaders, stakeholders and facilitators as they think about how to design and deliver a successful co-creation exercise. Alongside this sits a push for integration, as addressed in Part 2 of this book: The Practice Challenge. As Williams notes, while the integration of health and social care takes a number of different forms in different countries, in terms of both design and delivery across the world, choosing the right model for the right context remains a difficult issue to resolve in many countries. Some models have attempted to embrace both aspects within a single organisation, whereas others attempt closer working along a broad continuum from sharing information/co-location to coordination to complete merger of services. The proliferation of 'co' work necessitates a concern for boundaries.

Fourth, there has been, in many liberal democracies, systematic disinvestment in the public sector, which has manifested in some contexts as a decrease in public sector spending and in others greater externalisation (or outsourcing) of government functions to other sectors through a wide range of mechanisms. In the latter, greater amounts of public money may be available but it is not going to public bodies. This means that some types of boundaries pose more risk than before. Temporal boundaries are particularly relevant here. Time, and how boundaries change or remain constant in different contexts, has not been well examined in public administration (Pollitt, 2013). However, these are critical sources of risk; for example, in not paying attention to temporal boundaries we lose corporate knowledge and capacity inside the public sector (due, in part, to the increasing use of consultants) and become more prone to path dependency. While not as prominent in the literature as co-creation, new public management or new public governance, this is a critical issue facing the public service. Temporal boundaries and the risks they pose for capability development and sustainability, and innovation require more scholarly attention. Currently, this is an under-examined area in the boundary literature.

While each of these drivers represents a significant trend in public administration, it is worth considering the devil's advocate position. Is interest in boundaries merely fashion? Particular concepts in public administration move in and out of discourse over time. Boundary spanning, for example, was the topic of much discussion in the 1970s (Marmor, 2004). Similarly, policy implementation (which requires us to confront boundary issues) was also of keen interest at this time, only to fall away and re-emerge in recent years (Moon et al., 2017). It is possible that boundary issues are having 'a moment,' while acknowledging that they have been a topic of discussion in the past (Perri 6, 1997). Yet, the challenges captured in the boundary literature and this book are very real and, while the context is shifting, many are long standing. This suggests that even if the terminology of boundaries is transient, the problems it seeks to capture and explore are not.

2. *What Types of Boundaries Are There?*

Ideas are "claims about descriptions of the world, causal relationships, or the normative legitimacy of certain actions" (Parsons, 2002, p. 48). Ideas about what boundaries matter play a role in terms of what we see as problematic, why we decide to intervene and what form that intervention takes. As Béland (2007, p. 2) argues, "Ideational forces can become an independent variable that must be understood within specific institutional arrangements." That is, ideas are not just about what constructs enter the policy process and agenda setting phase of policy. Ideas about processes also shape what we see as problematic and what actions we should take in response (Béland, 2007; Carey, Buick, et al., 2017). Carey, Buick, et al. (2017), for example, describe the ways in which discourses on collaboration and joined-up government have created isomorphic pressure on public institutions. Those governments that are seen to be actively tackling boundary problems, they argue, are often lauded for the way they are attempting to 'future proof' policies and tackle complex policy problems. Simply put, ideas about the nature and form of public sector problems actively shape the processes that determine how governments think about and seek to address boundaries. These ideas highlight a range of different boundaries which exist and are identified in this book,

The most prominent boundaries receiving attention in the literature are the various forms of social and physical boundaries that exist between groups. Linked with these are subsequent boundaries in culture, language, ideas, values and norms. These cultural boundary problems are receiving growing attention (Buick, 2014; Buick et al., 2018; Williams, 2002). Buick et al. (2018) argue that efforts to address boundaries issues must include a focus on cultural integration. Similarly, Dickinson and Sullivan (2014) argue that cross-boundary issues are not simply a matter of finessing structural arrangements, but also addressing social and cultural dimensions, which means grappling with language, symbols and objects, emotions and identity. Research has shown that too much attention to structure leads us to miss the important ways in which human agency can produce boundary bridging practices, or the ways in which structure can interrupt such practices if considered in isolation (Carey, Buick, et al., 2017). As argued by numerous authors in this book, there is a need to take account of both in any consideration of boundaries.

Other important boundaries to emerge from this book include contextual boundaries, such as professional practice, incentive structures and power—that differ across and between organisational settings. As Williams notes in his chapter (p. 70), "while actors may manufacture outcomes, the parameters of their capacity to act—the constraint and opportunities—is set by the structured context in which they operate." These contextual factors necessarily contain elements of cultural norms and values—highlighting the interdependency of many, if not all, types of boundaries. Similarly, boundaries are also mental and cognitive. As a result of the cultural and contextual nature of boundaries, they can be highly subjective, as noted in the Practice Part of this book. Boundaries may be evident to some but not others. If we can't see a boundary, it is likely to go unaddressed.

Boundary objects and spaces are also starting to appear with greater frequency within the literature—physical and social entities, or mechanisms, which emerge at the intersections between groups, cultures and so forth where boundary problems come to the fore. Boundary objects and spaces can function as critical in-between elements where boundaries and boundary problems can be discussed and bridged. For example, these might take the form of working groups, committees or inter-sectoral initiatives that seek to actively surface and challenge boundary issues. Flynn provides a comprehensive list of boundary objects, which can include physical spaces (co-location of services in building), to managerial/leadership interventions (working groups) through to statutory instruments (pooled budgets). At present these boundary objects are treated within a normative frame of reducing boundary tensions. However, these very same boundary objects may also act to reinforce cultural difference and inflame tensions if not well managed, where, for example, negative stereotypes can be reinforced. For example, artificial intelligence can form a boundary object—monitoring and reporting software is now used by a whole host of actors in the delivery of public services overseen by government. However this software, and the algorithms that underpin it, can still be developed from a middle-class (and often white and male) normative perspective—inadvertently shaping the ways that services are delivered, received and monitored by individuals which may reinforce unconscious bias and stereotypes. Similarly, translation software, which is increasingly used by governments is developed from a normative frame of race—that has implications for how citizens and services interact. Hence, boundary objects are not apolitical in the sense that they have no meaning independent of human subjectivity (Bennett, 2004), but rather, function in a mediating and performative fashion (Fong et al., 2007; Gal et al., 2004).

A key theme in this book is a need to more deeply explore the interplay of structure and agency in order to understand how boundaries and boundary spanning efforts might act to reinforce or challenge boundary issues. That is, as covered in the Conceptual Part, when considering the major determinants of social phenomena, social theorists often distinguish between social structure and individual actions (human agency). Contest comes about in terms of the relative importance of these factors. In the Parsonian view of boundaries, social structure is seen as the crucial factor in creating boundaries within systems. In the socio-cultural perspective of boundaries, there is more room for agency—that is, the volitional and purposeful nature of human activity. This observation is important because social structures have typically been viewed as having a constraining effect on human activity, while agency is seen as a way of individuals to act independently of these constraining structures. As Dickinson (2014b) argues, the literature on public service collaboration is dominated largely by structural accounts, often making little room for agency (see also Dickinson and Sullivan, 2014). Although in more recent years, as Williams explores in the Part 2, the literature has attempted to draw greater attention to issues of agency through an interpretive turn associated with decentred governance (Bevir and Rhodes, 2003). There are many different views and permutations associated with this turn but, as Williams argues, most tend to emphasise that while actors may manufacture outcomes, the parameters of their capacity to act—the constraint and opportunities—are set by the structured context in which they operate. We agree that such a position is a step in the right direction, as we explore further. On the whole, however, in the academic literature, boundaries largely remain situated within a structuralist paradigm.

Each Part of this book is, in its own way, an attempt to integrate structure and agency when theorising boundaries. This is clear in both the Conceptual and Methodological Parts, which emphasise that boundaries are simultaneously a function of the activity of the system and a product of the strategy of description involved. A position that forces us to centre the relevant *agents*, their understandings and practices as an object of analysis. The key point here is that boundaries are not seen either as a purely 'real' or an 'imagined entity' but are both/and. Boundaries are emergent properties of the interaction of structure and agency and therefore inseparable from either. In considering the operation and impact of boundaries in public policy and public management, it is therefore important that consideration is given to both potential facets of boundaries and they are not seen as simply residing at either end of the structure/agency, cage/network continuum. The growing emphasis of interpretive research and new institutionalism is seeing advancements in this area (Dickinson and Sullivan, 2014; Kay and Daugbjerg, 2015)

3. Why Do We Care About Some Boundaries More Than Others?

When considering the boundary literature as a whole, there is uneven attention given to different types of boundaries. That is, we appear to be concerned with some boundaries more than others. It is worth noting that this may not reflect a hierarchy of how problematic boundaries are in any objective sense.

Structural boundaries appear to dominate research and practice, with some consideration of cultural boundaries. This has been the focus of most efforts to address boundary issues (Buick, 2014; Buick et al., 2018). In particular, most efforts to address boundaries focus on structural boundaries with only some paying attention to the interwoven cultural dimensions (Buick, 2014; Buick et al., 2018). However, as we note, a much greater range of boundaries exist including temporal and cognitive boundaries. Arguably, temporal boundaries represent a considerable and often overlooked risk to the public sector.

Our preoccupation with structural boundaries is likely to reflect the fact that some boundary 'problems' seem more amenable than others. Moreover, a structural change can quickly answer widespread calls for change (though do little to address the actual problems). This can be seen in Machinery of Government changes, where the election of new governments is typically followed by a major reorganisation of departments (Buick et al., 2018; Halligan, 2005; Pollitt, 2013). Similarly, problems within complex institutions may also drive structural change. For example, the NHS has been the subject of major top-down driven structural change, while underlying problems remain (Kieran Walshe, 2010). Thus, initiating a structural change is common, if not straightforward, but matters of culture, cognition and temporal challenges are more slippery. An alternative explanation for this uneven attention may be that we tend to focus on the things that are the most observable—cognitive and temporal challenges are more opaque. Cultural boundaries can be obvious to those experiencing them but invisible to others.

Given that, as we note early, all boundaries are likely to contain pieces of each other (i.e. structural boundaries include cultural elements, cognitive elements and so forth) our efforts to address boundary challenges are likely to be limited if they focus on only one dimension. This has been shown in the case of structural and cultural boundary interventions (Buick, 2014; Buick et al., 2018). As Buick and colleagues have shown, when we make structural changes but do not give attention to culture, we can end up reinforcing cultural boundaries, leading to dysfunction (Buick, 2014; Buick et al., 2018). This begs the question, what do we miss when we focus on some boundaries over others? And are some boundaries more problematic than others?

As noted earlier, there is a normative approach to boundaries whereby they are seen as problematic. However, it is worth considering whether rather than removing boundaries in some cases it may be a question of how can we generate and extract the most value from them?

Broader literatures suggest that boundaries are not just constraining but may 'also constitute gateways' (Rumford, 2006, p. 135); i.e. boundaries have a constitutive capacity, rather than simply just constraining activity and practice. O'Flynn (2016) notes that much attention to the 'boundary issue' has focused on how to create collaboration and consensus. However, recent research has highlighted the importance of difference and diversity in policy implementation and that engaging in different ways of knowing, being and doing can produce better outcomes (Carey, Dickinson, et al., 2017; Dickinson and Sullivan, 2014).

Finally, different methodologies construct those boundaries in different ways. That is, the ways that both researchers and practitioners come to understand a given boundary—their practices of data collection, analysis and dissemination—are intertwined with ways of seeing and enacting boundaries. This point might seem counterintuitive, but a raft of scholarship has shown that data never merely represents an objective reality, but rather intervenes to create such a reality (Coopmans et al., 2013; Lynch and Woolgar, 1990), privileging particular ways of seeing and interacting with the world (Haraway, 1997). As such, the notion that a particular boundary exists absent our engagement with it is a false one, as Craven et al. explored in Part 4 of this book. Instead, boundaries are actively created and enacted by researchers and practitioners in specific, situated ways, which are intertwined with the methodologies they use.

The key point here is that while the public policy and management community undoubtedly give a disproportionate amount of attention to particular types of boundaries, we can transform this. As noted, the interpretive turn in public administration is seeing a greater focus on symbolic boundaries (Dickinson and Sullivan, 2014), while work in historical institutionalism is driving more interest in temporal boundaries (Mahoney and Thelan, 2010). Our aim in this book has been to show how new approaches to understanding and crossing boundaries are possible by taking stock of the disparate and multi-disciplinary literature on the four boundary 'Challenges' around which it is structured. There is a value in remaining committed to critically examining the boundaries between disciplines, their normative standards and approaches to knowledge, and how these might be overcome in order for us to capture, examine and progress the boundary problems faced by practitioners and policy makers.

4. What Are the Impacts of Different Boundaries?

Parts 1 and 2 note that it is difficult to ascertain what the impacts of different boundaries are. This is largely because of a lack of evidence that links good outcomes with changes to boundaries. Dickinson and Smith note this lack of evidence in the field of collaboration, and Williams makes a similar observation in relation to partnerships and integration.

Arguably, we need to create models that do more justice to the types of boundaries that exist. This would provide a basis to:

- map evidence against where it does exist and can inform practice (for example, structural boundaries)
- identify where there hasn't been enough attention (e.g. symbolic and temporal boundaries)

Only with this information can we improve practice. Carey, Dickinison, et al. (2017) and Dickinson and Sullivan (2014) argue that researchers focused on understanding boundary spanning need to 'dig into' the practices of individuals where boundaries appear (i.e. in collaborations, in implementation etc.) to understand how they are performed socially and culturally, why they exist and are maintained, and their historical basis. Only from a deeper anthropological understanding can we truly understand the impact of boundaries as well as why some are surmountable, some are not and some we may not want to remove because they bring value.

However, there is a distinct lack of existing evidence on this point and we suggest that more research is required on methodological approaches to understand boundary crossing, as Craven et al. explored in Part 4. As they argue, currently much of the research on boundary issues reflects more general limitations in studies on wicked and complex policy problems. The field is predominately comprised of single case studies, from which the authors hope to generalise. In addition, research is often caught between being too specific or nor specific enough, describing cases without in-depth and nuanced investigation into the social practices that sit at the core of boundary work. A key methodological challenge here is how we come to understand what works or what might work in collaborative settings. That is, given a particular understanding of a problem, how can we generate knowledge about the craft of working across boundaries in public policy? Part 4 outlines that there are a range of strategies that can simultaneously address the generalisation challenge while maintaining a level of fidelity to the context of particular boundary spanning initiatives, such as meta-synthesis and meta-analyses, but that the boundary spanning research community has been slow on the uptake of these methodologies. As argued in Part 4, the challenge of developing methodologies to understand boundary crossings requires researchers and practitioners to cross boundaries through interdisciplinary research. Just like boundaries in other forms of practice need to be interrogated, we must reach across disciplinary boundaries in order to understand public policy challenges and provide knowledge which can assist in navigating emerging boundary problems.

5. What Do We Want to Do with Boundaries?

As Williams notes in his Part (p. 73): "There is a need to engage, at the very outset of potential cooperative action, in a hard-headed assessment of its appropriateness to particular circumstances and objectives." There is, indeed, a propensity to act on boundaries without first seeking a thorough understanding of them, including their different dimensions (cultural, symbolic and so forth) and the interplay of structure and agency in creating and maintaining them through context. Dickinson and Smith note (p. 15) that "Where boundaries appear in the public policy and public management literatures it is typically alongside a discussion of their inherently problematic nature. This line of argument has somewhat of an enduring quality over both time and space. What we find in the public policy and public management literature is that boundaries are described as being exceptional." However, as these authors go on to point out, boundaries exist all around us—they are a fundamental part of the organisation of society. This begs the question, why we are more focused on the removal of boundaries rather than their generative capacity?

Boundaries can be both 'good' and 'bad' in terms of their effects; however, they help us make sense of an inherently complex world. They are useful because they help us understand things. However, in some contexts they present barriers to action. Given the mixed nature of boundaries, we need to tease out when a boundary is problematic and when it is generative, and when the investment in addressing a boundary is worthwhile.

Both the literature and the contributions to this book indicate that there is no clear boundary solution. As noted in Part 1 of this book, attempts to address boundaries often fail. In fact, due to the interdependent and varied nature of boundaries, when we remove one we often produce new boundaries. Moreover, we can extract value from boundaries in terms of knowledge creation. Hence, we argue that rather than focus on the removal of boundaries (while noting that some are indeed problematic), practitioners should seek ways to derive value from boundaries, and come to understand their generative capacity and potential. But this likely requires a shift in mentality in the boundary-spanning community, catalysed and supported by academic research that explores what these best practices might look like. For these changes to stick, more work is needed to build a nuanced understanding of what motivates boundary spanners and how they conceptualise their craft, a point that was emphasised in each of the Parts.

6. *What Do We Need to Know About Those Who Cross Boundaries?*

A number of contributions to this book focus on the characteristics of individuals who work to bridge and span boundaries. This is consistent with the broader literature, in the sense that it positions boundaries as problematic. In the broader literature, the focus on the negative impacts of boundaries has led to a positive framing of those who traverse them. So-called boundary spanners are reticulists, interpreter/communicator, coordinator and entrepreneur—all of which have positive connotations. This is where the contributions in this volume depart from the broader literature—they challenge the normative positive framing of boundary spanners.

Part 3 introduces the notion of 'dark' boundary spanners, questioning whether all boundary spanners produce institutional gains and are motivated by altruistic factors. Meanwhile, Flynn (Part 3) highlights the potential for boundary spanners to be punished. Together, these contributions suggest that just as we require a more nuanced understanding and conceptualisation of boundaries themselves, so too do we need a more holistic analysis of the individuals who span them.

Across the four Challenges, it is clear that there remain a number of gaps in the literature about boundary spanners that need to be addressed if this work is to most effectively support organisations and practitioners in doing effective boundary work, namely:

- What motivates boundary spanners and how this impacts their practice and the outcomes it produces?
- How, when and why boundary spanners play negative, or self-interested, roles that do little for institutional change?
- What methodologies and other forms of data do boundary spanners use to navigate different boundaries and support their practice?
- Which forms of boundaries do boundary spanners tend to privilege in practice and why?
- How can we bridge, or balance, the structure-agency gap in our understanding of boundaries and boundary spanners?
- How can we supportive practices that harness the generative capacity of boundaries and limit negative effects?

Again, methods matter here. As Craven et al. showed in Part 4, a range of methodologies have been used to understand boundary spanners. They found that current research tends to use single-N case studies, social network analysis and other socio-metrics and 'practice as method.' As we suggested earlier, the studies reviewed in Part 4 make it clear that the research on boundary issues reflects more general limitations in studies on the complexity of policy problems. The field is predominately comprised of single case studies, from which we hope to generalise (Macaulay, 2016) and is often caught between being too specific, creating challenges for generalisation, or nor specific enough. If we are to begin to address these gaps and tackle the broader Challenges, we must think critically and creatively about what methods are best placed to do so. As Craven et al. show, a business as usual approach is unlikely to be enough.

7. *What Is the Process and Practice of Crossing Boundaries?*

The four parts of this book provide insights into what it means to cross boundaries. As Williams notes in his Part, boundary crossing often occurs in collaborative arenas: "Williams (2002, 2012) refers to the importance of boundary spanners and boundary spanning behaviours in collaborative arenas where activities, processes and tasks permeate, bridge and cut across conventional boundaries of organisation, profession, sector and policy." However, the Craft section demonstrates that boundary crossing is also deeply individual—driven by different motivations (as Carey and collaborators demonstrate), and leading to highly personalised practices, as shown by Flynn.

Williams usefully argues that before taking action to cross, alter or manage a boundary, we need to first analyse what the boundary challenge is. Too often we proceed without a thorough analysis and, as shown by the literature on structural boundaries (Buick, 2014; Buick et al., 2018; Carey, Buick, et al., 2017), this can have serious unintended consequences. In one such case, Carey, Buick, et al. (2017) demonstrate that this lack of analyses led to structural change and the creation of practices which were highly dysfunctional and decreased the robustness of policy advice in central government agencies. To prevent such issues, Williams suggest that practitioners generate contingencies before embarking on any strategy or activity that seeks to alter boundaries. In particular, Williams suggests that time and trust are key and interdependent. Indeed, too often action on boundaries is rushed and this, combined with limited understanding of the implications of change, erodes trust (Buick, 2014; Buick et al., 2018; Carey, Buick, et al., 2017).

Consistently research has shown that boundary crossing is resource intensive (Carey and Crammond, 2015; O'Flynn, 2011). As Williams argues (p. 80): "An important lesson for all forms of collaboration is to acknowledge that the process of this form of governance is demanding and requires effective resourcing." This resourcing must be monetary, temporal and relational. As Williams and Flynn suggest, we must give particular attention to leadership and management: building and sustaining effective relationships, servicing joint decision making structures, communication, networking and all the bureaucracy that is involved in the collaborative machinery and infrastructure is critical. This is likely to require dedicated personnel and time to co-ordinate and administer any joint arrangements added on to managers and leaders roles. Williams also notes (p. 80) that in paying greater attention to the temporal dimensions of practice, might also begin to recognise when it is time to let go of collaborative/boundary crossing endeavours: we must judge "when to call time on collaborations that are clearly not working and/ or have achieved their purpose(s). Some collaborations are perpetuated for cosmetic rather than productive purposes—actors not wanting to signal failure or damage potential future collaborations". This is consistent with systematic reviews of the literature which have emphasised that boundary crossing is dynamic, and our practices need to be equally dynamic (Carey and Crammond, 2015). Particular approaches (such as interdepartmental committees, for example) might be more appropriate at different stages of boundary crossing. What works initially may come to impede efforts down the track (Carey and Crammond, 2015).

The Flynn and Williams Parts emphasise leadership in a general sense, while the typology presented by Carey and colleagues together with Dickinson and Smith's Part suggest that distributive forms of leadership should be supported. Working across, generating value from or removing boundaries requires actors at all levels and in all positions to engage in leadership activities (Dickinson and Carey, 2016). Distributive leadership spreads duties within and across organisational levels over time, and sometimes across organisational boundaries (Dickinson and Carey, 2016). This form of leadership is more likely to enable cross-boundary working and change, as different actors are empowered to be more adaptive in their response to the changing context.

Flynn argues that crossing boundaries or breaking boundaries down is often done best through the creation of new spaces. However, when individuals leave these spaces, boundaries reform (i.e. in their own organisational homes). This speaks to the intractable nature of some boundaries. However, we must not forget that boundaries often exist because they are essential to the business of the public sector—governments need departments, for example, in order to organise the vast task of governing. This brings us back to the earlier question of what is it that we want to do with boundaries? Together, the contributions in this book suggest that we need to: recognise boundaries exist, map their various dimensions, appreciate the ways that they both add and subtract value, work towards supporting their effective operation or subvert them to produce institutional gain as appropriate. Ultimately, the question 'What do we do with boundaries?' is impossible to answer without identifying which boundary do we want to change, for what purpose, and to benefit whom and why.

Where Next for Boundary Research and Practice?

Methodologically, this book challenges researchers to go beyond the usual suspects when it comes to designing and conducting research. When we adopt case study models, how can we make sure they capture enough nuance to be truly informative? Beyond empirical research, how can we aggregate existing knowledge and systematically map the evidence? Combining qualitative methods such as ethnography with new and emerging socio-metrics such as network analysis and systems modelling can help us to more fully capture the interdependent nature of boundaries. Meta-synthesis and realist reviews can, in turn, help us to overcome the single case study challenge. However, these are merely starting points. More methodological innovations can, and should, emerge in the boundary spanning space.

Conceptually, drawing on the discussion of the challenges that have emerged from this book, we contend that a more dynamic account of boundaries is needed than currently exists in the academic literature. That is, we need an account that recognises their varied dimensions, interdependencies and also their ability to generate both positive and negative forces. Moreover, such an approach needs to integrate a range of perspectives—from the structural agential, to the cultural and social and temporal—in order to more fully understand boundaries and how they work.

Put simply, boundaries are complex, and we need to do more to actively address that complexity in research, policy, and practice. There is no doubt that accepting boundaries and boundary work as complex raises its own set of challenges, many of which we have discussed here, but ultimately this is no cause for alarm. An approach that takes complexity seriously, while remaining critical and reflexive about what we know and how, can help move us toward an understanding of boundaries to address these challenges. David Byrne (1998, p. 7) puts it well when he notes that, "the point about complexity is that it is useful—it helps us to understand the things we are trying to understand" by not abstracting them to the point of oversimplification, whereby our models no longer reflect reality in a useful way.

From a practice perspective, if we start with trying to appreciate the true complexity of a boundary issue, our analysis will be more nuanced and our plan to tackle the boundary more rounded. Similarly, in recognising the complexity of boundaries we also note their adaptive capacity—as we have shown throughout this conclusion, boundaries are inherently dynamic and multi-dimensional. In approaching boundaries from this perspective we are more likely to develop practices and initiatives that are more flexible and adaptive themselves and in turn, more likely to achieve their aims.

These three domains are of course interdependent. Changes in practice need to be studied and, ideally, can draw on the rich insights driven by methodological innovations. However, both of these need to start from a more robust conceptual basis that takes account of the multi-dimensions and dynamic nature of boundaries and boundary work. Without a robust conceptual starting point, research and practice will continue to miss critical elements of boundary problems. We anticipate that the contributions found in this book will help advance our conceptualisations of boundaries and in turn, drive innovation in both research and practice.

References

6, Perri., 1997. *Holistic Government*. Demos, London.

Béland, D., 2007. Ideas and institutional change in social security: Conversion, layering, and policy drift. *Social Science Quarterly*, 88, 20–40.

Byrne, D., 1998. *Complexity Theory and the Social Sciences*. Routledge, Oxon.

Buick, F., 2014. The culture solution? Culture and common purpose in Australia, in: O'Flynn, J., Blackman, D., and Halligan, J. (Eds.), *Crossing Boundaries in Public Management and Policy. The International Experience*. Routledge, Oxon, pp. 78–91.

Buick, F., Carey, G., and Pescud, M., 2018. Structural changes to the public sector and cultural incompatibility: The consequences of inadequate cultural integration: structural changes to the public sector and cultural incompatibility. *Australian Journal of Public Administration*, 77, 50–68. https://doi.org/10.1111/1467-8500.12262.

Carey, G., Buick, F., and Malbon, E., 2017. *The unintended consequences of structural change: When formal and informal institutions collide in efforts to address wicked problems*. www.tandfonline.com/doi/full/10.1080/01900692.2017.1350708.

Carey, G., and Crammond, B., 2015. What works in joined-up government? An evidence synthesis. *International Journal of Public Administration*, 18, 1020–1129. https://doi.org/10.1080/01900692.2014.982292

Carey, G., Dickinson, H., and Olney, S., 2017. What can feminist theory offer policy implementation challenges? *Evidence and Policy*, https://doi.org/10.1332/174426417X14881935664929

Coopmans, C., Vertesi, J., Lynch, M. E., and Woolgar, S., (eds.), 2013. *Representation in Scientific Practice Revisited*. MIT Press, Cambridge, MA.

Dickinson, H., 2014. *Performing Governance: Partnerships, Culture and New Labour*. Springer, London.

Dickinson, H., and Carey, G., 2016. *Managing and Leading in Inter-Agency Settings*, 2nd Edition. Polity Press, Birmingham.

Dickinson, H., and Sullivan, H., 2014. Towards a general theory of collaborative performance. *Public Administration*, 92, 161–177. https://doi.org/10.1111/padm.12048

Fong, A., Valerdi, R., and Srinivasan, J., 2007. Boundary objects as a framework to understand the role of systems integrators. *Systems Research Forum*, 2, 11–18.

Halligan, J., 2005. Public management and departments: Contemporary themes—future agendas. *Australian Journal of Public Administration*, 64, 25–34.

Haraway, D., 1997. *Modest_Witness@Second_Millennium.FemaleMan©_Meets_Oncomouse: Feminism and Technoscience*. Routledge, New York.

Gal, U., Yoo, Y., and Boland, R.J., 2004. *The Dynamics of Boundary Objects, Social Infrastructures and Social Identities*. Case Western Reserve University, Cleveland, OH.

Kay, A., and Daugbjerg, C., 2015. De-institutionalising governance? Instrument diversity and feedback dynamics. *Asia Pacific Journal of Public Administration*, 37, 236–246. https://doi.org/10.1080/23276665.2015.1117176

Lynch, M., and Woolgar, S., (eds.), 1990. *Representation in Scientific Practice*. MIT Press, Cambridge, MA.

Macaulay, A.C., 2016. *The Epistemological Evil of Wicked Problems*. IRSPM, Hong Kong.

Mahoney, J., and Thelan, K., 2010. *Explaining Institutional Change: Ambiguity, Agency and Power*. Cambridge University Press, Cambridge.

Marmor, T. R., 2004. *Fads in Medical Care Management and Policy*. TSO, London.

Moon, K., Marsh, D., Dickinson, H., and Carey, G., 2017. *Is all stewardship equal? Developing a typology of stewardship approaches*. Public Service Research Group, UNSW, Canberra, Australia.

Nicolini, D., Mengis, J., and Swan, J., 2012. Understanding the role of objects in cross-disciplinary collaboration. *Organization Science*, 23(3), 612–629.

O'Flynn, J., 2009. The cult of collaboration in public policy. *Australian Journal of Public Administration*, 68, 112–116. https://doi.org/10.1111/j.1467-8500. 2009.00616.x

O'Flynn, J., 2011. *Some Practical Thoughts on Working across Boundaries*. Occasional paper no. 14. Australian and New Zealand School of Government, Victoria, Australia.

O'Flynn, J., 2016. From headline to hard grind: The importance of understanding public administration in achieving health outcomes: comment on "understanding the role of public administration in implementing action on the social determinants of health and health inequities." *International Journal of Health Policy and Management*, 5(7), 439.

Parsons, C., 2002. Showing ideas as causes: The origins of the European Union. *International Organization*, 56(1), 47–84.

Pollitt, C., 2013. Context in Public Policy and Management: The Missing Link? Edward Elgar Publishing, London.

Rumford, C., 2006. Theorizing borders. *European Journal of Social Theory*, 9(2), 155–169.

Walshe, K., 2010. Reorganisation of the NHS in England: There is little evidence to support the case for yet more structural change. *BMJ*, 341, 160–161.

Williams, P., 2002. The competent boundary spanner. *Public Administration*, 80, 103–124.

Williams, P. 2012. *Collaboration in Public Policy and Practice: Perspectives on Boundary Spanners*. Policy Press, Bristol.

Index

academia *see* research
Africa: West Africa and colonial
  borders 36–37; *see also* Zimbabwe
agency 25, 36, 41, 53–54, 70, 80,
  91, 213–214, 245–246; *see also*
  Bourdieu, Pierre; structure
aims *see* values
America *see* United States
artificial intelligence: as boundary
  object 245
austerity 99
Australia 48, 171; Australian
  Public Service 154; Northern
  Territory 184; public satisfaction
  with democracy in 18; South
  Australia 83, 105; Victorian Royal
  Commission into Family Violence
  2015–2016 48; and young people
  91–92
Axelrod, Robert 225, 229

beliefs *see* values
borders 39; *see also* Africa;
  boundaries
boundaries: and borders 30; and
  the caring professions 36; and
  child protection 29; classification
  23, 26, 27; and cognition 245,
  247; and collaboration 29;
  composition of 29; and constraint
  29–31; and cross-cultural
  relations 37; eliminating 34; and
  geography 145; and knowledge
  17, 35; and organisations 24–25,
  36; Parsonian view of 23–25, 29,
  246; re-drawing 34; sociocultural
  perspectives 24; strictness of
  28–29; and virtuality 28; *see also*
  collaboration; cross-boundary

and inter-sectoral work;
  systems; time
boundary blurring 14, 20, 33–34, 95;
  negative aspects 36
boundary breakers *see* boundary
  spanners
boundary bullies 51–52
boundary devices 41
boundary events 50–51
boundary infrastructure 6, 93
boundary intermediaries *see* boundary
  spanners
boundaryless organisation 34
boundary management 67, 88, 92–93,
  109–110
boundary marker 50–51
boundary objects 41–44, 48–50, 93,
  121–122, 142, 146, 148–149,
  245–246; acronyms as 151;
  individuals as 150
boundary spanners 39, 46–47,
  83, 85–86, 98, 104–105, 119,
  121–122, 137, 181–182, 185, 241,
  249, 251; and Bourdieu 125–134;
  and collaboration 186; and elites
  126, 130; as facilitators 7, 150; and
  filtration 142; and methodology
  191–192, 195–197, 200–210
boundary work 29, 38–41; and
  systems 39; and technology 38
Bourdieu, Pierre 16; capital 123–124;
  doxa 123, 127, 129, 131; habitus
  122–123; theory of fields 121–125
Britain *see* United Kingdom
Business Process Modelling 50
Byrne, David 25, 211, 254

care work *see under* boundaries
Carlile, Paul R. 43, 97

child protection 159–160; *see also* boundaries

Christie Commission 69, 107

Cilliers, Paul 25, 29, 211–218

code of conduct *see under* values

cognition 13, 15, 35; and socialisation 16; *see also* boundaries; mental models

collaboration 5–7, 13, 17, 29, 31–33, 42–44, 46, 64, 67–71, 73–77, 119, 136–144, 165–185, 244, 251–252; and blurring boundaries 34; and colonial borders 36–37; and governance 78–81; and government 35, 86–87; and knowledge 43; and leadership 82; and methodology 193; in multicultural contexts 184–185; and power and identity 152, 155–156; and Six Circle Model 147, 149; *see also* facilitation; joined-up government

collaborative action 105

collaborative competency 90–91

collaborative working 19–20

communication 91, 165; *see also* values

complexity 10, 17, 69–70, 119, 136, 143, 194, 226, 254; British School of 25, 211; Cynevin approach to 144; and design 170–171; and facilitation 175–180; and public policy 154; and systems 211–216; *see also* wicked problems

conceptual modelling *see* mental models

confidentiality 183

conservation 51

corporate governance 79

craft 7, 119–120, 135, 153, 163–168, 175, 186, 250; and strategy 75

cross-boundary and inter-sectoral work 1–3, 6–7, 63–64, 75, 78, 81, 84, 88, 95–96, 104–105, 110, 119–120, 135–138, 141–142, 144, 149, 152–153, 155–156, 158–159, 163–167, 169–173, 178–179, 183–185, 195, 198, 243–244, 253; *see also* boundaries; interdisciplinarity

credibility 155; *see also* trust

Dalmau Network Group 180

databases 17, 38, 196

decentred governance 4, 25, 246

design model 168–170

drugs and alcohol 50

Durkheim, Emile 16

education *see* learning

emigration 20–21

emotion *see under* facilitation

epistemology 193–194; and methodology 202, 210

ethics 50; and competency 91; and facilitation 143, 155

ethnography 33, 110, 194, 198, 200, 205–207, 253

EU Dublin Regulation 20–21

European Union 20; UK decision to leave 21

evaluation 99–101

evidence-based policy making 99

facilitation 119–120, 136–137, 141–144, 147, 149, 231–232; and boundary objects 150–151; and boundary-spanners 165–167, 176; and emotion 175; facilitator qualities 152–153, 155–156, 159–164; sabotage of 173–174

family violence 50

Feldman, S. Martha 23, 29, 36, 29–40, 142

feminism 50

fuzzy cognitive mapping 224–225; *see also* mental models

gender 46, 48, 50; *see also* drugs and alcohol

generalisation challenge 8

geology 50

Giddens, Anthony 26, 28–29, 35, 121–122, 124–125, 194

Gieryn, Thomas F 16, 24, 38

Gladwell, Malcolm 166

governance 63–65, 67–68, 70, 73, 76, 78–80, 104; and collaboration 86–87, 108, 110; and epistemology 193–195

government 1–2, 18–19, 63, 129–132, 156–159, 193–194, 242–243, 244; and academia 106; and boundary blurring 19; and collaboration 184; trust in 18; and wicked problems 19; *see also* Machinery of Government

governmentality *see under* power

Great Britain *see* United Kingdom

Green Line Model *see* Six Circle Model
Griesemer, James R. 41, 94, 142
grounded theory 226
group model building 229, 231

Haraway, Donna 217–218, 248
health and social care 89–90, 243;
    integration of 93–94
Hernes, Tor 5, 13, 20–21, 24, 27–30,
    35–36, 53
human resources 17, 38

identity 26, 28, 39, 138, 146, 148,
    180; and uniforms 152
integration 139, 166, 243; *see also*
    collaboration
interdisciplinarity 6, 41, **44**, 54, 80,
    96, 137, 153, 165
inter-organisational practice 64,
    67, 139; *see also* learning;
    organisations
interpretivism 194–195; and public
    administration 246–248
inter-professionality 80, 88–91
Israel: American-Israeli cross-cultural
    relations 37

joined-up government 35, 105, 244
joined-up working 127, 134
joint working 106; *see also*
    collaboration; joined-up working

Keast, Robyn 139, 142–143, 168,
    178, 180–182
knowledge 95–99, 204, 214, 219;
    of self 153; social construction of
    193, 248

language 16, 39, 41, 143, 146, 150–151,
    154, 165, 169, 232, 244–245; and
    boundaries 15, 24–25, 28–29; and
    facilitation 158, 161, 178
Latour, Bruno 41
leadership 26, 65, 80–83, 95–99,
    119, 137, 144–145, 147–148, 151,
    166, 176, 178–179, 253; *see also*
    facilitation
learning 6, 8, 30, **47**, 79, 82–83, 86,
    90, 95–99, 139, 141, 147, 166,
    176, 180, 184, 200, 202–203,
    207, 220; action learning 194;
    experiential 104, 106; and
    facilitation 151, 163–164;
    inter-organisational 64; strategic

76; and training 65, 104–106;
    see also knowledge
Lefebvre, Henri 27–28
liminality 141–142
listing trap 226

Machinery of Government 247
management 76, 84–87, 104–105,
    108–110; *see also* public
    management
markets 35, 67–68, 150, 243
Marx, Karl 16
Marxism 194
materiality 41, **44**, 53
McIvor, Robert Morison 218
mechanism: in methodology 202
mental models 220–222,
    224–226, 232
meta-analysis 203–204, 253
methodology 8, 232–233, 248,
    251; and complexity 217–220;
    and context 200, 202, 207; and
    ethnography 200, 205–207; and
    systems 196, 205, 211, 220–221
mission statements *see* values
mixed methods 200–202, 219
modelling 9, **33**, 41–42, 77–79, 97,
    178–179, 186, 192, 211, 232, 243,
    249, 253–254; and complexity 144,
    216–219; and design 168–171;
    and learning 106; and systems
    216–218, 220–226; *see also* group
    model building; mental models; Six
    Circle Model; Theories of Change
Moran, Terry 154
motivation 32, 67
multi-cultural contexts *see under*
    boundaries; collaboration; Israel;
    values
multidisciplinarity *see* interdisciplinarity
mutuality *see* trust

networked governance 195
new institutionalism 246
New Public Governance 35, 242–243
New Public Management 17–18, 35,
    166, 195, 242–243
New Zealand 102, 109, 111
NHS 247
North America *see* United States

objectives *see* values
O'Flynn, Janine 2–3, 5, 9, 13, 15, 18,
    19, 29, 34, 38, 195, 241, 248

organisations 64, 75, 141, 147–148; culture of 124, 148–149; theory of 46, 48; *see also* values

Parsons, Talcott 23–24, 244, 246
partnership fatigue 79–80
partnership health checks 105
Paulsen, Neil 5, 13, 18, 20–21, 35–36, 53
performance 31–33, 99; and borders 39; targets 102–103
positivism 101–102; *versus* realism 195
power 42, 68, 81, 89; Bourdieu's theory of 130, 146; and governmentality 90; and learning 97; and uniforms 152
practitioner 165–166; *see also* facilitation
principles *see* values
private sector 77; *see also* public sector
process disturbance 173
professionalism 88–89; *see also* inter-professionality
public administration 1, 5, 51, 86, 121, 125, 143, 154, 166, 196, 203–204, 242–244; *see also* interpretivism
public management 1, 3–4, 7–8, 13–22, 26, 29–31, 33, 38–39, 54, 63, 70, 82, 84, 108, 138, 156, 166–169, 186, 241–243, 246, 250; and facilitation 119–120, 135; and learning 104, 106; and structure 41; *see also* New Public Management
public sector 68, 74, 96, 138–139, 141, 168, 243; and private sector 68, 156–159

quantitative and qualitative methods 9, 48, 100–101, 109, 147–148, 192, 194, 197–198, 200–204, 206, 208–209, 211, 220–222, 225–226, 229, 253; *see also* methodology
Quick, Kathryn S. 23, 29, 36, 39–40, 142

race 51
Ragin, Charles 209, 213, 218
realism 195, 202, 253

reciprocity *see* trust
reflexivity 127
relational sociology 25
reputation *see* trust
research 2–4, 16, 31, 65, 122, 141, 151, 165, 169, 180–182, 185, 191, 207–208, 247–250, 253–254; and facilitation 6, 8–10; and policy-making 100, 106, 109–111, 154, 158–160, 162–164; *see also* academia; complexity; methodology; quantitative and qualitative methods
respect *see* trust

safe space 7, 135, 171, 182–183; *see also* trust
Scanlon Foundation 18
Schengen Agreement 20, 34; *see also* European Union
Seven Circle Model 180
Silicon Valley 37
single-N case studies 198–203, 251
Six Circle Model 147–148
social media 16
social network analysis 198, 204–206, 251
software 17, 245
space 16, 20–21, 28, 34, 51, 138, 141–142, 245, 253; and collaboration 144, 152; as field 123; *see also* Lefebvre, Henri
specialisation 17, 101–102, 242
stakeholders 7, 75–76, 136, 139, 141, 143; role in collaboration 150
Star, Susan L. 41, 94, 142
strategy 172; *see also* learning
structuration theory 26; *see also* Giddens, Anthony
structure 53, 70, 92; and agency 25, 36, 64, 97, 109–110, 119, 202, 246–247, 251; Anthony Giddens' theory of 121–122, 124–125; *see also* agency; Bourdieu, Pierre
sub-cultures 138, 142, 158
Sullivan, Helen 15, 18, 25, 29, 31–33, 41–43, 50, 63, 73, 75, 82, 94–95, 99, 111, 193–195, 207, 244, 246, 248–249
sustainable development 95
Syria 20

systems 5, 9, 23–25, 32, 36, 39, **49**, 88, 101, 130, 147–149, 151–152, 161, 169–170, 180, 192, 217–226, 229, 246, 253; Anthony Giddens' theory of 123–125; as boundary objects 93; and complexity 29, 212–215; as fields 127; and modelling 192; and oppression 68; *see also* boundaries; methodology
systems maps 225–229, 232
systems thinking *see* mental models

technology 31–32, 41; as barrier 32; and boundaries 17, 20
terminology 14, 38, 46, 50–51, 71, 196, 244
Theories of Change 101–102
third way politics 35, 194
time 13, 34, 37, 51, 78, 82, 96, 99, 152, 155, 170, 176, 243, 247, 250, 252–253; and boundaries 16–17, 21, 26, 248; and complexity 212; and habitus 93; and modelling 200, 220; and partnership fatigue 79
training *see* learning
transdisciplinary knowledge processes 119; *see also* interdisciplinarity
trust 7, 18, 30, 75, 77–78, 82, 86–89, 91, 96, 101, 127, 136–137, 143, 152–153, 155, 157–159, 163, 174, 177, 178–179, 182–183, 194–195, 208, 252; *see also* safe space
T-shaped person 167

United Kingdom 15, 67; and health and social care 29; and New Labour 194; public services 64; Scotland 69, 107; Wales 42–43, 74, 94
United Nations Convention Relating to the Status of Refugees 20
United States 88; Federal Government 76, 88; Government Accountability Office 70

values 29, 32, 43, 73, 77, 81, 90–91, 106, 124, 130, 137, 141–143, 151, 155, 157–158, 173, 179–180, 207, 220, 244–245; and code of conduct 89; and multi-cultural contexts 184–185; and organisations 148–150; *see also* boundary marker
visioning *see* values

wicked problems 8–9, 19, 133, 210–211, *216*, 221, 226, 233, 249; *see also* complexity

Zimbabwe 51